Sustainable
Travel

by Lee Mylne

A Wiley Brand

Sustainable Travel For Dummies®

Published by: **John Wiley & Sons, Inc.**, 111 River Street, Hoboken, NJ 07030-5774, www.wiley.com

Copyright © 2024 by John Wiley & Sons, Inc., Hoboken, New Jersey

Media and software compilation copyright © 2024 by John Wiley & Sons, Inc. All rights reserved.

Published simultaneously in Canada

For general information on our other products and services, please contact our Customer Care Department within the U.S. at 877-762-2974, outside the U.S. at 317-572-3993, or fax 317-572-4002. For technical support, please visit https://hub.wiley.com/community/support/dummies.

Wiley publishes in a variety of print and electronic formats and by print-on-demand. Some material included with standard print versions of this book may not be included in e-books or in print-on-demand. If this book refers to media such as a CD or DVD that is not included in the version you purchased, you may download this material at http://booksupport.wiley.com. For more information about Wiley products, visit www.wiley.com.

Library of Congress Control Number: 2023951274

ISBN 978-1-394-21510-2 (pbk); ISBN 978-1-394-21512-6 (ebk); ISBN 978-1-394-21513-3 (ebk)

SKY10062799_121523

Contents at a Glance

Introduction 1

CHAPTER 1: Treading Carefully While Exploring the World 5

CHAPTER 2: Preparing to Travel Sustainably 17

CHAPTER 3: Getting There and Around Sustainably 35

CHAPTER 4: Packing to Save the Planet 57

CHAPTER 5: Where to Stay and Dine Sustainably 69

CHAPTER 6: Shopping for Sustainable Souvenirs 87

CHAPTER 7: Cultural Sensitivities 101

CHAPTER 8: Enjoying Ethical Animal Encounters 119

CHAPTER 9: Escapes That Are Easy on the Earth 153

CHAPTER 10: Making a Difference by Volunteering 177

CHAPTER 11: Learning on the Move 195

CHAPTER 12: From Sustainable to Regenerative Tourism 207

CHAPTER 13: Ten Ways to Travel Sustainably 217

CHAPTER 14: Ten Places to Go and Still Travel Sustainably 223

Index 231

Table of Contents

INTRODUCTION... 1
   About This Book 1
   Foolish Assumptions... 2
   Icons Used in This Book.. 3
   Beyond the Book 3
   Where to Go from Here 4

CHAPTER 1: Treading Carefully While Exploring the World.. 5
   Sustainable versus Responsible Travel — What's the Difference? 6
   Understanding Why We Should Care about Sustainable Travel 7
      Flight shaming and climate change 8
      Is all travel bad for the environment? 10
      Why does traveling sustainably make sense? 11
   Weighing Some Financial Costs of Sustainable Travel................. 11
      Offsetting your carbon footprint 12
      Slow travel — at what cost? 13
   Making Sustainability Your Choice in Travel 14

CHAPTER 2: Preparing to Travel Sustainably................................ 17
   Where to Go? 18
      Consider staying closer to home 18
      How to avoid contributing to over-tourism....................... 19
      Taking a sustainable tourism pledge.................................. 22
   Choosing a Sustainable Travel Provider 27
      What to ask your travel provider 28
      Sustainable travel insurance 30
      Checking sustainability credentials 30
      How to sniff out greenwashing... 31
   Traveling Sustainably as a Family... 32
      Budget tips for sustainable travel....................................... 32
      Teaching children the benefits of sustainable travel 33

CHAPTER 3: **Getting There and Around Sustainably** 35

Discovering the Joys of Slow Travel 36
Choosing Sustainability by Land, Air, or Sea 38
Flying as sustainably as you can 38
Cruising the ocean 39
Riding the sustainability train 42
Sustainable Road-Tripping 49
Public Transport Is Your Friend 50
Biking from Here to There 52
Going off the Beaten Track 54

CHAPTER 4: **Packing to Save the Planet** 57

Travel Products That Are Easy on the Planet 58
Choosing the best luggage 58
Sustainable travel clothing 59
Packing reusable items 62
Taking Just the Right Amount of Stuff 65
Traveling light 65
Packing tips to fit all your necessities 67

CHAPTER 5: **Where to Stay and Dine Sustainably** 69

Knowing Your Options for Sustainable Stays 70
Homestay with the locals 71
Eco-friendly accommodations 73
Indigenous-owned lodging 74
Finding a sustainable luxury hotel 75
What to ask your accommodation provider 78
Considering Where Your Food Is Coming From 79
Selecting sustainable seafood 80
Counting your food miles and reducing your "foodprint" 81
Eating like a local 82
Knowing what not to eat 84

CHAPTER 6: **Shopping for Sustainable Souvenirs** 87

Finding Sustainable Souvenirs 88
Spending your money locally 88
Checking for fakes 90
Mastering the art of bargaining 92
Staying plastic-free 94
Avoiding Purchases That Harm Animals 95

Palm oil products 96
Skins and furs 96
Seashells and coral 97
Turtle products 97
Snake wine 98
Ivory 98
Exotic "medicines" 98
Seahorses 99
Other Things to Watch Out For 99
Clothes and other fabric items 99
Wood products 100
Heritage items 100

CHAPTER 7: Cultural Sensitivities 101
Respecting Local Laws and Customs 102
Behaving in a respectful way as a visitor 103
How to interact with communities in a more
meaningful way 104
Speaking the same language 108
Getting Snap-Happy 110
Can I take your photo, please? 111
Photographing children 112
Connecting with First Nations People 114
Why it's important to take a cultural tour 115
Finding and choosing a cultural tour 116

CHAPTER 8: Enjoying Ethical Animal Encounters 119
Choosing a Reputable Wildlife Tour 120
Going on safari 121
Walking on the wild side 125
Whale-watching and other aquatic encounters 129
Cuddling up to koalas 134
Avoiding Unethical Animal Experiences 137
Elephant encounters — the good and the bad 138
Saying no to bullfighting and rodeos 142
Beasts of burden 144
What about zoos and aquariums? 145
What More Can You Do? 148
Taking time to have your say 149
Looking for other options 149
How to be an animal-friendly tourist 149

CHAPTER 9: **Escapes That Are Easy on the Earth** 153
   Choosing a Nature-Based Adventure 154
   Away with the Birds.. 155
   Diving Deep... 157
   Being Botanical 160
   Hiking and Trekking Adventures 162
      Getting started with shorter walks 163
      Longing for more distance and adventure...................... 163
      Taking sustainability on the trail 167
   Dark Sky Places.. 168
   Sailing on the Wind 170
   Freewheeling on Two Wheels 172

CHAPTER 10: **Making a Difference by Volunteering**.................... 177
   Introducing Voluntourism 178
      Combining travel with volunteering 178
      Near or far? Deciding whether to volunteer
      at home or abroad.. 180
      Paying to volunteer.. 181
   How to Choose Your Volunteering Experience........................ 183
      Deciding where to go.. 184
      Picking a volunteer activity 185
      Evaluating a voluntourism operator.................................... 189
   Addressing Common Concerns... 190
      Am I really helping?.. 191
      Avoiding orphanages.. 192

CHAPTER 11: **Learning on the Move**.. 195
   Getting an Education While You Travel 196
   Language Schools.. 196
   Road Scholar.. 198
   Photography Tours and Workshops 199
   Art and Cultural Tours 200
   Getting Sporty... 202
      Golf 202
      Sailing 204
      Surfing 204
      Yoga 205

CHAPTER 12: From Sustainable to Regenerative Tourism......207

Where To after Sustainability?......208

Leaving a Place Better Than You Found It:
Regenerative Tourism......210

Early leaders in regenerative travel......210

Being a nature-positive traveler......214

CHAPTER 13: Ten Ways to Travel Sustainably......217

Offset Your Carbon Footprint......217

Travel at Ground Level......218

Choose Sustainable Accommodations......219

Jump Aboard Public Transport......219

Take the Road Less Traveled......220

Connect with Cultures......220

Slow Down......221

Support Sustainable and Ethical Travel Companies......221

Be an Animal-Friendly Traveler......222

Buy from Local Businesses......222

CHAPTER 14: Ten Places to Go and Still Travel Sustainably......223

Costa Rica......224

Aotearoa/New Zealand......225

Borneo......225

Bhutan......226

Rwanda......226

Finland......227

Slovenia......227

Argentina......228

Greece......228

Scotland......229

INDEX......231

Introduction

Traveling is an integral part of my life — and quite possibly yours. As an avid traveler all my adult life (even before I became a travel writer), I have been to extraordinary places, seen things I'd never dreamed of, and met people with wonderful stories to tell. There seemed no end to the lessons that the world could teach me through travel. And then came a global pandemic. Borders closed, airlines were grounded, and it seemed that the world fell silent. And I started to learn some important new lessons — lessons I'd like to share with you.

Staying at home gave me time to reflect and reminisce about all those wonderful places I'd been. I was already aware that travel is not without its downside. Climate change had become a big issue, with talk of "carbon footprints" and the damage that carbon emissions from flights were doing. I calculated my own carbon footprint for the flights I had taken in the year before travel halted temporarily — and was shocked. Although I already had a reasonable awareness of "treading lightly," the results of that exercise made me determined that my future travel would be different.

Now travel is back, with a vengeance. Many travelers are making up for lost time, booking holidays and longer trips and hitting the road with joy in their hearts. And that's a wonderful thing! But this greater awareness that everyone has about the effect of mass travel on the environment is sharper now. "Overtourism" is another issue, as some of the most incredible places in the world — I'm looking at Machu Picchu and Venice in my mind's eye as I write this — are being loved to death.

So, what's the solution? The good news is that you can help. It won't always be easy, but it's possibly easier than you think. You certainly don't have to stop traveling; there are so many benefits to seeing the world and broadening your knowledge of it! By simply making some thoughtful changes to the way you travel, your impact on the planet can be less damaging. I hope this book will help show you how.

About This Book

This book is the culmination of decades of traveling — and many mistakes I've made along the way (elephant riding being just one of them). I've written countless travel articles for publications around the world as well as about a dozen guide books. I've visited 65 countries, lived in six of them, and undertaken some big overland adventures in Europe and the Middle East. Some of those travels — and mistakes — you'll read about in these pages.

I've taken a global approach to writing this book, knowing that some of you will be reading this in the United States, Canada, the United Kingdom, Australia, or New Zealand. And you'll all be looking to travel in different parts of the world, making your way to every continent as you explore our beautiful planet.

This book aims to get you thinking about how and why you travel and how you can travel in a way that leaves a positive impact on the places you go. It is a book for all ages and levels of travel experience.

Foolish Assumptions

While writing this book I've made the assumption that many of you know nothing about sustainable travel. I know that's foolish, but it's the easiest point to start from and is not in any way meant to be condescending. The truth is, researching this book has taught me a few things, too — and I'm keen to pass them on to you if you aren't already ahead of me!

I also assumed that, like me, you already have a deep love of travel but you want to know how to do it in a way that doesn't put added stress on the environment or harm, in any way, the people and creatures that live in the places you so desperately want to see. That's why you are reading this book.

I've assumed that you are not a selfish traveler, that you are interested in learning about the world and deepening your understanding of how other people live, and that you want to do it in a way that won't leave you with regrets.

Broadly speaking, I believe the advice in this book will be useful to all kinds of travelers, whether you are just starting out or have been traveling for years. You might be a solo traveler, a couple, or a family. You may be young and fancy-free, hitting the backpacker trail or planning to be a digital nomad. You might be an older adventurer with more time (and money) to take a deeper look at your chosen destination. More specifically, you're

>> A thoughtful traveler, someone who wants to travel in a more sustainable way but doesn't quite know what that means or where to start.

>> Someone who wants to travel lightly and make a positive impact on the place and people you see along the way.

My goal is to help you achieve all those things while making a positive contribution to the people who welcome you into their lives and their part of the world.

Icons Used in This Book

Throughout the book, I use a handful of icons to point out various types of information. Here's what they are and what they mean:

TIP

I've found a lot of ways to make some aspects of travel easier. These tips should help you, too!

REMEMBER

This is an important point that's key to sustainable travel or travel in general. It's a nudge to think about something you probably already know but need reminding of. Sometimes it's just about common sense.

WARNING

A heads-up about something that might cause an issue, put you in danger, or is worth avoiding if possible.

FIND ONLINE

This icon points out helpful online resources as well as items you can find on the resources page at www.dummies.com/go/sustainabletravelfd.

Beyond the Book

I've put together an online resources page to help you find more information about some of the accommodations and organizations that can tell you more about being a sustainable traveler. Here's just some of what you'll find:

>> Links to websites with more background info on sustainable travel

>> Links to tourism businesses that have a commitment to sustainable travel

>> Visa, passport, and other important travel information

Simply go to www.dummies.com/go/sustainabletravelfd. Be sure to bookmark the site so you can easily find it later.

Where to Go from Here

Start planning your next trip! Being concerned about sustainable travel certainly doesn't mean staying home. Armed with the knowledge you'll glean from this book, you'll be ready to travel with a new mindset.

Where you should go *in this book* is an easier question. You can start at the beginning and read it straight through if you want. There's lots of info throughout and even if it's a section you're not sure you need, there might be some tips and tricks in there that might be useful.

If you're just beginning to explore the concept of sustainable travel, start with Chapters 1 through 4. They'll give you a framework about what sustainable travel is and how you can plan and execute a trip based on sustainable principles.

If you prefer, you can dip in and out of chapters that grab your interest or seem relevant to the travel you're planning. If you're heading to Africa on safari, take a look at Chapter 8; if you're a souvenir-hunter, Chapter 6 will help you make sustainable choices. Do you want to learn more about First Nations cultures? Turn to Chapter 7.

If you're planning on full-immersion in a different culture or destination for an extended length of time, read Chapters 10 and 11. Everything else between can apply to trips of all kinds, as being a sustainable traveler isn't reliant on any particular style of travel. You can even apply it to luxury escapes!

Start planning your next trip now. Thanks for reading this book first — and happy travels!

Chapter **1**

Treading Carefully While Exploring the World

Times have changed. Travel has changed. And travelers are changing, too. People are traveling more than ever before — some are making up for lost opportunities during the pandemic years, while others are continuing a life-long love-affair with exploring as many corners of the Earth as possible. But for many — including me — there's a new awareness around *how* you travel and a desire to tread more lightly and to plan more thoughtfully.

Sometimes the imprint left behind is invisible, a barely perceptible trail in the sky or a temperature rise of just a fraction of a degree. Climate change became an emergency while the world was looking the other way. In other cases, the impact of mass tourism is shocking and in-your-face. Perhaps, like me, you're rethinking the need to go somewhere, anywhere, just because you can. Staying at home is not a palatable option for most inveterate travelers, who already know what they would miss out on by doing so. Whether you travel afar or close to home, getting out into the wider world opens up your life to new experiences that test your boundaries, expand your understanding of how other people live, and create lasting connections with the people you meet and communities you visit. But if you travel, you should do so mindfully.

In this chapter, I explain the impact your travel choices can have and how you can plan to lessen that impact to the best of your ability.

FIND ONLINE

For links to all the web addresses mentioned in this chapter, along with other helpful resources, visit www.dummies.com/go/sustainabletravelfd.

Sustainable versus Responsible Travel — What's the Difference?

You have to get over the semantics first. What is "sustainable" travel, and how is it different to "responsible" travel? Can you be a sustainable *and* responsible traveler — or is it really just the same thing with a different name?

There's a subtle difference. Put in its simplest terms, sustainable travel is travel that imparts a neutral or, preferably, a positive impact on the environment (including greenhouse gas emissions) as well as the local community and economy. It is about trying to promote the benefits of tourism to communities, achieving sustainable outcomes, promoting cross-cultural understanding, preserving culture, and protecting the environment and all living things.

Responsible travel is about what you can do to make travel more sustainable, putting the onus on travelers to ensure tourism provides that positive impact, asking travelers to take responsibility for changing and improving how tourism affects all those it touches, and ensuring it benefits communities and destinations.

The concept of "responsible travel," which first emerged in the 1980s as the impacts of mass tourism began to be noticed, was first defined in the **Cape Town Declaration on Responsible Tourism in Destinations** at the Earth Summit which preceded the United Nations World Summit on Sustainable Development in 2002. The declaration outlined the characteristics of responsible tourism as:

- » Minimizing negative economic, environmental, and social impacts
- » Generating greater economic benefits for local people
- » Enhancing the well-being of host communities
- » Improving working conditions and access to the industry
- » Involving local people in decisions that affect their lives and life chances
- » Making positive contributions to the conservation of natural and cultural heritage, to the maintenance of the world's diversity
- » Providing more enjoyable experiences for tourists through more meaningful connections with local people and a greater understanding of local, cultural, social, and environmental issues
- » Providing access for people with physical challenges
- » Being culturally sensitive
- » Engendering respect between tourists and hosts
- » Building local pride and confidence

These are all principles that are now applied to sustainable travel. Quality of life for all those involved in tourism and travel ventures — whether human, plant, landscape, waterway, or other animal — is at the heart of sustainable and responsible travel. Sustainable travel is just what the name suggests: it should be able to sustain itself well into the future, for generations ahead to enjoy the same experiences in an environment that has not been depleted or degraded by selfish or thoughtless travel practices. You're hearing more about sustainable travel now than ever before because the effect of travel — such as greenhouse gas emissions — is being recognized as a contributor to climate change.

Understanding Why We Should Care about Sustainable Travel

Changing times call for changing ways. Recognition of the impact that people are having on the world's climate — much of it related to travel — is causing a shift in how people see the world.

Sustainable travel is a way in which you can continue to celebrate the beauty and diversity of the world, while trying to limit the harm you do. Rather than checking off another sight on a must-see-before-I-die list, it's about choosing travel experiences that will bring you joy, safe in the knowledge that you are not contributing to loving the planet to death.

Traveling allows you to see the world's most beautiful, fragile, and precious places. By employing sustainable travel practices, it's possible to still do that while ensuring those places stay protected for the next generation of travelers — and those that come after them. Similarly, taking care of the unique wildlife that shares this planet ensures that the children of today's children will still be able to see elephants, tigers, koalas, and other threatened species when they set out on their own travel adventures.

REMEMBER

Sustainable travel is sometimes called *eco-tourism, responsible tourism,* or *ethical tourism.* These terms all have slightly different meanings — and are subject to misinterpretation, misuse, greenwashing, and exploitation — but all intrinsically have the common aim of reducing travel's negative impacts and preserving the joy of meaningful travel.

This book explains how to tell the difference between the truly sustainable and the green-wash facade and how to travel sustainably.

Flight shaming and climate change

With plenty of time on my hands when travel halted during the pandemic, I began to think about how much I had traveled in the past, the places I'd been, and where I might go when the world set itself right again. But in this new quiet space, a world without travel, many people began to see a silver lining: streets, skies, and seas emptied, allowing the natural world to recover from the impact of mass travel and tourism.

I watched as social media and news reports showed changes being wrought by the halt in travel. Reduced air pollution was reported around the world. Clearer skies above northern India made the Himalayas visible from Delhi for the first time in 30 years and pollution levels in New York and China dropped significantly because of less traffic and factory shut-downs. Seismologists around the world found fewer tramping feet, rumbling vehicles, and roaring jet engines enhanced their ability to hear seismic signals from deep inside Earth. Without cruise and container ships, the oceans, too, became quieter, a change that researchers said would lower stress levels for marine life.

Without people around, wildlife became bolder, reclaiming their territory. I laughed when I read that more than 100 wild goats living on a headland outside Llandudno in Wales had invaded the town. Elsewhere, other animals, free of the presence of humans, took the chance to expand their territory and breed more successfully. It was almost like witnessing a different — dare I say, better — world.

Climate change and over-tourism were already worrying issues. A new word had emerged: *flygskam* or "flight-shaming." It was coined in 2018 in Sweden and popularized by celebrities, including musician Malena Ernman, the mother of teenage climate activist Greta Thunberg, who pledged to stop flying. Within a short time, it was being widely used around the world to describe the practice of discouraging air travel in order to lower carbon emissions.

Aviation is responsible for an estimated 2 percent of global greenhouse gas emissions — and growing. Most of this is from fossil fuel burned during each flight, which results in the release of carbon dioxide and other gases into the atmosphere. But as travelers rush to make up for lost time after the pandemic, it seems that flight-shaming is not something that will influence all travelers — at least in the short term. European travelers have the advantage of being able to avoid flying by using extensive rail networks or by driving to other countries; for travelers in more remote and isolated locations, such as the South Pacific, getting anywhere else except by flying is a much more difficult proposition. Global travel patterns seem likely to change, with implications for the tourism industry in more far-flung destinations.

A *carbon footprint* is the term used for the total amount of greenhouse gas (GHG) emissions (including carbon dioxide and methane) that our actions generate, expressed in metric tons.

While it's difficult to pinpoint the emissions created solely by travel, the average American has a carbon footprint of around 16 metric tons, while the average footprint globally is around 4 tons. People living in developed countries — such as the United States, Canada, Europe, the UK, and Australia — generally have a much higher carbon footprint than those in developing nations where people have less access to energy supplies.

In flight terms, one person making a round-trip flight from New York to San Francisco creates a carbon footprint of about 0.9 metric tons. In the next section, I explain how you can compensate for the emissions from your travel by contributing to environmental projects.

Is all travel bad for the environment?

Should everyone just stay at home? If you are reading this book, the chances are you won't think so — and neither do I. To stop traveling and stay home is almost unthinkable after you've had a taste of what the world can offer. Each travel experience opens our minds and hearts to new possibilities and allow us to see how other people live.

While there are well-founded serious concerns about the impact that travel, especially mass travel, has on the environment, the answer is not to stay home, but to travel differently. Slow down and rethink your travel plans and look at ways in which you can make a positive contribution to reducing or eliminating detrimental impacts on the planet or the people whose lives you might be disrupting by your presence.

Instead of flying on every trip, consider alternatives. Train travel has a far less heavy carbon footprint than air travel, as does traveling by road. Why not take a vacation where you are walking or cycling instead of taking a bus tour — it's better for you and the environment. Be proactive in helping restore ecosystems by volunteering on conservation projects, combining a holiday with a chance to do good. As well as helping the natural world, it will give you a greater connection with the destination you visit and the people who call it home.

Staying closer to home is another option. You may not see the Eiffel Tower if you choose to go to Quebec, but you will still get the chance to practice your French and indulge in some French culture. Instead of an African safari, think about an American safari where you will see bears, wolves, and other wildlife. Thinking outside the box might bring unexpected rewards.

Why does traveling sustainably make sense?

You might be traveling for business or for pleasure to relax on a tropical beach that looks like it belongs on a postcard or to attend a convention or meeting. Everyone's reason for traveling is different, but the way that you travel can make you stand out from the crowd. It can also set an example for other travelers and for your children.

Travel offers a world of opportunities, both for travelers and those who welcome them into their lives, in places sometimes distant and unfamiliar and sometimes not so far from home. But there's no doubt that in the world today, travel has negative impacts on people, wildlife, and the places they live in. Communities, economies, and environments are sometimes at the mercy of the desire of others to travel.

The impact of tourism can be devastating, and as travelers you have a responsibility to help combat those negative effects if you want to continue to see the world. Understanding how to travel sustainably is one step toward achieving that. I'm sure that, like me, the most memorable travel experiences are those that benefit the lives of others in some way and that have deeper meaning than just ticking a "been there, seen that" box.

REMEMBER

Traveling sustainably, responsibly, and ethically is the only way that makes sense in our changing world if we want to continue to explore the world and to enable future generations the same privilege.

Weighing Some Financial Costs of Sustainable Travel

Some aspects of sustainable travel may be discouraging. Will it cost more than if you blithely continued without a thought for *how* you travel? Possibly. Some things might cost you more, but others will be cheaper — or even free! If you walk, rather than driving a short distance, it will cost you nothing. If you go camping in a national park, it will be much cheaper than staying in a hotel. Each flight or hotel you book, each step you take when planning your vacation, will have some cost both to your hip-pocket and to the planet. That's why it's so important to approach your travel plans mindfully, weighing the impact your travel will have on the places you go and the people or animals you encounter, as well as the cost.

Offsetting your carbon footprint

Every time you buckle your seat belt on a plane, you're about to create a carbon footprint. There's no exception and no way around it. The size of your footprint is calculated using the length of your flight, the type of aircraft you are flying on and the cabin class you are seated in (yes, Business Class creates a higher footprint).

The good news is that you can offset your carbon footprint. What does this mean? Simply, it is a way of paying to either reduce (offset) or balance out (neutralize) the carbon emissions created when you travel. Carbon offsetting is usually associated with flying but can also be applied to other forms of travel — and other aspects of life — that create emissions. Offsetting is an easy (and inexpensive) way to make a difference.

Fly direct if you can, as stop-overs add to emissions. Take-off and landing are the most polluting times of your flight.

TIP

Offsetting through your airline

The easiest way to offset your flights is through the airline when you are making your booking. The option is usually presented toward the end of the booking process. Just tick the box that asks if you want to offset your flights and the cost will be added to your booking (with some airlines, you can use frequent-flier points to pay for your carbon offsets). Some airlines use a calculator that allows you to put in your flight details separately and then click to buy.

It is usually only a few extra dollars, and the airline will send you a thank-you email outlining the projects your money has gone to. For example, after booking a recent flight with Qantas, my receipt explained that my carbon offset payment would be invested into one of more than forty carbon offsetting projects around the world, such as restoring native vegetation in Australia or building wind turbines in India. It's common for airlines to partner with projects in various parts of the world. For example, you could fly to Australia, but your offset may go to a project in the Amazon.

Airlines are as prone to greenwashing as hotels are. Several airlines have faced criticism — and litigation — for false advertising over misleading environmental claims. Before choosing your airline, check the claims it makes on its website. Is there specific detail about carbon offset programs or just vague promises? Is the airline trialing sustainable biofuels? Are they reducing single-use plastics? Be skeptical about any claims to be "carbon neutral" or "climate-friendly" — it's just not possible yet.

Using other offset companies instead

Generally, you're not able to choose which projects or suppliers your payment is allocated to. If that's important to you, or if the airline you are traveling with doesn't provide offset options, you can offset your flight emissions by using other offset companies. This may enable you to contribute to projects that directly benefit the place you are traveling to.

Do some research before you choose an offset company, as there are hundreds to choose from. One good website with lots of information about carbon offsets is **8BillionTrees** (www.8billiontrees.com). A popular US-based offset company is **Terrapass** (www.terrapass.com), which has a strong focus on funding US projects like reforestation and wind farms. Others include **Carbonfund.Org** (www.carbonfund.org), **South Pole** (www.southpole.com), which has more than 700 projects to choose from, and **Carbon Offsets to Alleviate Poverty** (www.cotap.org).

Carbon-offsetting is a good step toward mitigating the impact of your travel — particularly your flights — but it's not entirely a get-out-of-jail-free card. It's better than doing nothing, but the reality is that if everyone continues as normal, but pays to offset their flights, emissions will still be created. Reducing your need to fly by taking other forms of transport is something to seriously consider.

Slow travel — at what cost?

It's difficult to put a price on travel of any kind. The rich rewards that it brings are indeed priceless, but the reality is that all travelers have a budget. While you might love nothing more than the idea of throwing in your job and daily grind and setting off on an endless journey of personal discovery as you travel the world for a year — or more — the reality is usually different.

Slow travel, in reality, is more a state of mind than a long, unfettered journey. Your trip might be a week or two, or even just a few days, but the *way* you travel is the key to slowing down. Slow travel need not necessarily be any more expensive than the way you used to travel — it just depends on how you approach it.

Remember to balance all aspects of your trip planning. For example, you might decide to travel by train to lower your carbon emissions. It's true that some train fares — especially if you are booking a sleeper — can be more expensive than cheap flights. However, bear in mind that you are saving on a hotel room by taking an overnight train, and the fare includes meals.

TIP

Traveling by bicycle or by foot is a great way to enjoy slow travel. It's free or almost free, and the only negative is that you won't cover as much ground as you would in other forms of transport. But think of the back streets you can explore! You'll need more time, of course, but good planning will ensure you see and do everything you want to within the bounds of your vacation time. Staying in one place means you will explore it more fully and come away with a greater understanding of it.

Another aspect of slow travel is to plan your travel in the shoulder or offseasons, avoiding the most popular tourist times and avoiding crowds and queues. These times also have the cheapest prices for flights, hotels and restaurants, saving you a considerable amount of money (with which you can stay longer!). You might also be lucky enough to score the best house-sit or Airbnb.

REMEMBER

From time to time, here and there, slow travel might be marginally more expensive than normal travel. I doubt that the cost will be significant. What will be significant is the reduced impact on the planet that your actions in choosing slow travel will have. You can't put a price on that.

Making Sustainability Your Choice in Travel

Sustainable travel, as you'll discover as you browse the pages of this book, has many benefits. Done well, tourism provides jobs and opportunities for communities, creating income from sources that do not harm the environment or creatures that share it with them. It provides the means for children to have better health and education and for communities to retain their cultural heritage.

Choosing a destination that is a little off the beaten path, away from the most popular — and overcrowded — places will help to spread that income around as well as taking pressure off the busiest places. As a traveler, you'll benefit from a closer connection with those you encounter, who are likely to be more open to visitors and welcome the benefits your presence brings.

Being thoughtful about how you travel, embracing slow travel as a way of getting around, has the benefit of expanding your world. Slowing down, using public transport or your own energy to get around, and going to fewer places for a longer time all help to deepen your knowledge of a destination. You're more likely to meet people, be invited into someone's home or given tips about places that only the locals know.

REMEMBER

The important thing is to think not so much about how travel can benefit *you*, but how it will benefit the people you meet and the landscape you traverse as a visitor. This will help guide your choices as you plan your trip. Ask how your presence will benefit or improve the lives of those you will be observing or the ecosystems you visit. Instead of being a "taker," transform your travel experience into an exchange where you balance what you gain from it with what you give back. If you can do that, your visit is likely to be a benefit to your destination and its inhabitants — both the human and wild inhabitants — rather than a burden.

Learning to live alongside other species that share this planet, and to ensure that their habitat, as well as your own, is preserved for the future is essential to sustainable living. As a traveler, you should respect the homes of others — be they human or other living beings — as they tolerate your presence. Traveling to new places and becoming, even for a short time, part of the life there should be of benefit to those who live there as well as to yourself.

TIP

As you put some of the suggestions in this book into practice, you can also become an advocate for sustainable travel. Share your knowledge and your experiences with your friends and fellow travel addicts and provide feedback to the travel providers you interact with. Spread the word far and wide — it will make a difference.

Chapter **2**

Preparing to Travel Sustainably

Traveling can be hard. Sometimes, making sustainable travel choices might seem as if it's just making everything even more difficult. But with careful planning and sound research, making a difference to the planet need not be onerous. In fact, once you start looking at the options for sustainable and ethical travel, making those choices will soon begin to come naturally.

In this chapter, I show you how some simple planning can help you continue to travel while reducing your impact on the environment. There are many ways in which you can do that, and plenty of people to help you, from travel agents and tour companies to destinations that are making their own moves towards a more sustainable future.

FIND ONLINE

Be sure to check out the list of online resources I've put together at www.dummies.com/go/sustainabletravelfd, which includes links to the web addresses mentioned in this chapter, as well as other helpful resources.

Where to Go?

Traveling sustainably is not about depriving yourself of your wish list of dream destinations. It doesn't mean that you have to forego that trip to Paris in favor of camping in a national park near home. The world is still your oyster, but an important part of being a thoughtful and sustainable traveler is making decisions that will have minimal detrimental impact on the world we live in — and instead think about places to go where you can have a positive impact.

As travelers, deciding where and when to go, how to get there, and the decisions you make on the ground when you arrive can make you an influencer in the best possible way. Consider alternatives to the big-name destinations. Avoid popular places that are suffering — or in danger of being overwhelmed — by overtourism and explore off-the-beaten-track places, both at home and abroad. Look for destinations that you can explore in a sustainable way, by foot or bike. How will you get there, and what will the impact of your mode of travel be? Travel out of peak season to ease the burden on local resources and avoid the crowds.

Traveling sustainably is also choosing eco-conscious attractions or those that give back to the communities that surround them. Look for places that will help teach your children about nature, conservation, and the dangers of pollution.

Consider staying closer to home

There's absolutely nothing wrong with vacationing close to home. International travel isn't for everyone, and by limiting the distance you travel you are also reducing your carbon footprint. If there's one thing that closed borders taught us during the COVID-19 pandemic, it's that there are many great places to discover within easy reach of our homes. Prick up your ears when friends start talking about weekend getaways and think about which places you could easily go and still have an exciting and stimulating vacation.

Outdoor activities like hiking, ocean swimming, or cycling are often within easy reach of big cities, and there's nothing like some fresh air to blow away the urban fog. Look at your hometown's website for ideas of what's around that you might have been ignoring and plan to visit places as if you were in an unfamiliar destination. Playing tourist in your own town — something we usually only do when we have visiting friends or relatives — can be an eye-opener!

How to avoid contributing to over-tourism

Crowded places and long lines to get into major tourist attractions are never the highlight of a holiday. But it's much more than that . . . mass tourism has put unsustainable pressure on many lovely destinations to the point where they are no longer lovely. Too many tourists not only put pressure on existing infrastructure but are also a strain on the people who call it home.

In the past decade or so — long before the pandemic halted mass global travel — some places were in danger of being loved to death. Venice is one of them, and Peru's stunning Machu Picchu, pictured in Figure 2-1, another.

Lee Mylne

FIGURE 2-1: Machu Picchu.

Remember that gorgeous beach that starred in the Leonardo DiCaprio movie *The Beach*? In reality, it is Maya Bay on Thailand's Phi Phi Leh Island in the Andaman Sea. When the movie was released in 2000, everyone wanted to be there — and so they went. What had been depicted as an isolated, unspoiled and idyllic island became a nightmare with up to 5,000 tourists arriving by speedboat every day. The impact on the coral reef and marine life in the bay was devastating and the government of Thailand had to take action. In 2018 Maya Bay, which sits in Krabi's Hat Noppharat Thara-Mu Ko Phi Phi National Park, was closed to tourists to give its marine life time to recover from the onslaught. Although initially closed for four months, this was later extended and Maya Bay and Phi Phi Leh Island did not open to tourists again until March 2022, with strict controls on boat traffic, visitor numbers, restrictions on swimming, and a timed length of stay for tourists.

Similar caps on visitor numbers have been introduced in the picturesque Croatian walled city of Dubrovnik, in Barcelona, in Venice, and iconic destinations, such as Machu Picchu and the Greek island of Santorini.

REMEMBER

Researching how to make sustainable, responsible, and respectful choices while traveling should be part of your trip planning no matter where you plan to go, but it is especially important when visiting UNESCO World Heritage Sites. These amazing places are protected for a reason — so people can enjoy them — but their very status means they are prime targets for hordes of tourists. The Taj Mahal, Angkor Wat, Stonehenge, or the Acropolis all spring to mind. The brochures and postcards bear little resemblance to the reality.

Of course, it's understandable that everyone wants to see these wonderful places. So, I'm not saying that you shouldn't go, but rather, I'm encouraging you to think about when you go and how you approach your visit.

Skipping peak season

If you can, avoid peak season for any destination. This will help to support the local economy year-round and give you a more relaxed and enjoyable experience. There will be less people, prices are likely to be lower for both flights and hotels, it will be easier to find a rental car, and you will not have to fight for a table at a restaurant.

WARNING

Keep in mind, however, that the offseason might be the least popular time to travel to that destination for a very good reason. Maybe it's the weather, maybe it's because restaurants and attractions close in winter, or for cultural reasons. Some forward planning and research will give you the answers and help you make an informed decision.

Getting creative with time of day and other options

Think outside the box when you are going to popular destinations. For example, when you go to the Great Wall of China, don't follow the crowds or take a tour to the most popular — and very crowded — sections of the wall, such as those that start at Badaling or Mutianyu. Instead, find a tour company that can provide an English-speaking guide to take you to the wild, unrestored sections of the wall where you are likely to encounter few tourists.

Consider the time of day you might visit a major attraction — it is featured in all those Instagram posts for a reason (sunrise, sunset), but your experience might be more memorable without jostling for position with other tourists at a different time of day.

Considering a similar, less-known location

Exploring somewhere that's just as interesting and significant as the more famous attractions can be just as satisfying — and these days may even give you bragging rights when you return with tales of a place your friends have not heard of. If Stonehenge appeals to you but you're put off by the crowds, the need to book your spot to avoid lining up, and the fact that you are kept away from the Stone Circle and can only admire from a distance (unless you book a special time and pay extra), consider the fact that there are many more Neolithic standing stones scattered around the UK. I once found myself the sole visitor at the Calanais Standing Stones — which are older than Stonehenge — one misty morning on Scotland's Isle of Lewis. Entry to Calanais is free and although there is a visitor center, there is none of the hoopla that surrounds Stonehenge. I've never been to Cambodia's famed Angkor Wat, which attracts around 2,000 foreign visitors a day, but got my fix of ruined Khmer Empire temples at Wat Phou, outside the town of Champasak in Laos, pictured in Figure 2-2. Wat Phou is one of the oldest places of worship in Southeast Asia and was given UNESCO World Heritage status in 2001, but still attracts far fewer visitors and you will likely find yourself almost alone.

FIGURE 2-2: The ruins of Wat Phou, near Champasak in Laos.

Taking a sustainable tourism pledge

Making a conscious decision to travel sustainably is the first step towards actually doing it. Many countries are asking you, as a visitor, to think about how you travel by suggesting you sign a tourism pledge, a public stance that outlines your commitment to respecting the culture, environment, and wildlife in the place you are visiting.

Signing a pledge is not only your own personal declaration of your intentions, it can also be helpful in signaling to tourism authorities that travelers really do care about sustainable travel initiatives — and encourage them to keep up the good work they are already doing.

TIP

A pledge can be a good starting point for your travel plans. Does your chosen destination have one? If not, ask them whether they intend to do so in the future. You might just be starting something!

Share your good intentions too; spread the word on social media to inspire others to find out more about these pledges or just to raise awareness. Talk to other travelers to see if they have signed the pledge, too, and even if they haven't, start conversations about the benefits of doing so. Become a sustainable tourism advocate!

Many pledges use words and values from First Nations people, in beautiful and poetic language. The following sections cover various destinations that offer pledges (and the list is growing all the time).

USA

Like some other countries, most of the pledges in the United States are localized, usually in tourism hotspots. Hawai'i is the leading light, with several of the islands having their own pledges. The island of Hawai'i has the **Pono Pledge** (www.ponopledge.com). Pono means "righteous" and the pledge is based on the concept of *malama* (care for) the land, the sea, wildlife, and yourself. Tellingly, one of its lines addresses the dangers that some travelers put themselves in: "I will not defy death for breathtaking photos, trespass, or venture beyond safety."

The islands of Kaua'i (www.alohapledge.com) and Maui (www.mauitourism.org) also have their own pledges. When you take the **Aloha Pledge** on Kaua'i, you are addressing the island's children. It also acknowledges social media influence with the line: "I will protect special places by never geo tagging them on social media."

Both the Aloha Pledge and Maui County's **Malama Pledge** (which takes in Lana'i and Moloka'i) end with these words, "The land is a chief, man is its servant," written in Hawaiian and English.

Likewise, the adventure destination of Sedona, Arizona, asks those who sign the **Sedona Cares Pledge** (visitsedona.com) to promise that "I won't risk life or limb (human or sapling) for more likes. I won't get killed for a killer photo."

Like other pledges, those of the Colorado ski resort towns of Aspen and Telluride are shaped to fit the environment and activities that visitors will be experiencing. Telluride's **Tell-U-Right Pledge** (www.telluride.com) urges visitors to "care more about ourselves than the selfie" and to "keep the mountain pristine by bringing out everything that we brought in." **The Aspen Pledge** (www.aspenchamber.org/pledge) is an initiative of the Aspen Chamber Resort Association (ACRA), which donates $18.80 for each pledge signed to one of two environmental organizations (you get to choose).

Others regions in the United States that ask visitors to sign a pledge are California's Big Sur (www.cabigsur.org/big-sur-pledge), Bend, Oregon (www.visitbend.com/the-bend-pledge), North Tahoe (www.gotahoenorth.com/sustainable-travel-pledge), and Washington's San Juan Islands (www.visit sanjuans.com/san-juan-islands-pledge).

Canada

The Thompson Okanagan region of British Columbia, which takes in more than 120 communities, including 33 Indigenous communities, has a **7 Generations Pledge** (www.totabc.org/regional-pledge) based on the philosophy that decisions made by individuals today have an impact for seven generations to come.

Canada's Haida Nation are custodians of the Haida Gwaii archipelago, off the coast of British Columbia in Canada. The **Haida Gwaii Pledge** (www.haidagwaiipledge.ca) uses traditional Haida values such as *yahguudang* (respect for all beings), *ad kyaanang* (ask permission first), and *tll yahdah* (making it right) to impart its message of respectful and responsible travel.

Vancouver Island's North Island **Wild Pledge** (www.vancouver islandsnorth.ca/takethepledge) is a promise to practice responsible tourism when visiting communities, forests, and oceans.

Iceland

Iceland was the first country in the world to create a tourism pledge, in 2017. **The Icelandic Pledge** (www.pledge.visiticeland.com). One of the shorter pledges, it focuses on respect for the environment.

Finland

The **Sustainable Finland Pledge** (www.finlandnaturally.com/sustainability) asks visitors to "be like a Finn." That means "slowing down from within" and is written as a poem.

Australia

Like the United States, Australia's vast expanse seems to have led to a scattered approach to sustainability pledges, with only a few destinations yet to launch them. In New South Wales, the Central Coast (www.lovecentralcoast.com/sustainability-pledge) and Byron Bay's **Byron Way Pledge** (www.byronpledge.com.au)

ask visitors to commit to sustainable travel, as does uninhabited Maria Island in Tasmania (www.eastcoasttasmania.com/maria-island-pledge) where you are asked to "keep it wild and pristine" and to respect the furred and feathered residents, particularly wombats. On Queensland's Great Barrier Reef, Lady Elliott Island's pledge (www.ladyelliott.com.au) is all about protecting the fragile ecosystem of this beautiful coral cay.

New Zealand

The **Tiaki Promise** in Aotearoa/New Zealand draws on the Maori word *tiaki*, which means "to protect, guard, and care for." New Zealanders are connected to nature because they live so close to it — in this island nation you are never far from the sea or the forests. The Māori people, the *tangata whenua* (people of the land), believe every mountain, river, and tree has a story and the guardians Ranginui (sky), Papatūānuku (earth), Tāne Mahuta (forest), and Tangaroa (oceans) look over the lands and waters.

The Tiaki Promise asks everyone to make a commitment to care for New Zealand, for present and future generations, to act as a guardian and protector. It's three tenets are:

» Care for land, sea, and nature, treading lightly and leaving no trace.

» Travel safely, showing care and consideration for all.

» Respect the culture and local communities, traveling with an open heart and mind.

Palau

The Pacific islands nation of Palau asks all visitors to become a "trusted friend" by taking the **Palau Pledge** (www.palaupledge.com). Unlike other pledges, this one is not voluntary. If you want to visit Palau, an archipelago in Micronesia, you must sign the pledge, which is stamped in your passport on arrival and is part of the country's immigration laws. Legislation introduced in 2018 means your travel agent or tour operator will have a talk to you about the pledge and ensure you understand its importance.

A lovely aspect of the Ol'au Palau pledge is that it is addressed to the nation's children, some of whom helped draft the pledge. It begins: "Children of Palau, I take this pledge as your guest, to preserve and protect your beautiful and unique island home . . ."

In Palau, you can also use the **Ol'au Palau app** (www.olaupalau. com) to earn reward points while visiting. Sign the pledge, off-set your carbon footprint, visit culturally significant sites, or use reef-safe sunscreen and use the points to access places and experiences usually off-limits to visitors, such as meeting elders and visiting villages.

Philippines

In 2018, the president of the Philippines declared "a state of calamity" for the popular island of Boracay, describing it as "a cesspool." The tiny island, inundated by more than two million tourists a year, was closed to visitors for six months while beaches were cleaned, the sewer system was upgraded, and illegal structures removed. Since reopening, with visitor limits in place, tourists are asked to sign an **"Oath to a Better Boracay."** It begins: "I hereby solemnly swear, as a visitor of Boracay island, that I will, to the best of my ability, help ensure its preservation and sustainable development, and follow/observe environmental laws and regulations" and outlines rules about waste disposal, alcohol, smoking, bonfires and parties on beaches.

Other pledges

There are also other pledges that you can take to signal your commitment to sustainable and ethical travel. You can promise to reduce your carbon emissions by become an "infrequent flyer" by avoiding air travel for a year (or longer) by taking the **Flight Free Pledge** (www.flightfree.org). This small but globally expanding campaign has branches in the United States, UK, Sweden, France, Australia, Slovenia, and Peru and says flying is the most polluting thing most people ever do, with aviation responsible for 5.9 percent of human-caused global warming. It advocates rail travel — especially where the trains are electric — as the most sustainable form of travel apart from cycling or walking.

If you are a wildlife lover, there are animal-friendly pledges. On the **World Animal Protection** website (www.worldanimalprotection. org.au), you can pledge to make animal-friendly choices including shunning elephant rides and not taking animal selfies. The **Gorilla Friendly Pledge** (www.gorillafriendly.org) is an initiative of the International Gorilla Conservation Programme to raise awareness among tourists who travel to see the mountain gorillas of Uganda and Rwanda.

If you are a scuba diver, this one's a no-brainer. The Professional Association of Diving Instructors (PADI) wants you to be an Ocean Torchbearer and sign the **Save the Ocean Pledge** (www.padi.com/conservation/save-the-ocean-pledge). With this global pledge, you'll be promising to protect sharks, clean up ocean plastics, and free entangled animals as well as undertaking actions that help leave ecosystems in better shape than you find them.

Choosing a Sustainable Travel Provider

You're committed to being a sustainable traveler, but don't want to plan everything yourself. Perhaps you want to leave the itinerary in the hands of a travel agent, or you want to book all or some elements of your trip with a tour company. There are definitely benefits to doing this, particularly if you want advice on where to go or the trip is likely to be logistically complicated. A good agent or tour operator will not only offer helpful suggestions on places that suit your interests but also do the hard work for you, keeping on top of changes to bookings.

But how do you know if they share the same commitment to sustainable travel as you do? "Sustainability" is the word on everyone's lips in a post-pandemic world, so how do you know which operators' claims are really true?

REMEMBER

When dealing with a travel agent to make your bookings, it is perfectly acceptable for you, as their client, to request that they only book you into attractions or tours that have a stated commitment to responsible travel. If they are reluctant, or do not understand what you mean by that, it might be a good idea to take your business to one who does.

If you are booking directly with a tour operator, look for companies which are transparent about their commitment to the "quadruple bottom line" of sustainability — climate action and environmental, economic, and social sustainability — and which have clear sustainability statements (including emissions reductions targets and strategies) and/or codes of conduct on their websites.

This means they are actively taking measures within their own businesses — both in their head offices and in the field — to measure (as far as possible) and minimize their carbon emissions and offset any residual emissions.

The United Nationals World Tourism Organisation's **Glasgow Declaration on Climate Action in Tourism** (www.unwto.org/the-glasgow-declaration-on-climate-action-in-tourism), which asks signatories to commit to halving emissions by 2030 and reaching Net Zero before 2050, has been signed by more than 450 organizations (at the time of writing). Ask your tour operator if they have signed! Another website to check up on which travel companies have committed to reaching net zero by 2050 is **Tourism Declares a Climate Emergency** (www.tourismdeclares.com/who-has-declared).

You can also use a travel aggregator such as **Responsible Travel** (www.responsibletravel.com), which bases its business model on only listing trips that meet its strict responsible travel criteria. That means you can be sure it's not sending you to a place that deals in unethical animal experiences, such as elephant rides, or to orphanage tourism, for example. And its website has clear information about its philosophy, history, and actions to promote sustainable tourism. Another example is UK-based **Byway** (www.byway.travel), a flight-free travel company that creates bespoke holidays based on your interests. Each itinerary will include several stops, with inclusions that fit your style of travel. **Book Different** (www.bookdifferent.com) is another travel booking platform that lists sustainability options for destinations, hotels, transport, and meals.

What to ask your travel provider

As well as a commitment to climate action, sustainable travel goes hand in hand with ethical travel. So it's not just about being green, but about being a thoughtful, responsible traveler who considers the people and environment you may be impacting. And, of course, you want the travel providers you work with to be in tune with those values too.

Again, it's about transparency. Any tour operator that's serious about operating ethically will spell out the measures it is taking on its website in a Responsible Travel or Sustainability policy. Don't be taken in by vague but worthy-sounding statements like, "We care about the planet." If they care, what are they doing about it?

Ask for details on how a tour company works with local communities in the places they will take you to. Do they employ local guides and contribute to the community in other ways? What is their approach to environmental conservation? Don't be afraid to ask questions like these:

>> **Does the company have an animal welfare policy?** If you can ride, touch, feed, or take a selfie with a wild animal, or see it perform tricks, stay away (read more in Chapter 6). **World Animal Protection** (www.worldanimalprotection. org) has information to help you assess if wildlife sanctuaries or animal experiences are ethically run.

>> **Does the tour operator ensure that money spent stays in the local community?** Are the owners of the tour company part of the local community, or do they employ local workers to ensure the money you pay benefits the whole community? Is your accommodation owned by locals, rather than investors who are based elsewhere? Ethical tour operators often support not-for-profit foundations that help them give back to the communities they visit.

>> **How big is the tour group?** Small group tours, of around ten people, are able travel more responsibly and have less impact and a greater connection to people and places they visit.

>> **Are the workers looked after well?** It's important to ensure that people who are helping you — for example, trekking porters or local tour guides, are properly paid, trained, equipped, and supported.

>> **Is the company taking positive action to reduce plastic waste?** Do they offer filtered water to guests so they can refill their own reusable bottles? Do they take part in any cleanups as part of their tours?

>> **What are their policies around waste, water, and other resources?** How do they minimize and dispose of waste, do they recycle water or use grey water where possible?

>> **Do they have an environmental impact policy?** Are travelers required to abide by rules to ensure the environment is left in the same — or better — condition as before they arrived?

>> **What is their policy around respect for First Nations and other cultures, cultural interaction, and preservation?** Do their tours demonstrate their respect and understanding of the culture you are learning about? Do they employ indigenous or local guides?

>> **Does the trip cost include carbon offsets?** While this is still unusual, some companies are moving to include offsets as part of the price of your travel. Global adventure tour companies Intrepid Travel (www.intrepidtravel.com) and World Expeditions (www.worldexpeditions.com) are two that already do this.

Sustainable travel insurance

It can't be said too often: If you can't afford insurance, you can't afford to travel. Insurance is always your best investment in protecting yourself when the worst happens. And that applies even when traveling lightly. But are all travel insurance providers going to meet your standards of sustainability — and how can you tell? A few simple questions will give you the answers.

Ask your insurance company if they donate to or work with any environmental or socially responsible organizations. Do they practice sustainable travel within their own company? Do they offer digital "paperwork" to help reduce paper use and save trees?

TIP

World Nomads (www.worldnomads.com) is one travel company that sells insurance coverage to its clients — and gives them the chance to give back, not to the company, but to one of the many community development projects that World Nomads supports. When you buy travel insurance, you can add on a micro-donation to the price of your policy — typically only $2 or $3 — which is collected and passed on to these projects through World Nomads' **Footprints** program. So far, around one million travelers have donated, to raise more than $3 million. World Nomads absorbs the administration costs, so 100 percent of the donations goes to the projects.

Checking sustainability credentials

Among the hundreds of certifications, awards, badges, and other ticks of approval for travel companies that are doing the right thing for the planet, how do you know which ones are legitimate — or at least worth taking notice of? Each country has its own certifications — sometimes more than one — so it can be confusing.

However, there are a few key places to start when you want to check how well your chosen travel provider stacks up in the sustainability stakes. First, you can check if they're certified by the **Global Sustainable Tourism Council** (www.gstcouncil.org/for-travelers), which sets the global standard for accreditations.

The other highly reputable certification is **B Corp** (www.bcorporation.net). Companies with this certification are global leaders in the move towards positive impacts on all stakeholders in their company — workers, communities, customers and the planet. Certification measures their entire social and environmental impact and scores them out of 200 (80-plus is the benchmark for certification). **Intrepid Travel** (www.intrepidtravel.com) is the travel industry's largest global B Corporation.

Several large travel aggregators are also labeling the products they sell with badges indicating a level of green-ness. Booking.com has verified travel sustainable badges on accommodations while **Google Flights** (www.google.com/travel/flights) and **Skyscanner** (www.skyscanner.com) have similar eco-certified labels. Look for similar logos wherever you are booking.

It's important to remember that high level certification is a complicated and often costly process for companies to undertake. This often hinders small travel companies or accommodations from gaining them, but does not necessarily mean they are not following sustainable practices or "doing the right thing" by working on reducing emissions and offsetting any that can't be eliminated. That's where your own research, questions, and instinct come in.

How to sniff out greenwashing

You've heard about whitewashing, right? But do you know about *greenwashing*? It's a term coined in the 1980s by New York ecologist Jay Westerveld, that refers to marketing-speak — or spin, if you prefer — to give the false impression of what is now called sustainability. Westerveld used the example of hotels who disguised a cost-cutting measure — the reuse of towels — as a way of helping save the environment. More widely, it has come to mean the practice of spending time and money marketing a company as environmentally friendly, rather than actually taking steps to becoming so. It's misleading and deceptive.

So how do we spot it? Usually, it's around language that doesn't mean too much, like "eco-friendly" or an inability to back up claims. Perhaps it's a hotel that touts its farm-to-table menu but still provides bottled water on the bedside table. Inconsistency around sustainable policies and an inability to back up claims with details are warning signs.

Not all greenwashing is intentional. Some companies just don't fully understand that they are doing it; what they do understand is that travelers are looking for sustainable options and for companies that fit the ethos.

Well-informed travelers have the ability to help change, influence, and educate travel companies about changing expectations around sustainable travel. Use that influence by using online platforms to share your views or write directly to companies that need to be aware that their policies aren't hitting the mark.

Traveling Sustainably as a Family

Planning a family holiday that's sustainable is not as hard as you might imagine. One of the key elements of sustainable travel is slowing down, and as any parent knows, small children are very good at taking their time. Staying for longer in one place is something the whole family will appreciate — and may be something you already do, as it is undeniably an easier way to travel as a family. This helps reduce your family's carbon footprint without even changing the way you travel (you may already be a family that travels sustainably, without being conscious of it).

Look for a travel agent or tour company that hangs its hat on sustainable travel for families. One that does is **Global Family Travels** (www.globalfamilytravels.com), based in Seattle.

Budget tips for sustainable travel

Being a sustainable traveler doesn't need to bust your budget. While some sustainable choices can be expensive, in many ways traveling lightly in itself is a way to keep your travel costs down. When you're a family, that's even more important if you're to stretch the budget.

Try these tips for saving money while still enjoying everything you can on your trip:

- **Avoid flying.** Not only is it cheaper, especially for a family group, but it's easier on the planet.

- **Take a reusable water bottle, a water filter, and water purification tablets.** Buying bottled water can be ridiculously expensive in some places; impossible to find in others.

- **Eat and drink locally.** Stay clear of fast-food joints and head to the local markets. It's healthier, cheaper, and a new experience — try that weird-looking fruit!

- **Go camping!** You'll still have to get to your destination — probably by driving — but once you have pitched your tent and rolled out your sleeping bags, your carbon footprint will be much less than that of anyone staying between four walls. And the cost of your accommodation will be negligible.

- **Book your train travel ahead of time.** The closer the time comes, the more expensive the tickets can be.

- **Rent bikes.** The kids will have fun and it's good for your health.

- **Stay longer in each place.** There are often savings on accommodation for longer stays and you save on transport costs by not moving around.

- **Stay in hostels where you can share a room.** The kids will like the bunk beds and the costs will be considerably cheaper than a hotel or motel.

- **Try house-sitting.** Some people will also need a pet-sitter, which could be fun if you don't have one of your own.

Teaching children the benefits of sustainable travel

Children are like sponges, soaking up information with their ever-growing brains. So grab the chance while they are young and start instilling the principles of treading lightly as soon as you can. Good habits are as hard to break as bad ones, so starting early is likely to establish a lifetime commitment to looking after the planet.

If camping isn't your thing, look for places where you can combine holiday fun with some lessons in conservation or sustainability designed for young ones. Plenty of eco-resorts run nature-based programs for children that teach them about the natural world as well as how to conserve and protect it.

And if your commitment to educating your children on this topic early is really strong — and you are up for a long-term adventure — consider enrolling them at a **Green School** (www.greenschool.org). This innovative school system is designed to teach sustainability as part of a holistic education model founded by entrepreneurs John and Cynthia Hardy in Bali, Indonesia, in 2008. Now there are schools in South Africa and New Zealand, with another opening in Mexico in 2026.

Green School Bali is the location for the short-term Green Camp (www.greencampbali.com) which runs three- and five-day family camps that focus on the environment, using Bali's beaches and jungles as the backdrop. Activities include kite-making, organic gardening, and bamboo raft building (and the chance to try them out) as well as learning about Balinese culture. Leave your phones behind.

REMEMBER

The most important thing you can do for your children is to lead by example. If they grow up traveling sustainably with you, it will be second-nature to them. Practicing sustainability at home and while on the road will be something they take for granted, a natural part of their lives.

Chapter **3**

Getting There and Around Sustainably

How you get to your chosen destination may well depend on where you are going. Stay close to home, and the options are fairly simple. Travel any distance — whether at home or abroad — and you will need to consider the impact that your travel has. Will you fly or take longer and travel by train? Is a long road trip going to be more sustainable than other means of transport (with the benefit of having wheels when you get there)? With thought and planning, the most sustainable options will be clear.

Solo and independent travelers, or those with unlimited time, will have easier decisions to make. Families may be constrained by the number of people traveling and the length of time available.

On arrival in your destination, look for the best way to get around and still tread lightly. Walking tours, or just walking on your own, are the best choice but are not always feasible because of distance. Hire a bike, take an organized tour, or take public transport — these are all going to help keep your carbon emissions low.

Feeling a little lost? This chapter helps you figure out how to make the best and most sustainable transportation choices for your travels, whether it's figuring out how to get to your destination or getting around once you're there.

Go to www.dummies.com/go/sustainabletravelfd for a handy list of links to the web addresses mentioned in this chapter, as well as other helpful resources.

FIND ONLINE

Discovering the Joys of Slow Travel

Slow travel isn't only about the pace you set. In many ways, it's about the mindset you approach travel with. Of course, it can be about a lack of speed or the length of your trip — stretching it out as you choose slower and more sustainable methods of travel — but it's also about rethinking your style of travel so it becomes more meaningful and thoughtful.

Slow travel is about connection. It's about taking time to delve deeper into a destination and seeking experiences that truly allow you to gain an insight into the place, its people, wildlife, landscape, and history. It's about spurning the idea of ten-countries-in twelve-days whistlestop tours to tick off famous attractions and instead staying put in one place and getting to know it well.

While slow travel isn't a new concept, its appeal has grown with a new awareness of the impact of travel since the pandemic. Lockdowns, restricted movement, and social distancing highlighted the importance of connection and raised questions around how we travel and how we can explore the world closer to home. New trends emerged as travelers sought to avoid crowds. The effect of less travel — particularly by air and sea — on the environment was demonstrated clearly, and thoughtful travelers began to reassess their transport choices in order to reduce their carbon emissions.

I first came to experience the joy of slow travel on a yacht owned by friends, sailing a section of the northeast coast of Australia some years ago. I had wondered if I would be bored but it was quite the opposite. Instead, nature wove its magic, and I became enthralled with everything around me — the sea, the sky, the wildlife that occasionally popped up from the water, the sunsets, the birdcalls. Life seemed to slow down, to take on a different rhythm on the sea, as in Figure 3-1. At times like this, time stretches, the noise and clutter of the everyday falls away and mind and soul restore themselves. Everyone sometimes needs this.

FIGURE 3-1: Life at sea slows down.

As contemporary life, especially city life, seems to become ever-busier, taking the path of slow travel can provide a reset that's often much needed. Embracing slow travel will help you engage with the world around you, with the added benefit of keeping your carbon footprint low.

REMEMBER

While time constraints might seem an obstacle to taking the slow road, you really don't need to travel for weeks or months to experience slow travel; it's all about the way you travel. A few days, spent in the right place, with the right mindset, can be as restorative as a longer holiday. Throw away the idea of planning an itinerary jammed with must-see or must-do items to tick off your list and idle away some time in the backstreets of a village where the locals outnumber the tourists. Make space in your plans for the spontaneous or serendipitous. Be open to adventures you hadn't planned on.

The result of embracing slow travel may well be that you create a shift in your whole life, adopting some or all of the philosophy of slow travel as part of everyday living on your return home. And that can't be a bad thing.

Choosing Sustainability by Land, Air, or Sea

Staying close to home is the most sustainable travel choice you can make, but there are times when we do need to travel long distances — sometimes across the world — and yet we still want to minimize our carbon emissions. Your mode of transport will depend on where you're going, the time you have available, and your commitment to traveling sustainably. If you have unlimited time and are as free as a bird, you can take long overland journeys, but for most travelers that's not an option, however wonderful the idea might be.

Whether to fly to your destination, take a leisurely cruise to see unfamiliar parts of the world — or to reach a destination — or to board a train for similar reasons, is a decision that will take all these factors into consideration. Of these options, rail is the most sustainable form of travel — and to my mind, the most enjoyable — and is much more carbon-efficient for short journeys.

In the following sections, I set out some of the factors that you can consider for sustainable options when planning your travels.

Flying as sustainably as you can

If flying is the best (or only) option for your travel plans, you can still take steps to make your trip as sustainable as possible. The first is to choose your airline carefully; if there are several airlines flying to your destination, check out their eco-credentials before booking.

Newer planes are likely to have lower emissions than older ones. Check out the aircraft you'll be flying on and do some research into which airlines are using biofuels (produced from seaweed, vegetable oils, trees, or organic waste) or upgrading their fleet. Newer planes such as the Dreamliner 787, the A350 XWB, and the A321Neo produce around 25 percent lower emissions than older aircraft. They burn less fuel and have aerodynamically designed wings that cut drag and fuel consumption. These planes are used by many airlines, including Cathay Pacific, Malaysian Airlines, Hawaiian Airlines, Qantas, United Airlines, Air New Zealand, American Airlines, Etihad, Singapore Airlines, and more. Airlines are also using advanced navigation systems to map fuel-efficient flight paths based on weather data. Flight comparison site Sky-scanner (www.skyscanner.net) lists carbon-efficient fares by aircraft type, seat capacity, and number of stops. Take a nonstop flight if you can; landing and takeoff create extra emissions.

Now for the bad news. While it might be much more comfortable for those long-haul flights, flying business or first class is much worse for your carbon footprint than flying economy class. Why? Simply because a seat in business or first class takes up more room, reducing the number of passengers who can fly (and more of them are usually empty). According to some studies, business class emissions are between 2.5 and 4.3 times great than those for economy.

The best thing that you can do if you choose to fly is to always offset your carbon emissions. This means paying a small amount — sometimes only a few dollars — in addition to your fare to contribute to certified programs that counteract, or offset, the emissions you've created. Every airline now offers this option when you are booking your seat (see more on this later in this section).

Do your bit to reduce onboard waste by taking your own reusable water bottle, coffee cup, and cutlery. Use them at the airport, too, and avoid buying food that comes in plastic packaging.

Cruising the ocean

The cruise industry is huge — and growing in popularity all the time, as travelers love the idea of taking a slow boat to some beautiful parts of the world and not having to unpack and repack every time they get to a new port.

Sadly, most large cruise ships are just about the least sustainable choice you can make for a holiday.

The **Cruise Lines International Association** has set a target of achieving net-zero carbon cruising by 2050 — but that's a long time away and you need to consider how to cruise sustainably *now*. A 2022 study published in Science Direct's Marine Pollution Bulletin (www.sciencedirect.com) said large ships produced three times more greenhouse emissions than long-haul planes, and a large ship could have a greater carbon footprint than 12,000 cars. **Friends of the Earth** publishes an annual Cruise Ship

Report Card (www.foe.org/cruise-report-card) that ranks 18 major cruise lines and 213 ships according to their environmental impact (sewage treatment, air pollution, water quality, and transparency). Take a look at it before you book your cruise.

Of course, it's still possible to have a vacation at sea without boarding a massive cruise ship. Think small: Look for small ships, expedition cruises, or yachting charters. Look for small cruise companies that follow traditional seafaring methods, usually under sail. You should still do your due diligence with these companies but they are much more likely to be following sustainable practices. Expedition cruise ships typically carry far fewer passengers — anywhere from 50 to 200 — and are focused on exploring the environment in which you are sailing, rather than on their onboard entertainment. They also usually have a marine biologist, historian, or other relevant experts on board to provide the context of what you are seeing and provide shore excursions, such as the one I capture in Figure 3-2.

Lee Mylne

FIGURE 3-2: Going ashore in Zodiac boats on an expedition cruise.

Look for a cruise company that has a stated commitment to sustainability and where environmental education about what you are seeing around you is part of the program and the ethos. One example is **Aurora Expeditions** (www.auroraexpeditions.com.au), founded by explorer Greg Mortimer, which runs expeditions to Antarctica and the Arctic. Aurora is one of 100 members of the **International Association of Antarctica Tour Operators** (IAATO), committed to safe and responsible travel to one of the planet's most fragile and threatened environments. Travelers with Aurora can also act as citizen scientists, collecting data on whales, seabirds, weather patterns, microplastics, and more.

Another expedition cruise company that's leading the way is **Lindblad Expeditions** (www.expeditions.com), which became 100 percent carbon-neutral in 2019 by offsetting emissions that can't yet be eliminated. Lindblad partners with National Geographic, with its experts joining some expeditions to share their knowledge and research in the fields of oceanography and wildlife biology with passengers.

While innovative ship building is already underway to address emission concerns, it will be some years before this is the norm. **PONANT** (www.ponant.com) is one cruise operator that's ahead of the game, with an expedition sailing yacht, a switch from fuel oil to low sulphur marine gas oil across its fleet of 13 ships to reduce sulphur dioxide air pollution, and the launch in 2021 of a hybrid-electric ship powered by liquified natural gas.

REMEMBER

As part of your trip planning, also look at the ports that your cruise ship may be stopping at. Many of the popular destinations are suffering from over-tourism, in large part because of the influx of cruise passengers on shore excursions. Venice and Dubrovnik are two that spring to mind.

If you're feeling really intrepid, and have plenty of time, consider getting to your overseas destination by cargo ship or freighter. Some ships have limited numbers of cabins for usually four to twelve passengers. It won't be the most luxurious cruise you've ever made — but I guarantee it will be memorable! My experience of this was four days aboard a supply ship from Mangareva in the Gambier Islands, 1,000 miles southeast of Tahiti in French Polynesia, to Pitcairn Island, one of the most remote places in the world, in the South Pacific. Pitcairn has no airport, so ship is the only way to get there, and apart from a few cruise ships that anchor offshore from time to time, the regular way of getting there (and staying for more than a day) is on the supply ship. It was one of the most interesting trips I have ever made, with long conversations with a well-traveled and interesting crew and a few other passengers.

TIP

Pack seasick pills. Your ship may be in the high seas and rough weather can be an issue. With luck, anti-motion-sickness pills will help stave off the dreaded *mal de mer.*

Cargo ship travel can be booked through specialist companies and can be expensive (depending on your destination). And it is a sustainable option; the ship will sail whether you are on it or not, so your carbon footprint is negligible. But be prepared to be flexible as departure days are not set in stone. Some companies that facilitate these journeys are Cargo Ship Voyages (www.cargoshipvoyages.com), SlowTravel (www.langsamreisen.de/en/freightertravel), and Freighter Trips (www.freightertrips.com). Be prepared to potentially share a cabin, eat simple but hearty meals with the crew, and have almost no entertainment — apart from books, movies, and conversation.

WARNING

If you opt for freighter or cargo ship travel, check that your travel insurance will cover you.

Riding the sustainability train

The romance of riding the rails has never gone out of fashion, thankfully, and I've long been a fan of this form of slow travel. So when you are looking for sustainable options to travel, look no further than trains. Every budget is catered for, the frequency is usually excellent, and a long-distance rail journey is an adventure in itself.

TIP

The International Railways Union's calculator (www.ecopassenger.org) enables you to see the difference train travel will make, comparing the emissions made by train, car, and plane travel.

Unlike overnight flights or tedious night coaches, a railway journey allows you to stretch your legs whenever you feel like it, even if you are only in a seat all night. Train stations are always in the center of a city, and you can turn up around 30 minutes before the whistle blows for your departure. And your luggage won't be weighed!

REMEMBER

Book international and long-distance train and boat journeys well in advance. Long-distance train tickets will likely be cheaper if you book ahead but have less flexibility if you want to change your plans.

Book an overnight train if you can; it will save you the cost of a hotel room at the same time as it whisks you to your destination. Overnight trains usually arrive at their final destination early in the morning, giving you a full day of exploring on day one! If you have limited vacation time, this is a bonus. On sleeper services, you can typically choose from a lie-back chair (the cheapest option), a couchette — where your seat folds out into a dorm-style bed — or a private cabin with a bathroom. Many long-distance trains offer a high level of luxury, making the journey as memorable for the accommodations as for the scenery beyond the windows, and almost all have Wi-Fi.

TIP

The Man in Seat Sixty-One (www.seat61.com) is a terrific website for anyone looking for rail travel options anywhere in the world. It has basic how-to information.

The following sections cover what you should know about rail travel in various locations across the globe.

Europe

Europe is a leader in rail travel, with trains becoming more efficient, affordable, and accessible all the time. France is ahead of the game in the sustainability stakes, banning short-haul air travel for distances that can be covered by train or bus in two-and-a-half hours or less, such as between between Paris-Orly and Bordeaux, Nantes, and Lyon, in an effort to reduce carbon emissions.

Whether you book a sit-up-all-night seat, a couchette bunk bed in a cabin with others, or book a private space for you and your companion(s), there are many choices to travel Europe by train. **Rail Europe** (www.raileurope.com) is a one-stop shop for information and bookings across the continent, for all budgets, as is **Eurail** (www.eurail.com), which offers rail passes to 30,000 destinations in 33 countries.

TIP

Make sure you book ahead. In Europe, make your booking at least two months before you plan to travel. Remember that winter (November to January) are busy months.

When I think of luxury rail travel in Europe, I'm back in the world of Agatha Christie on the **Venice Simplon Orient Express** (www.belmond.com/trains/europe/venice-simplon-orient-express), the epitome of glamor and style. Leave London's

Victoria Station aboard the luxury British Pullman train, cross the English Channel on the Eurostar, before joining the Orient Express in Paris for the overnight journey to Venice. Of course, there are many other less expensive ways to experience rail travel in France, but few so elegant.

Night train options in Europe are extensive, from **Intercites de Nuit** (www.sncf.com/en) in France to Sweden's **Snalltaget** (www.snalltaget.se/en) or EuroNight's **Kalman Imre** (www.eurail.com) from Munich to Budapest. Nightjet's network (www.nightjet.com/en) covers a large expanse of Europe, from Brussels to Vienna, Florence, Rome, and Zurich — and places in between. The trans-alpine Nightjet from Budapest to Zurich passes through five countries, including tiny Liechtenstein, in 11 hours and 40 minutes.

TIP

If you're a solo female traveler, look for trains that provide compartments close to the conductor, reserved for women traveling alone or with young children. One that does is the French SNCF night trains; look for the **Espace Dame Seule** (solo female space).

The **SJ EuroNight** (www.sj.se/en) from Berlin to Stockholm is a really sustainable choice — this Swedish sleeper train is fueled by 100 percent renewable energy. It travels from Berlin to Stockholm via Hamburg and Copenhagen.

Don't forget Italy and Spain! The **night train from Milan** in the north of Italy to the south includes a ferry crossing to Sicily — in your train carriage — before you arrive in Palermo (www.trenitalia.com). The whole trip takes around 20 hours — but make sure you take provisions as there is no bar or restaurant carriage (you can restock at the ferry café if necessary). For a slow exploration of Spain by train, board **Al Andalus** to journey from Seville to Granada and back over six nights.

In northern Europe, families will love Finland's **Santa Claus Express** (www.vr.fi/en/santa-claus-express), a 12-hour night journey that runs year-round from the capital, Helsinki, to Rovaniemi in Finnish Lapland. The trip offers the chance to see the midnight sun or the northern lights (depending on the season) and to visit the home of Santa Claus in Rovaniemi (it's everything you would expect!). Cabins on the lower deck share bathrooms but are a good choice for families as adjoining rooms can be linked. The cheapest ticket is a seat only, and there's a restaurant carriage for drinks and snacks. This, too, is a great sustainable choice, as almost all VR trains run on hydro-electric power.

If you've always dreamed of traveling on the Trans-Siberian Railway, you may have to put that dream on hold. At the time of writing, all international trains to and from Moscow and Russia were suspended because of the war between Russia and Ukraine.

United Kingdom

You can travel almost anywhere in the UK by train — and it's so easy! Nothing is too far from the next place, but there are two long-distance trains worth considering if you're after more than getting from one place to another. The **Night Riviera Sleeper** (www.gwr.com) links London with Penzance in Cornwall. The train leaves London just before midnight, taking around eight hours to reach Penzance. The return train leaves earlier in the evening and gets into Paddington Station around 5 a.m. (but there's no rush to leave and you can have breakfast on the train after you arrive).

The **Caledonian Sleeper** (www.sleeper.scot) from London to Scotland has the unusual luxury of double beds — and it's also pet-friendly! It's expensive, but worth it for those two points alone for many people. The journey takes nearly 12 hours. There are several routes: the Lowland Sleeper travels to Edinburgh and Glasgow, and the Highland Sleeper to Aberdeen, Inverness, and Fort William.

USA

Amtrak trains (www.amtrak.com) criss-cross the continent to more than 500 destinations, so wherever you want to go, there's sure to be a rail route that will get you there. Amtrak also has 15 long-distance sleeper trains, but there is no complete trans-continental service. To achieve that, you'll have to plan a stop in Chicago or New Orleans. One of the most popular long-distance routes is the **California Zephyr**, which travels through the Rocky Mountains on its way from California to Chicago.

For a touch of luxury, **Rocky Mountaineer** (www.rockymountaineer.com) offers a three-night journey between Moab, Utah, and Denver, Colorado, through desert, rocky canyons, and mountain ranges.

TIP

Sign up for emails from Amtrak when sales are announced. Consider buying a United States or California rail pass to save money on your fares.

Canada

Long-distance trains in Canada are run by **VIA Rail** (www. viarail.ca), including **The Canadian** from Toronto to Winnipeg, Edmonton, Jasper, and Vancouver. With good planning, you can also hop off along the way at various places and jump on a train to somewhere else.

A trip on the **Royal Canadian Pacific** (www.royalcanadianpacific. com) from Calgary to Vancouver is aboard beautifully restored vintage carriages, with all the amenities of a luxury hotel. Three- or four-night tours pass through some of Canada's most jaw-dropping scenery — you'll be glued to your window. Then there's the fine dining, off-train excursions, and more. Expensive? Oh yes.

If the idea of rockin' and rollin' through the night doesn't appeal, the **Rocky Mountaineer** (www.rockymountaineer.com) from Vancouver to Jasper or Banff stops each night so you can sleep in a bed that doesn't move. A wonderful feature of this train is the glass-domed carriages, which allow forward views of the train and tracks and the huge windows next to your seat.

Australia

Australia has several long distance and trans-continental rail journeys. The longest is the 70-hour, 2,704-mile luxury **Indian Pacific** which travels between Sydney on the east coast and Perth on the west, crossing the deserts of the Nullarbor Plain. Equally epic is **The Ghan** which traverses the continent between Adelaide in the south and Darwin in the north. Pronounced "*gan*" and named after pioneering Afghan cameleers, it cuts through the vast Red Centre. Both these trains are run by Great Southern Rail (www. gsr.com.au) and offer similar five-star adventures, with plenty of stops at highlights along their routes. Another sister journey is **The Great Southern**, which runs in the southern hemisphere summer (December to February) between Adelaide and Brisbane, a three-day northbound trip or a four-day southbound — although strictly speaking it's a meandering route through the south-east corner of the continent, with plenty of off-train experiences.

In Queensland, the **Spirit of the Outback** journey runs between Brisbane and the outback town of Longreach, over 820 miles and 26 hours. Run by the state-owned Queensland Rail (www.queenslandrailtravel.com.au), this is a less luxurious trip, which can be made in a reclining seat if your budget doesn't stretch to a sleeper. Queensland has a number of other long-distance trains, including one from the capital, Brisbane to Cairns, the gateway to the Great Barrier Reef.

New Zealand

There are three long-distance train journeys in New Zealand (www.railnewzealand.com), all of them daytime services. The 11-hour **Northern Explorer** links the major North Island cities of Auckland and Wellington, and the **Coastal Pacific** train runs between Picton at the top of the South Island and Christchurch, taking six hours. The most spectacular, though, is the **TranzAlpine** five-hour journey from Christchurch on the east coast of the South Island to Greymouth on the west coast, which will afford you a view of the mountains of Aoraki/Mt Cook National Park, with stops along the way.

South Africa

Africa's most famous long-distance train is the **Blue Train** (www.bluetrain.co.za), which runs between Pretoria and Cape Town in South Africa across 900 miles of changing countryside over 48 hours. It's very posh; gentlemen are required to wear a jacket for dinner, and there is butler service. A twice-yearly special route travels to Kruger National Park, where guests stay in lodges and go on safaris. **Rovos Rail** (www.rovos.com) offers a range of luxury and bespoke journeys across the south of the continent, including the 3,600-mile fourteen-day trip from Cape Town in South Africa to Dar es Salaam in Tanzania.

There are other, much more affordable long-distance trains in Africa, too, but the pandemic played havoc with services and many were not running at the time of writing. For updates, check www.seat61.com.

Asia

Japan is famous for its *shinkansen* (bullet train), but rail travel here isn't all about speed. While the train may get you there in good time, the ability to sit back, relax, and watch the countryside goes by is the real joy. Buy a **Japan Rail Pass** (www.jrailpass. com) for convenience and likely the best deal, as train fares in Japan are expensive. However, it sometimes pays to make the comparison with normal tickets, just to be sure, if you're only going to make one or two trips. The pass can't be used on some of the bullet trains, but it's good for others and for the Narita Express between Tokyo and Narita airport. It will also allow you to travel on one of Japan's newest sightseeing trains, the **Two Stars 4047** (www.jrkyushu.co.jp/english), which runs in a loop connecting Takeo-onsen and Nagasaki on the island of Kyushu and is designed in Japanese style with lattice windows and sofa seating.

If it's luxury on rails you're seeking in Japan, take the **Seven Stars in Kyushu,** a sleeper service from Hakata to Miyazaki and back, on Kyushu (www.visit-kyushu.com/en/spots/seven-stars-kyushu). Book well ahead, as it is very popular and has only twelve sleeper cabins. The three-night journey travels through seven prefectures and includes one night at a ryokan (traditional inn).

Run by the same company as the Venice Simplon-Orient-Express, the **Eastern & Oriental Express** (www.belmond.com/trains/asia/eastern-and-oriental-express/) from Singapore to Kuala Lumpur, Langkawi, and Penang is just as luxurious and features an open-sided observation carriage from which to gaze out on the rice paddies as you go by. Off-train excursions have a sustainable theme, with visits to traditional villages and a look at the work of conservationists protecting the critically endangered Malayan tiger.

In Thailand, you can travel from Bangkok to Chiang Mai in comfort aboard the prosaically named **Train No. 9** (www.railway.co.th). The train leaves every evening around 6pm from Bangkok's Krung Thep Aphiwat Central Terminal (also known as Bang Sue Grand Station) and takes around 12 hours to reach Chiang Mai. First class is a private sleeper cabin with washbasin and television; second class separates your bunk from the rest with a curtain. Toilets for both classes are shared with other passengers. If you prefer to watch the world go by, **Train No. 7** follows the same route, leaving at 9am. Both trains are very popular, so book as far ahead as you can. Thailand has five major rail lines, making most parts of the country accessible by train.

Indian trains are a real experience. While there are luxury sleeper trains such as the **Maharaja's Express** (www.maharajaexpress.co.uk) from Mumbai to Delhi, traveling by train on a budget will bring you face-to-face with Indians traversing their country by the only means many have. India has a huge rail network (www.indianrail.gov.in) and you can take a train between almost any two places you want to go. Delays are almost certain to happen, causing confusion and distress (take it from me), but your train journey will most certainly be memorable. Fares are cheap, so book a first- or second-class ticket, which means your bedding will be provided for your berth; "sleeper class" (which I once braved) is in open-plan carriages, with no bedding provided (and no air-conditioning). Either way, you'll wake in the morning to the chai-wallah calling his wares.

Sustainable Road-Tripping

Road-tripping may be a more carbon-friendly option than flying, but there's no doubt that by jumping in a car you are still creating emissions. If you're renting a car, the best way to reduce those emissions is to hire an electric vehicle (EV) or a hybrid model. Most major rental companies now offer both options.

Not only are you helping save the planet, but a fuel-efficient car is also a cheaper choice in the long run. Charging costs will be only a fraction of the cost of gas.

WARNING

If you're going to be driving in a foreign country, make sure you find out which countries drive on the right-hand side and which drive on the left. Laws vary, with many countries driving on the left, including the UK, Ireland, Japan, Indonesia, Singapore, Malaysia, Thailand, Australia, and New Zealand.

Electric cars are powered by an electric engine and a battery. But you need to consider how easy it will be to charge the battery while you're on the road, especially if you have time constraints or are going to be traveling long distances. Most electric cars have a range of no more than 340 miles (550km), sometimes less. You'll also need to factor in the time you need to stop to charge the car; some charging stations are fairly quick (10 to 15 minutes, while you stretch your legs and have a snack) but others can take longer.

You'll also need to download an app (if you don't normally drive an EV) to manage the charging.

Having a car is a great way to set your own pace and give you maximum flexibility on your holiday. If you are traveling overseas, find out if you need an International Driving Permit (IDP) in addition to your own country's license. In some countries, your own driver's license will be enough to rent a car with, but others will require an IDP, which is a United Nations–sanctioned translation of your license in nine different languages. An IDP is valid for a year. If you stay in Europe longer than that, you may need a local license. Some countries require that you get a local translation of your license sooner than that.

TIP

Foreigners are not permitted to hire cars in China or Vietnam, as a local license is required to drive. And given the chaos on the roads in both places, that's something you'll be thankful for! Using public transport or hiring a car with a driver is a good option in these countries.

Public Transport Is Your Friend

Whether you've reached your destination by plane, train, ship, or car, public transport is your sustainable option for getting around. Even if you've driven, park the car and walk or get around the way the locals do. Look for areas that are pedestrian-friendly or where there are bike-share schemes — or jump on the local tram, bus, or train to do your sightseeing. By using public transport instead of hiring a car, you are saving on emissions.

Start as soon as you arrive — take public transport from the airport or train station to your hotel. This is likely to be much cheaper than taxi or ride-share fares, as will airport shuttle services that will take you right to the hotel door or very close by. Sometimes it's even preferable to take a train part of the way and do a shorter hop with your bags by taxi for the final part of the journey. If you can, depending on how much luggage you have, walk from the bus or train station to the hotel (for tips on packing light, see Chapter 4).

Public transport is one of the best ways of getting to know a new city. Instead of navigating unfamiliar streets, with all the stress of potentially getting lost — whether in a car or on foot — sit back on any form of public transport and watch the world go by. Make sure you know which stop you want to get off at or ask the driver or another passenger if in doubt.

TIP

Buses and trams are a cheap way to see the sights. Find out which routes offer the best sightseeing options, as many of them pass major landmarks.

So many cities have great public transport networks, it's easy to choose one — and even smaller places have some form of local bus service (this could be the highlight of your visit). In 2023, *Time Out* magazine surveyed more than 20,000 people living in 50 cities around the world to find out how they rated their public transport. These cities were the top ten:

>> **Amsterdam** has a great network of trains, trams, ferries, and buses. Buy an I Amsterdam City Card for unlimited use of public transport and free entrance to 38 museums and attractions over 24, 48, or 72 hours.

>> **Berlin,** for its comfortable, safe, and punctual U-Bahn, S-Bahn, buses, and trams. The U-Bahn (underground) is simple to navigate and efficient. Buy a day ticket or a seven-day ticket.

>> **Copenhagen,** for its reliable network of trains, buses and water buses. Buy a Copenhagen Card to get around the whole of the Danish capital.

>> **Hong Kong,** with an extensive network of metro lines, all accessible with an Octopus Card.

>> **Prague,** where you can ride the tram or take the metro, with three color-coded lines covering almost every part of the city. A 24- or 72-hour ticket also lets you ride the funicular to Petrin.

>> **Shanghai** has the world's largest metro system — and one of the most efficient. Trains, buses, ferries, maglevs, and taxis can all be paid for using the Shanghai Public Transportation Card.

>> **Singapore,** where the MyTransport.SG app makes planning your travel easy and the Singapore Tourist Pass pays for it all. Buses and MRT lines are easy to use and will deliver you to all the main attractions.

>> **Stockholm,** where your trips come with a serve of art and culture at *tunnelbana* (subway) stations adorned with paintings and mosaics. Transport options include trams, buses, and ferries to the islands.

>> **Taipei** has a an efficient MRT light rail system, with plenty of English-language signage making it easy to get around Taiwan's capital. It's all clean and comfortable and a large range of passes is available (keep them as a souvenir).

>> **Tokyo** sells the Greater Tokyo Pass for five days of unlimited travel on all train, tram, and some bus lines. Avoid the crush during commuter hours if you can. I found it easy as a non-Japanese speaker to work out the system, and everything runs like clockwork.

Also on the list are Beijing, Chicago, Edinburgh, London, Madrid, Montreal, Mumbai, New York, and Paris. I'd also add my own favorites: Vienna, Bangkok, and Melbourne. Wherever you are heading, check out the passes available, from tourist offers to daily, weekly, or monthly tickets that can add up to good savings and are infinitely more convenient.

TIP

Some train stations are also worth a visit in themselves for their stunning architecture or interior artwork, such as the spectacular Dome of Light at Formosa Boulevard Station in Kaohsiung, Taiwain, in Figure 3-3.

Biking from Here to There

According to researchers at England's University of Oxford — where bicycles are part of everyday life around the city — choosing a bike over a car for just one day a week would make a huge difference to transport-related emissions, with regular cyclists having 84 percent lower CO_2 emissions than people who did not cycle. What better reason do you have to jump on a bike?

TIP

In many major cities, bike share schemes allow you to hire two wheels for an hour or a day or more. Hundreds of cities across the United States and around the world have these schemes — some also including electric scooters — along with dedicated bike lanes or paths to take the stress out of dodging traffic and making it easy to incorporate pedal power into any style of holiday.

Lee Mylne

FIGURE 3-3: Formosa Boulevard Station's Dome of Light.

Cycling — whether along country lanes, canal tow-paths, or city streets — is a fantastic way to reduce your carbon footprint and save money on tours. Pick up a set of wheels from a bike-share scheme and pedal your way around for the cost of just a few dollars (mostly with a bond payment as well) for an hour or two or several days. When you have finished with the bike, just leave it at a docking station and pick up another one when you need it again.

On a bike, you're independent and in touch with the locals in a way that the cocoon of a car or bus prevents. Bike-share schemes are also great for families, often with the option of electric bikes or scooters. If you're traveling with young children, stick to bike paths and routes away from traffic.

European countries are among the most cycle-friendly in the world. Head to the Netherlands, Denmark, Germany, Sweden, and Norway, where bikeways will get you almost anywhere and cycling is part of most people's normal day's travel. Many European train stations have bike hire facilities to make your sustainable travel seamless.

In the United States, Minneapolis and Portland have great reputations as cycle-friendly cities. Minneapolis, with 98 miles (157km) of bike lanes, 101 miles (162km) of off-street bikeways and trails, and 16 miles (25km) of on-street protected bikeways, is rated as one of the best bike-friendly cities in the country. Portland has a 400-mile (644km) network of protected bikeways and 100 miles (160km) of greenways and multi-use paths. In some cities, like San Francisco, other forms of public transport have places for carrying bicycles.

As the popularity and recognition of the plain good sense of cycling increases, many cities are putting serious money into their cycling infrastructure, so wherever you travel, check out what's available on two wheels.

If you want to explore further than the city by bike, check out more on cycling holidays in Chapter 7.

TIP

Going off the Beaten Track

Roads less traveled are the way to go for sustainable travelers. While that means avoiding crowded cities and those places — both urban and natural — that are struggling with mass tourism, it also means continuing to make ethical choices. Finding alternatives to well-known places or routes can open up exciting and unexpected adventures.

Find a local guide who can show you the places you'd never find on your own. Better, make friends with locals and ask them where to eat, what to do and see, where the quietest beach is.

If off the beaten track to you means communing with nature, look for the least crowded national park or wilderness area. National Parks all over the world have had a surge in popularity in recent years, so seek out some of the less famous ones and you'll be ahead of the pack. When hiking or driving, stay on the main trail or designated road to avoid damaging delicate plants or disturbing animals.

Don't be tempted to stray from the path or step beyond any safety barriers — you could be doing damage to the environment by trampling delicate ecosystems, or worse, endangering yourself and those who may need to rescue you. No number of likes on Instagram or follows on TikTok are worth it! Sadly, there have been too many accidents — and deaths — caused by bravado and inattention by travelers chasing that top shot, usually a selfie. A 2021 study published in the Journal of Travel Medicine estimated that

WARNING

between 2008 and 2021 around 380 people had died while taking selfies.

Be an individual who doesn't need to follow the pack, who can find the most amazing spots that others miss, and who lives to tell the tale over the dining table for years to come.

TIP

Leave No Trace (www.lnt.org) lists sound principles (there are seven of them) for leaving minimal impact on the environment when you are discovering the great outdoors.

Chapter **4**

Packing to Save the Planet

raveling sustainably is not just about how you move from place to place and where you'll stay. Being a sustainable traveler starts from the time you pull your bag out and ponder what to pack. For a start, it should be all about traveling light. And while your sustainable travel life might be just beginning, choosing the right gear to take with you is important. Much of your travel kit will last you a long time, so getting it right at the start is, well, a good start.

Packing less enables you to avoid baggage fees, save time (no waiting around for checked luggage), never worry about lost luggage, and move more easily when getting on and off planes, buses, and trains. And if you have to carry your own bag any distance, the lighter it is, the happier you will be.

In this chapter, I help you choose the best sustainable luggage, clothing, and accessories to take with you, including things you can use over and over again on your current trip and in the future. As you wonder what to take and what to leave behind, I also share packing tips so you can fit everything you need into that small bag and never feel deprived.

FIND ONLINE

For a list of links to the web addresses mentioned in this chapter, as well as other helpful resources, go to www.dummies.com/go/sustainabletravelfd.

Travel Products That Are Easy on the Planet

Choosing travel products that are made sustainably is easier than ever. Many companies are looking to lessen their impact — and yours — on the planet by actively developing ways of making travel as sustainable as possible.

While you may not have a zero-carbon impact yet, aspiring to do so is the first step towards it. Your thoughtful choices can really make a difference.

This section covers the best luggage for your style of trip, how to adapt your wardrobe to your new sustainable travel ethos, and which items you'll be able to use again and again on your travels.

Choosing the best luggage

Your choice of luggage will depend on your style of travel. Are you going on safari to Africa, spending a month or two backpacking through Europe, or making a quick business trip to Detroit? Do you want a traditional-style suitcase, a backpack or duffel bag, or a carry-on only? Will your carry-on be a briefcase, laptop bag, or something slightly bigger that you can pack a lot into? Whatever you need, in today's market you can find a sustainable choice to suit.

REMEMBER

Of course, you may already have luggage, and if so, the best eco-choice is to keep it until it needs to be replaced. Using what you have for as long as you can is the best way to be sustainable and not add to a landfill. If you really need to replace your bag(s), consider looking at your local second-hand store (that's where I got my last one, for the bargain price of $20 — and a few years later, it's still going strong).

TIP

Another option for pre-loved bags is **Worn Wear** (wornwear.patagonia.com), a program that allows you to trade in or buy used Patagonia brand products, including packs, duffle bags, totes, and other gear, at cheaper prices than you'd pay for new. Buy online or check the website for store events in the United States where you can take your gear in or go along to buy. You can buy online from anywhere in the world, but returns are not accepted from outside mainland United States.

But maybe your old bag is no longer serving its purpose and you're planning to buy new but sustainably this time. If so, here are some tips and considerations:

» Look for luggage that's made of recycled materials or from plant-based materials.

» Is it biodegradable? Some polycarbonates are made from recycled material, and in terms of how they look, you'll be hard pressed to tell the difference between these stylish products and those that aren't made sustainably. If anything, some of them look better!

» Some soft-sided bags are made from recycled plastic bottles or fiber like jute or upcycled cotton. These are great options if you are going for duffle-bag-style luggage and don't need something that will stand up to being tossed around by baggage handlers and traveling in the hold of an aircraft with a whole lot of other sturdier bags.

» Chemical-free luggage is the ideal, but some bags will need protective coatings; in this case, look for polyurethane rather than PVC.

» Check out the manufacturer's supply chain and labor practices. Do they have a Code of Responsibility regarding child or forced labor, fair wages, non-discrimination, safe work environments, and so on? Most ethical companies also have a charity that they support, whether they are climate-related projects such as reforestation or social responsibility programs.

Most companies that are serious about their sustainability credentials will have all the information you need on their website. A little bit of research will tell you all you need to know.

Sustainable travel clothing

Landfills are a huge problem all over the world. Our consumer society has created mountains of waste clothing. According to the Council for Textile Recycling, the average US citizen throws away 70 pounds (31.7 kg) of clothing and other textiles every year. Wearing your clothes for as long as you can, recycling them, and buying sustainably crafted garments can help prevent this problem growing worse.

Ideally, don't rush out and buy a vacation wardrobe. Chances are you'll never wear these things again (even on another holiday), and they'll also end up being tossed out of your wardrobe in a year or two. If you really need new items for your trip, buy basics that will have a long life and be useful additions to your everyday wardrobe when you come home.

You may have heard of slow fashion. But what does it mean? Basically, it's all about wearing clothes that are made of sustainable and durable fabrics that will last you a long time. When it comes to your travel wardrobe, that just makes sense; I certainly don't want to be buying new gear every time I hit the road, and shifting shopping habits can really make a difference to the world. The money you save on clothes can be better spent on those travel experiences! Buying good quality is always a better bargain.

WARNING

Many cheap clothing brands keep their prices low by employing workers, including children, in countries like Bangladesh, India, Vietnam, Indonesia, the Philippines, China, and South America. These workers are often employed in terrible and dangerous conditions and are paid a pittance. Avoiding these brands and really thinking about what you buy and where it is made is a good start to improving conditions and helping the environment.

Check out the Fashion Transparency Index (fashionrevolution. org), a review of 250 of the world's largest brands and retailers, ranked for their public disclosure on environmental policies, practices and impacts, and human rights record. The Fair Wear Foundation (fairwear.org) lists 134 brands that operate under safe conditions for their workers.

REMEMBER

As well as making sure your clothes and shoes are sustainable, take note of the packaging they come in!

Once again, Patagonia's Worn Wear program (wornwear.patagonia. com), may come in handy as an avenue to buy or sell pieces from your travel wardrobe. This system allows you to earn a store credit by trading in your pre-loved clothing — everything from kids' sportswear to cashmere sweaters and alpine jackets to parkas and snow gear. You can expect to get anywhere from $10 to $100 for your used items and can also buy in-store or online. (Note: if you're outside mainland United States, you cannot return goods after buying them.)

If you find you need a few new items for your travels, consider the following:

» Check the labels. It will help identify where the garment is made and what the materials are. The best options are natural materials such as organic cotton, hemp, responsibly produced fabric such as lyocell and modal (both made from wood fibers), or recycled synthetic fibers.

Stay away from acrylic, lycra, nylon, polyester, and spandex, if you can. And remember that the closer to home your clothes are made, the better it is for the environment.

» Clothing brands — especially those with sustainability goals — are increasingly looking to add social responsibility to their aims. Do your research to find out how the brands you like are prioritizing social impacts and how they contribute to making the fashion industry more sustainable.

» Hiking boots are likely to be on many travelers' packing lists — and if you're in the market for a new pair, consider vegan boots, that is, those that are not made of leather. There are many options around now, with even the big brand companies dipping their toes in the vegan boot pool. Inspect your chosen boots closely, do some online research and go for those that are made of materials like recycled or natural rubber, hemp, cork, or recycled plastic.

Big brands like Merrell shoes (which I have worn for years) and Adidas now make hiking boots and trainers from recycled synthetic materials such as plastic and fishing nets.

» Even your choice of accessories counts. Look for bamboo or recycled plastic sunglasses to ward off the sun's glare on your beach, island, or snow vacation.

Some companies also support campaigns to provide prescription glasses and sight-saving surgery to those who can't otherwise afford it. In the US, San Diego-based SOLO Eyewear (soloeyewear.com), born out of a San Diego State University class project, sells ethically sourced sunglasses made from bamboo, repurposed wood, and recycled plastic, and partners with organizations such as Flying Samaritans and Restoring Vision in 32 countries. And don't forget that many optometrists will take your old frames back to be sent to communities in need.

Packing reusable items

How much space you'll have will depend on your mode of travel. If you're off on a fabulous road trip, leaving from home in your own car, you can load up the trunk and the back seat (sorry, kids!) with as much stuff as you like — and that should include reusable items like coffee cups, straws, and other daily necessities. If you don't have tons of space, you'll have to pack smarter. This section includes some tips and suggestions for items that take up minimal space but are also extremely handy and environmentally friendly.

TIP

The one thing I never travel without is a sarong (Figure 4-1). It's a multi-purpose item that can be put to a multitude of uses: wear it (of course), hang as a curtain or privacy screen, wrap around fragile things in your packing, use as an under-or-over sheet, dry yourself off with it, tablecloth, picnic blanket . . . the list is endless. And it takes up no room at all.

Lee Mylne

FIGURE 4-1: A sarong is a multi-purpose packing item.

Reusable water bottle

A reusable water bottle should be at the top of everyone's packing list, even if you're only taking hand luggage or an overnight bag. Not only are you saving the planet, but you'll save money, too! While there are plenty of plastic reusable bottles available, I really like a stainless steel one, which keeps the water cooler for longer, is sturdier, and doesn't risk leaching synthetic particles into the water. If you like to drink with a straw, take a stainless-steel straw as well.

TIP

If you are traveling to a place where the water is not filtered and you need to think about purifying, look for a water bottle with a filter, such as those made by LARQ (livelarq.com). The purifying tech used means you can fill up along the way without having to resort to buying water in single-use plastic bottles. The filters will have to be changed from time to time, but that's a small price to pay for ditching plastic bottles.

Reusable cutlery and food container

Reusable cutlery is also good to have on the road, even if you're not camping. If you're not sure about the hygiene at that food stall in India, you've got your own fork at hand. Look for bamboo cutlery sets or use your own chopsticks, which can be slipped into a slim carry case to keep them together. You can also carry normal cutlery of your own, but be careful not to pack it in your carry-on if flying.

TIP

If you have space, consider carrying a reusable food container to carry leftovers in or to avoid plastic containers from street vendors or takeaway joints. Look for one that is insulated to keep food hot or cold. If you're on a budget it will prove invaluable and prevent food waste.

Reusable bags

A tote bag that packs flat in your luggage and takes up no room is an essential reusable item. Take it to the local market or supermarket, use it for going to the beach, or to keep items such as dirty clothes separate in your bag. For years, I've been carrying a hand-woven string *bilum* I bought in Papua New Guinea (Figure 4-2), which takes up no room but expands to carry almost anything and is so strong it's almost indestructible.

Lee Mylne

FIGURE 4-2: My creative choice for a tote bag, a string *bilum* from Papua New Guinea.

If you take a foldable lightweight but sturdy backpack as your carry-on bag, you can also use it again and again as your day pack. Make sure it's made of recycled material, has well-padded straps, plenty of storage pockets, and a spot for your water bottle.

Toiletries

In terms of toiletries, it may be tempting to buy those mini-version shampoos and conditioners, but they are just adding to the plastic nightmare (this also applies to hotel-supplied shampoos, but many hotels are thankfully moving away from these, too). Instead, invest in refillable bottles (under the 100 ml mark if you're flying) and fill them from your supply at home. Solid shampoo, cleanser bars, and deodorants are also a better option than liquids, soaps, and aerosols. When choosing toiletries, chemical-free or organic are the way to go, and make sure the packaging is similarly planet-friendly. Ditch the packaged face wipes in favor of a cotton face cloth that you can wash, dry, and use again. Similarly, a sustainably made quick-drying travel towel can also be used in myriad ways and is particularly useful if you're planning outdoor activities.

When you buy a new toothbrush for your travels (or any time) look for a biodegradable bamboo brush. According to the World Wildlife Fund, about 3.5 billion plastic toothbrushes — which take up to 500 years to break down — end up in landfills or in rivers and oceans every year.

TIP

Female travelers can also try to reduce the use of tampons and other disposable hygiene products by switching to menstrual cups or period pants. This is a particularly good idea if you are traveling to destinations where sewage and waste systems are not highly developed.

Taking Just the Right Amount of Stuff

How much is too much? Every traveler's needs are different, depending on the destination, the type of trip you are planning and how much you care about having a selection of clothes. You might also need equipment such as a laptop or large DSL camera. But bear in mind that packing light — especially if you are traveling by air — is good for the planet. In the case of flying, every little piece of luggage that you can avoid taking will help reduce the weight of the aircraft, meaning it will pump less carbon dioxide into the atmosphere. In simple terms, the heavier your luggage, the more fuel is needed for the plane to reach its destination.

Traveling with a carry-on only is the ideal. But always check your airline's latest carry-on rules, which are subject to change and will vary from airline to airline. And remember your bag must be able to fit in an overhead compartment or under the seat in front of you.

Traveling light

If you can get away with traveling with hand luggage only, you'll be doing yourself a favor. Not only will there be no chance of your luggage going to Johannesburg when you're in Jamaica, but there'll be no long wait at the baggage carousel at the end of your flight.

Color coordinate your clothes to minimize the amount you'll need to take. It's easier for men than for women, of course, but mix and match is the name of the game. Wear neutral shades — black, white, gray, beige, or navy, for example — and throw in some colored scarves to add a bit of variety. Choose items for their versatility, so you can wear them in different situations.

When you're traveling, nobody — except your travel companion(s) — is going to know or notice you've worn the same clothing again and again!

Layers are the key to packing for all weather eventualities. Pack clothes that you can put on or take off as needed. Rather than pack one bulky sweater, layer a short-sleeve shirt with a long-sleeve top. In cold climates, add a lightweight foldable jacket. Have a trial run before you leave home, to make sure the layers fit easily over each other and to see how each piece of clothing works with others.

Shoes take up a lot of room, so minimize the number of pairs you take and always wear the heaviest or bulkiest pair (hiking boots, probably) on the plane. Sneakers are a great choice, too. These are also among the most expensive and difficult things to replace if your bag goes missing or is delayed in transit.

Use a zippered plastic bag (I know!) instead of a larger toiletries bag. It takes up less room. Have a spare for wet swim gear.

One of the biggest space-wasters in anyone's luggage is electronics. Unless you are traveling for work or really need your laptop, leave it at home. After all, it's a vacation! And you'll save a whole lot of space without it and all the assorted chargers and accessories you might need for it. Most smartphones now do all the things that a computer does anyway (unless you're a real photography bug, also consider leaving your camera at home and using your phone only). A tablet or e-reader loaded with books and maps can also save weight and space. Pack a small storage device for downloading or backing up your photos or upload them to a cloud-based server.

However, if you really need to take your electronic gear with you, make sure you minimize the number and weight of chargers by packing chargers and cords that can multitask or can charge more than one device simultaneously.

Many travelers pack far too many toiletries and makeup. Not only does this take up space, but you may need to check your bag if you're carrying too many liquids. Keep liquid or cream beauty items, perfume, and sunscreen away from clothes, and if you are traveling by plane, remember that altitude and air pressure changes can cause products to expand, leak, or drip. Keep them contained to prevent them making a mess of the rest of the contents of your bag.

Buy toothpaste and makeup in travel sizes. Try to fit everything into a single, clear zip-up bag and keep it at the top of your carry-on. Think about what you don't need and leave it behind if you can buy it when you arrive or expect it to be provided by your hotel (soap, shampoo, and conditioner from pump packs and so on).

Packing tips to fit all your necessities

Seasoned travelers swear by packing cubes or cells. Staying well-organized will not only save you time looking for the clean clothes among the dirty ones, but will maximize the space in your bag. These are most useful if you are packing a large suitcase but come in different sizes and shapes. Look for cubes made from sustainable fabrics, such as recycled plastic bottles. If you're packing for more than one person, they also come in a range of colors for easy identification. Semi-transparent cells are a good idea, so you can easily find what you're looking for. Compression cubes, which can be vacuum pressed to extract the air from them after they are packed, are also useful.

Roll or fold? Most people adhere to either one or the other method (I'm a folder) but essentially it doesn't matter too much. Remember to put smaller items inside others, such as stuffing your shoes with socks or other small things. Pack a laundry bag that can be used to separate the clean from the dirty as your trip progresses. Leave belts flat; a rolled belt takes up more space.

Pack a lightweight, zippered collapsible bag. It can work for a beach tote, shopping bag, or an extra bag to bring souvenirs home.

Consider shipping souvenirs home. Can't resist that Turkish rug from Istanbul? In many cases, reputable stores will arrange shipping for you at an extra cost. For other items that you don't want to lug around with you as your travels continue, send them home ahead of you. If you think this is a possibility, check carriers and costs before leaving home.

Luggage can get delayed or lost. Be sure to keep these essentials with you in your carry-on bag: passport or other ID, money, glasses, medication, spare underwear, hairbrush, and toothbrush.

Never pack anything fragile in your checked baggage. Wrap it well in that handy sarong and take it with you in your carry-on.

Travelers to developing countries are often keen to help out by taking clothing, educational materials, medical supplies, books, and other items that are needed. It's a commendable thing to do but needs planning — and luggage space. **Pack for a Purpose** (packforapurpose.org) can help you find out what is needed and where. The organization's website lists what is needed by community-based projects in around 60 countries and advises travelers how to deliver them — usually to a hotel or tour company in that destination who will pass them on to the project. Supplies needed might range from pencils to stethoscopes or soccer balls (deflated for easy packing). The website also has handy tips for minimizing the space needed in your luggage for the items.

Save space and leave jewelry and valuables at home. They are safer there, and you are less likely to be a target for muggers and thieves.

TIP

Chapter **5**

Where to Stay and Dine Sustainably

The places you stay and where you eat on your travels will stay in your memories forever — or at least the very good ones and the horribly shocking ones will! Making the right choices when it comes to your accommodation and choice of restaurants means you can remember them fondly, knowing that you've contributed to the communities who have welcomed you as a visitor. Every time you book with or buy from a small business owner, you are helping to keep profits in the local economy.

In this chapter, I take you through some hard questions to ask your accommodation provider and look at some options that will not only result in a closer connection to your hosts but enrich your travels in other ways. Eating like a local may sometimes take you out of your culinary comfort zone — but it will be worth it if you approach it thoughtfully!

FIND ONLINE

This chapter is chock full of web addresses for recommended establishments and resources. Head to www.dummies.com/go/sustainabletravelfd for a list of quick links to them all.

Knowing Your Options
for Sustainable Stays

Large hotel chains, roadside motels, and homely bed-and-breakfasts — with perhaps a campsite or two along the way — are no longer the only options open to travelers. Whether you are traveling solo, as a family, a group of friends, or a couple, there are an increasingly large number of sustainable stays open to you. This section covers various options to consider based on your desires and your destination.

REMEMBER

Discovering how eco-friendly your accommodation is can be difficult sometimes — greenwashing is rife in the accommodation sector — but by asking the right questions and doing some research before you book, you *can* make the right choices and support those hosts who are doing their bit for sustainability. Look for accommodations where waste reduction, energy and water conservation, recycling programs, and other sustainable goals are clearly outlined on the website. If you can find such a treasure, choose a carbon-neutral hotel!

If you're heading to Europe, one way to connect with a community and see your dollars going to good use is to book with **Fairbnb** (www.fairbnb.coop). Operating only in Europe — Spain, Portugal, Italy, Germany, Slovenia, France, Belgium, the Netherlands, the UK, Austria, and Switzerland, so far — it's a cooperative which invests its profits back into the local communities you stay in. Similar to Airbnb, the difference is that neighborhoods are consulted about short-term rentals, and 50 percent of the commission fee goes into community projects — and you get to choose which one.

Rooms for Change (www.roomsforchange.com) is a non-profit hotel booking platform that offers you a chance to find the best rates on thousands of hotel rooms worldwide — everything from hostels to five-star luxury while contributing to a good cause. Rooms for Change contributes 100 percent of its profit to creating travel scholarships for disadvantaged youth, seniors, and veterans.

TIP

The website of the **Global Sustainable Tourism Council** (www.gstcouncil.org), which manages the global standards for sustainable travel and tourism, has an extensive list of the standards accommodation providers should meet. The list provides links to standards set by countries around the world as well as platforms like Booking.com. Check it out when you are choosing your hotel.

Homestay with the locals

Hotels aren't for everyone, and choosing a homestay is one of the most sustainable options you can book — because you are giving back to the local community's economy in a direct and tangible way.

After a homestay visit in Thailand, I once wrote: "Take a healthy appetite with you and be prepared to eat like you've never eaten before." My hostess was a terrific cook, as well as being a talented ceramic artist, and my memories of that stay at Don Kai Dee Village, about 46 miles (75 km) outside Bangkok are all good.

Of course, not all homestays include such feasts as I was treated to, but most do include meals with the host, often as part of a family. Homestays usually open doors to local experiences that you might otherwise miss and provide a real chance to connect with those who know your destination best. Another memory of that stay was jumping on the back of motorbikes driven by friends of our hostess to visit small local temples and other places my friend and I would never have found on our own.

One way of finding a homestay is through an organization like **Homestay** (www.homestay.com), which has 63,000 rooms in more than 175 countries and operates on the philosophy that staying with a local is an important part of exploring a destination. Many Homestay hosts expect stays of more than a week, giving you time to really get to know them. The other advantage is that it is also usually a very affordable option for budget travelers.

Homestayin.com is another simple, user-friendly website that lists homestay rooms across more than 1,200 cities in 85 countries. The majority of the hosts come from cities in the United States, Canada, the United Kingdom, Australia, New Zealand, and Europe.

Another option is to look for a company that incorporates homestays in their tours, although this is likely to only be a night or two.

G Adventures (www.gadventures.com) runs small group "local living" tours in Ecuador, Italy, and Croatia, for four to six nights with a local family, including meals (you may be invited to help with the cooking sometimes). G Adventures also includes home-stays in other tours. I highly recommend the Back Roads of Japan tour, on which I stayed with a Japanese family in the coastal city of Hagi on the island of Honshu. It was a rare glimpse into a century-old family home with tatami mat floors and bedrooms behind paper screen doors. Helping with the cooking, I learned to make the popular snack Takoyaki under the watchful eye of my hostess, Toshiko-san and her 89-year-old mother Satoko-san. Despite a language barrier with Satoko-san, there was a lot of laughter — and the end result was delicious!

Homestays in Japan are called *minpaku* and are usually cheaper than hotels but may not include meals. As *minpaku* are often in residential areas, respect for neighbors is important (no loud parties!) as is — according to the Japan National Tourist Organization — sorting and putting out the garbage. Some *minpaku* are not registered, but to find those that are, look at official websites such as **Stay Japan** (en.stayjapan.com) or Airbnb.

Cuba is another destination that has long offered tourists the chance to stay with local families. Since 1997, the Cuban government has allowed citizens to rent out rooms — and all who do so are state licensed to do so. Staying with a family is one of the best and cheapest ways to see Cuba and get to know its people. A private room, house, or apartment in Cuba is called a *casa particular,* and a useful website, www.casaparticularcuba.org, lists hosted rooms and some private apartments.

If you're looking for a rural experience, think about signing up as a WWOOFer (www.wwoof.net). This is the chance to stay on an organic farm, where you can work in exchange for room and board. It actually stands for **World Wide Opportunities on Organic Farms,** an online matching service connecting hosts and guests worldwide. The idea behind WWOOF is to create a way for people to learn about organic food, farming, and culture. While you're helping your hosts, you're also learning about growing food sustainably and rural life in your chosen destination. WWOOF operates in 130 countries, so the options are endless. No money changes hands between the guest and host, but you must pay a membership fee to WWOOF in the country you intend to visit — this is $40 in the United States, $55 in Canada, and from 10 to 35 euros in Europe, as a guide. You're free to work as little as a few hours a day, in agreement with your host before you commit, having time to also explore the place you're visiting. This is also open to families, with children welcomed by some hosts (check with them before signing up).

Eco-friendly accommodations

When you think about eco-friendly accommodations, the image of a treehouse in the jungle, a log cabin in the forest, or a safari camp in the desert might spring to mind. Often our mental picture is that the ecologically conscious accommodation must look like it fits with the natural environment around it.

WARNING

In reality, *eco-friendly* is a term that lends itself to greenwashing, with plenty of places jumping on the "eco" bandwagon without actually being environmentally sustainable.

Appearances are not everything and there is much more than the visual appeal to consider when staying in a place that claims to be eco-friendly. Finding a place to stay that combines sympathetic design with a true commitment to sustainable practices is the key. Design may be a factor in making the accommodation blend with its environment — and there's no doubt that eco-friendly accommodations come in a huge array of shapes and sizes, from five-star resorts on private islands to homestays in traditional villages; from family-owned B&Bs to backpacker hotels, glamping in the desert, and everything in between.

But to legitimately claim the eco-friendly label they must have a commitment to minimizing carbon emissions; tread lightly on their physical environment; have a positive impact on their local community; and provide a guest experience that makes a connection to the destination.

Ideally, they'll have a written Sustainability Plan and be certified by a recognized ecotourism certification body — though the onerous certification process is often beyond the resources of many micro businesses such as homestays.

Seeking out accommodation that has been thoughtfully designed and built and still gives a strong sense of place will enhance your stay. Even large hotel chains can commit to sustainable methods of building — using local, recycled, and sustainable building materials is just a start. But a step further is to incorporate elements of local culture into the design and décor, connecting the accommodation to the destination and giving it a personality of its own.

REMEMBER

When looking for eco-friendly accommodations, go beyond the visible and ask about carbon offsetting, sustainable use of natural resources, how they deal with waste, and whether the property supports the local economy by hiring local staff, buying produce from nearby growers, or contributing to the community in other ways.

Another important thing to consider is whether the accommodation is owned by a local family or business, ensuring that the profits will stay within the community you are visiting.

Indigenous-owned lodging

Learning more about the First Nations peoples of the world is a great step toward understanding the history and culture of places you visit. By staying in an indigenous-owned lodging, you'll not only be likely to meet and talk to First Nations staff but you'll also be helping to give vital support to their communities.

REMEMBER

Tourism is becoming an important part of First Nations communities' economies, helping to create jobs and keep cultural traditions alive, and many communities are developing accommodations — some of them boutique — that showcases their culture and provides an income.

Examples of this can be found around the world. In some countries, such as New Zealand and Pacific Island nations, it's easy to find First Nations accommodations, as many are family-run and Maori and Pasifika culture is part of everyday life. In other places you may have to seek it out. A few examples are:

>> **The View Hotel** (www.monumentvalleyview.com) at Monument Valley, Utah, is owned by Armanda Ortega, of the Navajo Kiy'annnii (Towering House) clan. It is the only hotel in the Monument Valley Navajo Tribal Park and offers guests the chance to take tours with Navajo-owned tour companies approved by the Navajo Nations Parks. This ensures you are getting an authentic experience, learning about local customs, culture, and history from indigenous guides. A Trading Post sells traditional crafts.

>> **Skwachays Lodge and Residence** (www.skwachays.com) in Vancouver is Canada's first indigenous art hotel. With only 18 rooms, it also incorporates the Urban Aboriginal Fair-Trade Gallery and an artist-in-residence program for

24 indigenous artists and is owned and run by the Vancouver Native Housing Society.

» **Spirit Bear Lodge** (www.spiritbear.com) is owned and operated by the Kitasoo Xai'xais First Nation in British Colombia. Guests can explore Canada's Great Bear Rainforest with indigenous guides to connect with the wildlife, culture, and environment that is celebrated here.

» **Sani Lodge** (www.sanilodge.com) sits near the Napo River in Ecuador and is owned and run by the Sani Isla Kichwa community of the Amazon. Indigenous guides lead bird-watching trips and rainforest hikes and demonstrate Kichwa hunting methods. The lodge partners with a social enterprise that supports local women to earn an income making and selling crafts.

» **Tangulia Mara** (www.tanguliamara.com) in Kenya's Maasai Mara National Reserve was the first safari camp to be owned by Maasai people. A stay at the camp includes cultural visits to nearby villages, walking safaris, and game drives led by Maasai guides. Camp co-owner Dominic Nchoe established Lemek Community Conservancy, a local organization dedicated to the protection of natural and cultural resources and limited the impact of tourism on the natural environment. It also trains rangers who patrol to protect animals in the reserve against poachers.

» **Ayers Rock Resort** (www.ayersrockresort.com.au) makes up almost all of the small desert town of Yulara, adjacent to the sacred monolith Uluru on the traditional country of the Anangu in Central Australia. The resort, adjacent to Uluru-Kata Tjuta National Park, is owned by Voyages Indigenous Tourism Australia, which also operates the Anangu Communities Foundation to fund projects to support local indigenous communities. Resort accommodation includes six hotels of varying degrees of comfort and luxury and a campground. Guests can take walks with indigenous guides, learn didgeridoo playing, join artists for painting workshops, or learn about traditional foods and medicines.

Finding a sustainable luxury hotel

While you might love the feel of those Egyptian cotton sheets with the high thread count that many luxury hotels boast about, thinking beyond your own comfort is the key to finding sustainable luxury. And yes, it *does* exist! Put simply, hotels that take sustainability seriously should be looking for alternatives to cotton bedding, such as hemp or bamboo. And that's just one of the things you should look for when choosing a hotel on any budget. Many luxury hotels are part of international chains, and the good news is that many of them are aware that their savvy guests are looking closely at their operations with an eye on sustainability. And it goes much further today than simply asking for your room to be cleaned or towels to be replaced less often, as shown in Figure 5-1.

Lee Mylne

FIGURE 5-1: Hotels are signaling their 'green' intentions.

At the top end of the market, hotels are setting new standards of conscious luxury and are making worthwhile contributions to their communities. Luxury travel generally comes at a high carbon cost so looking for carbon emission minimization and offset opportunities is essential. Places that work with local communities are also key — ensuring that every visit from a luxury traveler has a positive impact on the surrounding region. Properties that use renewable resources, such as solar power, have a significant impact on ensuring a stay with them is as environmentally positive as possible.

Denmark's **Arthur Hotel Group** (www.arthurhotels.com) lays claim to the title of the world's first hotel chain to achieve carbon-neutral status, in 2014 — but it is no longer alone.

At **Six Senses Shaharut** resort in Israel, (www.sixsenses.com/en/resorts/shaharut) guests can visit the "Earth Lab," which explains how the hotel was built on sustainable planning and management principles from the ground up. On a behind-the-scenes tour, guests can see for themselves elements of the hotel's sustainable design and construction, visit the organic kitchen garden, and learn about the resort's energy-efficiency and sustainable approach to food waste, use of cooking oil, and wastewater.

TIP

It can be daunting and time-consuming to research hotels yourself, but there are several well-regarded platforms that have done a lot of the legwork for you:

>> **Green Pearls** (www.greenpearls.com) is a useful platform for finding green hotels around the world. Members are chosen for their sustainability initiatives and green projects. Based in Germany, it considers all aspects of each property: from management systems to architecture, food, waste management, energy and water consumption, and commitment to local communities, social projects, and culture.

>> **Small Luxury Hotels of the World** (www.slh.com), which encompasses 540 independent hotels in more than 90 countries, has launched its Considerate Collection for "actively sustainable" luxury hotels "that go the extra eco mile." The 56 hotels within the collection have met criteria that align with the goals of the United Nations' Sustainability Development Goals and the Global Sustainable Tourism Council. A handy searchable map shows locations from Iceland to New Zealand.

>> Australian-based global booking platform for sustainable hotels **GoKinda** (www.gokinda.com.au) lists "stylish and conscious" hotels that are environmentally and socially responsible. GoKinda also supports the One Tribe rainforest protection project: For each booking made on the website, a donation is made to cover protection for five trees.

What to ask your accommodation provider

Before booking your accommodation, no matter what budget you are on or where you are going, it is perfectly acceptable to ask about the commitment to sustainability and eco-practices followed. Whether they are small family-run hotels, hostels, or belong to a large chain or marketing group, every hotel should be able to happily answer your questions.

Start by looking at their website. Is there any content about sustainability? If not, contact the hotel directly. Some questions you can consider asking include:

» **How does your hotel source and conserve energy?** Does the hotel use renewable energy sources such as solar panels, electric cars, or have heat-reflective windows? Do they have an energy-efficiency plan, using thermostats, lighting, timers, and other tools to cut their energy use?

» **How do you source, conserve, or recycle water?** It's not enough today for a hotel to give you the option of reusing your towel. Have they installed low-flow shower heads? Is rainwater collected for use on the hotel gardens? Are they still using plastic bottled water, or do they have a filter system? Do they recycle grey water?

» **What is the hotel's recycling policy?** How do they dispose of food, paper, plastic, and toxic waste — not only that used by guests but in the administration side of the business as well? Do they compost for the garden?

» **Are you reducing single-use plastic?** If there are still plastic straws and little cocktail umbrellas in your drink, it's not a good sign. Straws, stirring sticks, disposable coffee cups (and lids), plastic bags, and plastic wrap on food may not be banned everywhere (yet) but savvy hotels should be a step ahead of local laws in this area.

» **How are your bathroom amenities dispensed?** If those little plastic bottles are still in use in the bathroom, it's another point to press home. Pump dispensers are more common now, but not everywhere.

» **How do you support the local economy and community?** Sustainability is also about staffing, worker's rights, inclusivity, and the impact on locals. Does a portion of proceeds support local education, health or environmental programs? Many sustainability-conscious properties also instigate or support community projects such as arts and education. Do you hire First Nations people as staff or work with First Nations communities?

» **Do you have a current sustainability report?** More and more hotels are working toward becoming carbon neutral, through minimizing their greenhouse emissions and offsetting residual emissions. Some will cover the cost of purchasing offsets as part of their sustainability protocol, while others encourage guests to contribute. Either way, they should be systematically identifying and reducing their emissions and happy to tell you about their progress in cutting them and their aims. The best sustainable properties will have completed an independent certification process and produce an annual sustainability report.

» **Do you align your operation with the UN Sustainability Goals?** And have you achieved any recognized, independent sustainability certification, such as Green Globe (www.greenglobe.com) or Green Key (www.greenkey.global)?

» **Have you used sustainable building practices, design, and materials?** This might include using recycled plastic or timber, natural fibers in furnishings, locally made furnishings and artworks? Were local builders and craftspeople employed in the building process?

With the answers to these questions, you will be well prepared to make an informed choice about whether this is a hotel or resort you want to support with your tourist dollars.

REMEMBER

As a hotel guest, you have a great deal of influence. After your stay, remember to leave an online review that rates your accommodation's sustainability efforts. Whether it is positive or negative, your feedback will be valuable to the hotel — and will help other travelers to decide whether to stay or not.

Considering Where Your Food Is Coming From

If you're like me, eating is one of the great pleasures in life. And sustainable travel doesn't mean depriving yourself of the delights of tucking into local cuisine wherever you are — it simply means that stopping to think about where the delicacies on your plate have come from might alter the choices you make, both from the menu in front of you and in other places that you choose to dine at on your travels.

Wherever you travel, give thought to where your food is coming from. Are the eggs on your breakfast table organic, cage free, or free range? Look for hotels and restaurants that source their food locally — it's bound to taste better, too! Does the hotel have a kitchen garden where it grows its own organic produce?

Avoid hotel buffets. They generate large amounts of food waste.

Food choices that are good for the environment usually taste better, too! Buying produce that has been produced using organic or regenerative farming methods is likely to taste as if it had come from your grandparents' backyard vegetable patch. Another term to look for is biodynamic food; this is a type of organic farming that uses traditional methods that have a strong emphasis on environmental sustainability. Organic meat is free from hormones and antibiotics and is from animals that have been humanely treated during their lives.

Developing countries are likely to be among the easiest places to find fresh, organic food. In the Pacific islands, where importing food is expensive and difficult, hotels and restaurants source their fruit, vegetables, eggs, and other fresh food direct from local farmers.

Selecting sustainable seafood

If you love seafood, remember that more than 90 percent of the world's fisheries are either fished-out or overfished. Your choices at the dining table can help protect the ocean and its finite resources. Overfishing and other unsustainable practices are putting pressure on seafood stocks, along with loss of biodiversity. Some species, such as the cod which fed Newfoundlanders for generations, are vanishing, and others are in danger. When you're buying or eating fish, choose those that have been line or pole caught; avoid fish caught by trawling, ghost fishing, longlines, or explosives.

In North America, many hotels and restaurants now follow the guidelines from **Seafood Watch** (www.seafoodwatch.org), issued by Monterey Bay Aquarium, on which fish to avoid serving. The list is long, but includes a handy search function that breaks down each species into what to buy and what to avoid. The best idea is to eat locally sourced fish from small suppliers. Head to the local fish markets, or the dock where the fishing boats tie up to get the freshest fish.

PETA (www.peta.org) estimates that around 650,000 marine mammals — including dolphins, whales, and porpoises — are seriously injured or killed each year by commercial fishing. Seabirds, such as albatross, have been driven to the brink of extinction thanks to unscrupulous (and often illegal) large-scale, long-line fisheries. Switching to small, local, and sustainable fishing companies is a much better way to enjoy seafood, while reducing the amount of bycatch and lowering the threat to large marine life.

Counting your food miles and reducing your "foodprint"

Counting food miles is a way of trying to measure how far the food on your table — at home or in a restaurant on the other side of the world — has traveled before it gets to your fork. That distance will have had an impact on the environment — and it's one that you can take simple steps to counteract.

Buying and eating locally is the answer. It not only reduces that impact on the planet, but you are supporting local farmers and probably eating fresher food. If you are in the United States or Australia and you're eating bananas from Ecuador or apples from Chile, they have traveled a long way to be in your fruit bowl. It's so much better in every way to buy from a local grower. Think about the fossil fuels used to grow, process, store, transport, and cook what we eat, particularly in remote locations.

Be aware though, that some foods may appear to be from local suppliers but if bought at supermarkets, have probably toured the country between depots before arriving in the shop.

There are plenty of food mile calculators online. One you can use is www.foodmiles.com — it's an interesting exercise!

TIP A less familiar term might be *foodprint*. As you might guess, it's along the lines of your carbon footprint, but relating to food consumption. It's a little bit harder to calculate but is based on the impact the food you eat has on the environment, the welfare of animals and food or farm workers, and on public health. Your foodprint is based on everything it takes to get your food from farm to plate. Essentially, it's about eating ethically. FoodPrint (www.foodprint.org) is also the name of a US-based non-profit organization that delves into all these issues.

Keep in mind when you're eating out that as a responsible traveler making sustainable choices, you should be looking for SLOW foods — that's seasonal, local, organic, and whole.

REMEMBER

When you're browsing the menu in a restaurant — whether at home or on the other side of the world — ask the waiter these questions:

>> Where do you source your meat/seafood?

>> Is this dish in season right now?

>> What farms do you buy from?

>> Are the eggs organic?

Eating like a local

Keeping your food miles low can be fun. When you're traveling, try eating like a local. Check out the local supermarkets, visit farmers markets, and talk to locals about what the best things to eat in the region are. Don't be afraid of eating street food — in my mind, it's one of the joys of travel. Once you have overcome the fear of dodgy hygiene — and take sensible precautions, of course — the exotic tastes of unfamiliar food await at food markets and hawker stalls all over the world.

That unfamiliarity is what is so exciting — unusual colors (I'm thinking dragonfruit in Asia, with its bright pink skin and black-and-white flesh), smells, and tastes will add to your experience. Engage with the sellers — ask what things are (make sure you learn how to ask that question in the local language) and ask for tastes before you buy. From smelly cheese to aromatic pastries and bread, sausage, and other deli delights, food markets have something for every tastebud. If you don't fancy cooking for yourself, most food markets also have cooking stalls where you can snatch a snack, as I have often done (Figure 5-2).

Lee Mylne

FIGURE 5-2: Floating market near Bangkok, Thailand.

First Nations cuisine is also growing in popularity, with native ingredients making their way onto restaurant tables. Sign up for culinary tours or cooking classes to learn more about hunter-gatherer customs or traditions that have been followed for years, such as truffle-hunting in France. While you may never use those recipes again, the experience will teach you a lot. I've crunched my way through fried grasshoppers in Vietnam, gulped down a roasted witchetty grub (a kind of big white worm) in the Central Australian desert, and reluctantly dined on pigeon soup in Shanghai (just to be polite) to no ill-effects. I did, however, draw the line at eating the local delicacy *cuy* (guinea pig) in Peru.

TIP

Traveling Spoon (www.travelingspoon.com) can connect you with local cooks worldwide looking to share their culture with visitors. You can share a homemade meal with a family, learn to cook with your host in their kitchen, or take a market tour to discover the best local produce from someone who really knows (or combine all three experiences). Whether it's pasta-making in Italy or grinding spices in India, or a farm-to-table meal in California, there's something for every taste.

Knowing what not to eat

It's important to remember that "eat like a local" isn't a foolproof mantra. If you are tempted by a rare and special local delicacy, the likelihood is that an endangered species is being threatened or unimaginable cruelty has been wrought on an animal. Is the novelty of having tried a dish with those origins worth it?

Some foods to avoid as you travel include:

>> **Shark fin soup:** You are most likely to find this in China or Singapore. Apart from the fact that many shark species are already threatened, the fins are cut from them while they are still alive, and they are tossed back into the sea to wait for a slow and painful death.

>> **Turtle soup, meat, or eggs:** Turtles are endangered all over the world. While many countries ban the harvesting of turtles for food, turtle soup is still served as a delicacy in some places.

>> **Kopi luwak:** This exotic coffee — made famous in the movie *The Bucket List* — is produced from coffee beans that have passed through the digestive system of a civet cat. If that's not enough to put you off, consider that many of the civets are captured and caged in order to produce this most expensive coffee.

>> **Bird's nest soup:** One of the most expensive soups in the world, this is made from real bird's nest, a small swift's nest believed to have medicinal properties. Some are now "farmed" for their nest-building, but poaching is also rife. Many countries, including the United States and Australia, ban the importation of birds' nests.

>> **Whale or dolphin meat:** Japan is one of the few places in the world that still hunts whales and dolphins and where you can buy whale meat. Just don't.

>> **Beche de mer:** Tropical sea cucumbers are harvested from the ocean floor and dried for sale as a delicacy and health food in China and other parts of Asia. Mostly found in tropical waters, it's not illegal to eat them, but they play a vital role in ocean ecosystems and are in danger of being over-harvested and poached to extinction.

- » **Patagonian toothfish:** Overfishing of this fish, also known as Chilean Sea Bass, is depriving South American elephant seals of 98 percent of their diet. So there are two species in danger.

- » **Foie gras:** France's love of food is usually irresistible, but please don't buy or eat foie gras. This paté is made from the livers of ducks or geese that have been force-fed through a tube for months in a process called *gavage* (French for "to gorge"). It's hideously cruel.

- » **Pangolin:** Pangolins are the world's only scaled mammals. These ancient termite-eating creatures are on the verge of extinction because of habitat loss and poaching. Some Asian cultures believe the scales of the pangolin have medicinal and magical properties, and there is a huge black market trade for them.

As a responsible traveler, saying a resounding *no* to dishes like this a step towards helping to stop these illegal and unsustainable practices.

Chapter **6**

Shopping for Sustainable Souvenirs

angible memories that come in the form of souvenirs provide a wonderful way to remember your travels. As a responsible traveler, it's important to think carefully about what you buy and where it came from. Finding authentic and ethically produced souvenirs to take home will give you a lasting reminder of your trip that is rich and meaningful, and when you come home, you can show those souvenirs off with pride, safe in the knowledge that you've bought them fairly and squarely, to the benefit of those who sold them to you.

In this chapter, I guide you through some of the traps for unwary shoppers, show you how spot a fake, and help you perfect your bargaining style.

**FIND
ONLINE**

Find links to all the online resources mentioned in this chapter, as well as additional ones, at www.dummies.com/go/ sustainabletravelfd.

Finding Sustainable Souvenirs

On a visit to Thailand, I bought a souvenir photo of myself that was presented for sale already framed by quick and resourceful locals. The frame — which looked like cardboard or thick recycled paper — was made of elephant dung. Sustainable? Perhaps, but the Customs officials who spotted it when I came through the airport on my return home did not hesitate to confiscate it and consign it to the trash as potentially carrying harmful bugs (I got to keep the photo). Thankfully, I had declared it as I was uncertain about whether or not I could bring it back — and I was not heartbroken to lose it. But my experience is a good example of how careful you need to be about what you buy to bring home. And a reminder that while something might be made from natural materials, that doesn't necessarily mean it is sustainable or a desirable item bring back home.

This is a good reminder that as well as thinking about the product you are buying, it pays to also consider the packaging it comes in. Not that it will often be made of elephant dung — more likely plastic — but in many cases packaging is excessive and contributes to landfill.

TIP If traveling lightly — perhaps only with carry-on luggage — is your aim, ask yourself if you really need a souvenir at all. If the answer is yes, look at buying something very small but that you will treasure forever.

WARNING Avoid souvenir shops, and don't buy last-minute gifts at the airport. Not only will the prices be higher, but almost everything will be mass-produced.

Spending your money locally

Sometimes it seems that everywhere in the world is starting to look the same: Every big city has the same chain stores, big-name labels, fast-food joints or coffee shops. If you really want a souvenir that takes you right back to that fantastic trip to Africa or Argentina or the Azores every time you look at it, shop local. Look out for the national chains (think Printemps in France or Ripley in Chile) or mom-and-pop stores, or head to government emporiums or markets. After all, you don't need to buy something while you're traveling that you can easily buy back home.

Buying a souvenir direct from the hands of its maker usually means it has been made with love and is better quality than something that has been mass-produced. It also means that there has been little or no transport involved in getting it to the market, which reduces the carbon footprint of that item.

The following sections cover some great options for finding quality locally made items.

Local arts and crafts markets

Find out when the local arts and crafts markets are on and grab the chance to pick up authentic craft souvenirs direct from the hands that made them. Meeting a maker will give an added depth to your attachment to your purchase, as you'll hear the back story to how it came to be, what it means and more about the artist. You'll also be sure that your money is going straight to the person who put their time, talent, and effort into bringing it into being. What's more beautiful than that?

Museums and galleries

Museums and galleries are always great places to pick up souvenirs and gifts, with their stores often acting as outlets for the artists being shown.

WARNING

Beware of imported souvenirs — always check the label. My mantra for souvenirs is that they should be both useful and beautiful, and on a trip to Taiwan I found what I felt was the perfect memento in a most unexpected place. At the Fo Guang Shan Buddha Museum I bought a set of lovely earthenware cups perfect for serving green tea. At home, I unpacked them and discovered a label that said "Made in Indonesia."

Indigenous artisans

Indigenous art and craft pieces make wonderful souvenirs and are a growing segment of the art trade, benefiting First Nations communities in many ways. Not only do they create an income, they support the continuation of traditional customs. The **American Indian Alaska Native Tourism Association (AIANTA)** publishes an online calendar of native art markets where you can meet artists and learn about their work: https://www.aianta.org/shop-native/native-art-market. Other great websites include the

First American Art Magazine (www.firstamericanartmagazine.com/calendar), which lists fairs, markets, exhibitions, and other events by Indigenous peoples across the Americas.

There are lots of indigenous artisans and makers across Canada who can introduce you to authentic indigenous arts and crafts. Canada's **Destination Indigenous** (www.buyauthentic.ca) is a good source of information about where to buy.

Wherever there are First Nations people, there will be traditional art in some form or other. But making sure that what you buy is authentic and will benefit the artists directly is essential. (In the next section, I explain how you can do that.)

Checking for fakes

It's pretty easy to spot the fake Gucci handbags and cheap knock-off brands that proliferate many big markets, particularly in Asia and Africa. Apart from the workmanship, the price is usually a giveaway. But it's quite a lot harder to know if that artwork you're coveting for your wall or that beautiful woven basket you can't live without has really come from the hands of a local artist.

TIP

The best way to ensure you buy the real thing is by dealing directly with the artist, going to their exhibition or workshop where you can see the work being produced, whether it is art, pottery, metalwork, jewelry, rugs, or clothing. Sometimes, even market sellers are not the artists, so doing research and asking questions are two key things to do before you buy. If you're not buying from cooperatives or fair-trade marketplaces, where the artists are on hand, make sure you ask questions about the provenance of the work and ask for a certificate of authenticity or other evidence of where it was created and by whom, such as these labels attached to baskets in a market in Darwin, Australia (Figure 6-1).

First Nations art in particular is increasing in popularity and value, and in some countries fakes and forgeries are rife. Some of these are mass-produced in other countries — usually in Asia — and their production and sale are exploiting the traditions of indigenous communities and taking income away from them. The exploitation can also extend to the workers who are employed to create the fakes, who are potentially underpaid or working in poor conditions.

Lee Mylne

FIGURE 6-1: Baskets labeled with the artists name and image.

The materials used in fakes are often not sustainable, sometimes using wood such as bamboo or teak, made overseas, imported for sale as indigenous-made, and labeled to mislead. Some may even be polyester or plastic-based.

What is the solution? Some countries have vetting programs that label local products. In Canada, the **Igloo Tag** trademark (www.inuitartfoundation.org) has been used since the 1950s as a symbol of authenticity for art created by the Inuit peoples. In Australia, look for the red-and-black logo of the **Indigenous Art Code** (www.indigenousartcode.org) that provides a standard of ethical practice for dealers in Indigenous visual arts. India's **Craftmark** (www.craftmark.org) symbol helps shoppers distinguish authentic handmade craft products from replicated machine-made ones. In New Zealand, **Toi Iho** (toiiho.co.nz) is a trademark that indicates a product — particularly an artwork — is Maori-made (but does not apply to all genuine Maori-made products).

REMEMBER

Here's some tips to make sure your First Nations art purchase is authentic and ethical:

>> Check if the gallery or shop you are dealing with has adopted a Code of Practice or similar, with guidelines on the ethical sale of Indigenous art.

- » Ask for the details of the artist — where they come from, if they work as part of a co-operative, and take note that the work is signed.

- » Where and when was the work made? Is it contemporary? Is it a historic artefact?

- » The best way to buy is direct from the artist, so you are sure they are getting the full price. If buying from a gallery or arts center, ask what percentage of the sale of the artwork goes to the artist — some galleries will take a sizeable commission, sometimes up to 50 percent of the price. If you feel the artist isn't being fairly compensated for their work, buy elsewhere.

- » If you are buying from a gallery, ask about its connection to the First Nations community that its artists live in. Does it partner with community arts centers to ensure artists are fairly treated and paid and that income goes back to the community?

- » If buying carvings, look closely at a piece and physically handle it. Carvings that appear to be soapstone may actually be made of resin (the giveaway is that stone is cool to touch, plastic is warm). Stone is also usually heavier than plastic. Is it perfectly uniform or lacking in surface variations?

- » Gallery purchases may come with a certificate of authenticity, but genuine indigenous art should come with a community certificate of authenticity that states the artist's name, language group, community, and often the story behind the artwork. Lack of information about the artwork should be a red flag about authenticity.

Mastering the art of bargaining

Who doesn't love a bargain? In Western countries, shoppers flock to sales as if their lives depend on it. Most of the time, they happily pay the advertised price for anything they see in a shop or even at a market stall. Mostly, Western consumers accept that the price stated is what the item is going to be sold for; if they think it's too expensive, they move on without argument. But when faced with something you want to buy while traveling, there's often a different attitude toward paying the asking price.

In many countries, there's still an age-old tradition of bargaining. There's an art to it, and you can be sure that the vendor in a market where this is a way of life will be well-practiced. Let yourself be drawn into the labyrinth of a bazaar such as this one in Morocco (Figure 6-2), and test your skills against that of the master hagglers.

Lee Mylne

FIGURE 6-2: Wander into a bazaar and practice bargaining.

One of my great travel memories is of drinking endless small cups of tea as my partner and I haggled over the price of a Turkish rug in an Istanbul bazaar, to an outcome that satisfied all parties. Approach it with the right attitude, and it can be fun as well as an insight into how things are done in other cultures. If you've read the room wrong, and bargaining is not on the table, your efforts will be rejected quickly, clearly, and firmly.

TIP

Keep it friendly. Part of the fun of bargaining is that everyone knows it's a game. Bantering with the vendor may be one of the best stories you bring back from your vacation.

If you are interested in buying an item, spend some time asking the vendor about it. How was it made? How long did that take? How did you learn to do this? A little bit of small talk can go a long way toward making them feel friendly toward you — and maybe giving you a good price!

Before you haggle hard consider the true amount that you are bargaining over. Paying 24,000 Vietnamese dong might sound like a lot, but in reality, it's about one dollar — but the difference that dollar might make to the person you're buying from could be enormous.

It's important to pay a fair price, not just aim to get the cheapest price possible. Bargain hard by all means, but keep it polite and good-natured. It's a game you might not win, but can have fun trying. The end result should be a price that both you and the vendor are smiling about. And remember to say *thank you* — in the local language!

Always carry small change and low denomination notes. If a vendor can't give you change, you might miss out completely.

Staying plastic-free

The statistics are so astonishing and so horrific they should be enough to turn you off plastic forever. According to **Conservation International** (www.conservation.org), the Great Pacific Garbage Patch contains around 1.8 billion pieces of trash — and there are four other similar patches floating in our oceans. Add to that the mountains of plastic waste on land and soon the world will be drowning in it.

Avoiding single-use plastics should be high on your list of considerations when traveling and shopping. Single-use plastic bags have been banned in many places around the world, and you can help avoid them by always including a reusable shopping bag in your luggage (and in your everyday life).

When shopping for souvenirs, consider the packaging of anything you consider buying; so much plastic waste is from unnecessary packaging. Buy at markets and refuse offers of plastic wrap, bags, or packaging.

If you are likely to be buying take-out food on your travels, carry your own reusable containers and say no to the plastic ones. Take your own metal or bamboo straw for drinks.

Look for items made from recycled plastic. Some fashion brands are using recycled plastic to create fabulous clothing and jewelry. Seek them out and support those efforts.

Be mindful that developing countries don't have the recycling or waste management facilities of the developed world, and in these places, plastics are even more likely to end up in waterways, landfill, or the ocean. That's an even greater reason to limit your use of plastics and avoid them where possible when buying packaged goods.

In Africa, look for souvenirs that are made from recycled materials, such as wire sculptures or shoes with soles of recycled tires.

TIP

Avoiding Purchases That Harm Animals

You may already know that it's illegal to bring home elephant ivory, rhino horn, and tiger products, but some souvenirs that are unethical can sneak under your radar because their origins are not obvious at first glance. As a thoughtful traveler, you can help support conservation efforts by asking questions and taking care before you buy any souvenir that has originated from wildlife.

Just because an item is for sale does not mean it is ethical to buy it or legal for you to import it to your own country. You may need a permit for some products. Without one, you may be fined and your souvenir may be confiscated.

WARNING

Most countries protect their native species under national laws and as signatories to the Convention on International Trade in Endangered Species of Wildlife Fauna and Flora (CITES). This means they will not allow trade in wild animals or plants or products made from them which might endanger their survival. This can apply to a huge range of products, including leather goods, wooden carvings, musical instruments, or dried herbs.

The World Wildlife Fund suggests asking these questions before you buy any souvenirs:

➤➤ What is this product made of?

➤➤ Where did it come from?

➤➤ Does the country you are visiting allow the sale and export of this product?

➤➤ Do you need permits or other documents from this country (or your own) to bring this item home?

Some unscrupulous vendors may not tell you the truth, of course, but any hesitation or obfuscation should be taken as a sign that all is not what it should be. Let your instincts guide you and walk away if you have doubts.

There are some products or items, such as those covered in the following sections, that you should be particularly careful about, particularly those where the impact of your purchase may be hidden.

Palm oil products

Palm oil plantations are taking over some of the world's most important ecosystems, including habitat for orangutans, tigers, elephants, and rhinos. In some places, it is also displacing indigenous communities from their traditional lands. Large plantations are found in Malaysia (Borneo) and Indonesia, with Thailand, Colombia, and Nigeria also producing on a smaller scale.

Palm oil is the cheapest vegetable oil available, and it is widely used in snack foods, cosmetics, toiletries such as toothpaste and soap, candles, and laundry detergent, as well as in biofuels.

When traveling, you can help by visiting forests and national parks, spending money in local communities and supporting local tourism initiatives which create other income streams for local people. When buying — at home and while away — always check ingredient lists on labels and avoid buying anything that contains palm oil. Use alternatives such as sunflower, olive, or flaxseed oil.

The **Roundtable on Sustainable Palm Oil** (www.rspo.org) works to promote products which use palm oil farmed sustainably by branding them with the RSPO logo. You can download a PalmOilScan app created by the World Association of Zoos and Aquariums (www.waza.org) if you live in the United States, Canada, UK, Australia, or New Zealand.

Skins and furs

If you must wear fur, go faux. Buying animal fur or skin souvenirs is a risky business, wherever you are from. Few governments approve, whether it is the hide or hair of lizards, snakes, otters, seals, or tigers that you plan to bring (or wear) home. That goes for snakeskin shoes and belts, or that goatskin drum you learned to play in Haiti. Many nations, including China, South Africa, and the Philippines, require you to have an export permit for animal skins and fur products before you leave the country. Always check the local regulations and that the Customs regulations of your own country allow you to take it home.

There are a few exceptions. It is legal to buy genuine handicrafts made by Alaskan natives using polar bear or otter fur. In countries across Africa, Asia, and South America, as well as Australia, crocodiles are sustainably farmed for their meat and skins and it is legal to buy crocodile leather goods, but you may need a CITES permit in order to export it. Sustainable crocodile farming is carried out under regulations set down by the International Union for Conservation of Nature (IUCN) Crocodile Specialist Group (www. iucncsg.org), which works closely with CITES and is regarded as part of conservation efforts for the world's 23 species of crocodilians.

In New Zealand, it is perfectly fine to buy possum fur and fur/wool blend products because these introduced Australian marsupials are a feral pest destroying ecosystems necessary for the survival of native species. Possums are hunted and trapped, with the aim to eradicate them by 2050.

Seashells and coral

She sells seashells on the seashore . . . but thoughtful travelers will not buy! Nor will they beachcomb for pretty shells or pieces of coral as keepsakes to take home. Apart from being ecologically unfriendly, it might also be illegal as many countries ban their export — which is what you would be doing. Shell art is popular in many countries, but their export may not be. Do your research before you buy, and don't risk having your coastal souvenir confiscated at the airport.

Some corals and shells are listed as endangered species because the scale of collection has been so great. Don't forget that many shells — including the conch shells sold in the Caribbean — provide homes for live animals and by collecting shells or buying shell ornaments you are depriving them of their habitat.

Turtle products

Six of the world's seven species of sea turtle are threatened, and three of them are endangered or critically endangered, according to Earthwatch (www.earthwatch.org). Shiny hair clips, jewelry, and other tortoiseshell ornaments all come from these turtles. The importation, sale, or purchase of turtle products — including eggs, meat, and shells — is banned in the United States and many other countries. Also watch out for products such as musical instruments, turtle leather products, and anything labeled "tortoiseshell." And never order anything from a menu that offers turtle soup, eggs, or meat (in fact, my advice is to just walk away from the restaurant completely).

Snake wine

It's not uncommon to see bottles of wine with snakes inside them in some parts of Asia, particularly in China, Taiwan, and Vietnam. Although touted as having medicinal properties, this is highly unlikely (and in fact, is likely to pass on parasites if you drink it). Venomous snakes are usually used, and this too can cause health problems for those who imbibe. More often, it is bought by travelers for its curiosity value. Knowing the facts behind its creation is likely to deter you from any temptation to buy; often it is made by drowning the snake in the wine. A variation on snake wine is scorpion wine.

Ivory

By now, most people know that ivory from elephant tusks is banned by most countries, and buying ivory souvenirs is tantamount to supporting the poaching of these majestic and endangered animals. But there are still traps for the unwary: Avoid buying anything carved or made from the teeth or tusks of seals, whales, walruses, or narwhals. Buying walrus tusk carvings or engravings (also known as scrimshaw) is legal in the United States — but only if it has been created by native Alaskans. To be sure, you should ask for a certificate of authenticity and check the state laws where you live or are intending to buy.

Exotic "medicines"

Asian medicines — especially aphrodisiacs — are often made from rhino, tiger, or black bear products. Some black bears are milked for their bile in a cruel practice that sees them kept in cages, sometimes for years. According to Animals Asia (www.animalsasia.org), around 10,000 bears are kept on bile farms in Asia. Some are breeding farms, but bears are also poached from the wild as cubs. Farmed bears are starved and dehydrated as this stimulates bile production in their bodies. Bear bile farming is legal in China, and despite being banned in Vietnam since 1992, it still continues. The good news is that Animals Asia — which operates bear sanctuaries in China and Vietnam — is working with the Vietnam government to rescue all bears and close all farms by 2026.

Seahorses

Many of the world's 46 species of seahorses are endangered or vulnerable. Nevertheless, dried sea horses are often sold as souvenirs in places including China, Hong Kong, Singapore, and Taiwan. Although seahorses are now included in CITES agreements, Americans who buy seahorse souvenirs or dried seahorses for medicinal use can bring limited amounts (no more than eight items) into the country for personal use. However, you do need a permit from the country of origin. Find more information from the US Fish and Wildlife Service (www.fws.gov).

Other Things to Watch Out For

Apart from products that harm animals, there are other traps for the unwary souvenir buyer. Here are some of them.

Clothes and other fabric items

When it comes to buying clothing and textiles, natural fibers are usually better than synthetics but cotton and bamboo need water, energy, and chemicals to transform them into the fabric that you may be considering buying. Ask about where it has been grown and if it has been harvested responsibly (and consider this at home as well). While traveling in India, you might see expensive scarves and shawls made from *shahtoosh*, a fine wool that comes from Tibetan antelope called chiru. Poaching for their wool has made chiru a threatened species with an uncertain future.

TIP

Ask yourself if you'd really wear that colorful Nepalese jacket and matching pants when you get back home. What seems like a good idea while on holiday may just seem ridiculous when you get back to reality, like that Indian sari that has sat untouched in my cupboard for the past decade.

Wood products

Carvings and other wood products should be chosen carefully. Whether you are buying carvings, musical instruments, boxes, or other decorations, ask about the type of wood it is and where it has come from. Keep in mind it could be from rainforest or old growth forests. Ask if it has been sustainably harvested. All **rosewood** is protected worldwide under the Convention on International Trade in Endangered Species of Wild Fauna and Flora (CITES). Brazilian rosewood (also known as Bahia rosewood and is native to Belize, Guatemala, and Mexico) is used to make musical instruments and decorations often sold to tourists.

Heritage items

If your budget allows you to consider splashing out on something very old and valuable, make sure you take a good long look at it and ask some hard questions about its origins before parting with your cash. As a general rule, don't buy antiquities and don't be tempted to "souvenir" a piece of a nation's heritage. Make sure that any valuable items you take home have a documented history, aren't stolen, and can be legally exported. Historic religious centers are common targets of thieves and traffickers, so if it looks like it has religious significance, it's probably worth resisting. Similarly, items of cultural significance, such as traditional head-dresses or other artifacts, belong in their communities, not on your wall at home.

REMEMBER

Never take "souvenirs" from landmarks, ruins, or places with cultural or religious significance. Not only is it illegal in most countries, but many believe it can cause bad luck!

TIP

Think about making your own souvenir when you get back home. Choose the best of your hundreds (or thousands) of digital photographs and use an online publishing service to create a book that will serve as an easy and permanent reminder of a wonderful trip.

Chapter **7**
Cultural Sensitivities

Immersing yourself in a different culture, and in doing so learning how other people live, is one of the richest experiences that traveling can bring.

The first rule is to realize that you are not at home, and very different laws and customs may apply. And apart from sheer good manners, respect for the country you are visiting is essential if your vacation is not going to be marred by tangling with the strong arm of the law.

This chapter also looks at respectful ways of photographing people you encounter on your travels and how to engage and connect with First Nations peoples in order to learn about their cultures and lives.

FIND ONLINE

For handy links to all the web addresses provided in this chapter, as well as additional resources, check out www.dummies.com/go/sustainabletravelfd.

Respecting Local Laws and Customs

Being respectful, whether it is in an Asian temple or the quiet backstreets of a Greek village, will help ensure you are welcomed and accepted as a visitor. In today's climate of over-tourism, when many people are tired of their place and space being invaded by strangers, a respectful visitor will get a warmer reception than one who is oblivious to the differences they may encounter when stepping into someone else's world.

Every country will have its own customs and standards of polite behavior. In some cultures, it's impolite to look someone in the eye, to shake hands, or to point with your index finger.

Find out if it's acceptable to tip or if it's expected that small gifts will be exchanged with hosts. In some cultures, a small token gift that represents your home country in some way will be greeted with delight.

WARNING

What might be acceptable behavior or considered a misdemeanor at home might well land you in the slammer abroad. For example, in some countries, including Thailand, it's against the law to criticize the royal family. In Brunei it's offensive to criticize the royal family and illegal to criticize Islam. Ending your holiday with a trip to a foreign jail cell is not on anyone's travel wish list, but that can potentially be the penalty for failing to adhere to the laws and customs of your holiday destination.

FIND ONLINE

Do your research before leaving home; by that I mean more than just knowing the law that surrounds alcohol and drug use, however vital that is. The governments of the United States, Canada, United Kingdom, and Australia, among others, provide online advice for their traveling citizens (find links to those countries' pages at www.dummies.com/go/sustainabletravelfd) that includes information on local laws. These websites can also tell you what to do if things go wrong and where you can seek help from your embassy or consulate. Guidebooks and official tourism websites for the country you are visiting can also be good sources of advice and information.

REMEMBER

Appreciate the cultural differences between your own country and the one you are visiting. Don't expect everything to be the same as at home.

Knowing the best ways to interact with people of other cultures will ensure you get the best experience possible while traveling. How should you behave when you're invited to a private home? Is it okay to smoke? What pitfalls are there to avoid when meeting someone for the first time? The following sections cover the basics of being a respectful visitor as well as some specific areas you should research before beginning your travels.

Behaving in a respectful way as a visitor

One of the first rules of respect in other cultures is often around religion, and this's often most clearly shown in what you wear and how you behave. Make sure you know what is appropriate and what is not.

Do you need to cover your head, your arms, legs? Should you take your shoes off before entering a home? When is it necessary to be quiet? If you wouldn't call out to a friend in a church at home, think twice about doing it in a temple in Asia.

REMEMBER

If you're visiting a conservative or religious place, dress appropriately. No matter how hot it is, women should always cover shoulders, arms, cleavage/chest, legs, and sometimes head. I always pack a sarong or shawl that can fit into a day bag for unexpected times when it might be needed. This might be while visiting a Buddhist temple in Asia or any place in the Middle East where conservative dress is expected. Loose clothing is not only cooler in many places but also does not show the shape of your body.

Men should also be aware that in some places, bare legs are not acceptable, so pack some light long trousers just in case you need them.

In Thailand, huge billboards urge visitors to respect Buddhism — the country's largest religion — by not getting tattoos of Buddha or wearing jewelry or clothing with Buddha's image on them, or otherwise using the sacred image as decoration. "Buddha is not for decoration," the billboards read. In some Buddhist countries, the penalties can be harsh; in 2014 a British woman was deported from Sri Lanka because of a Buddha tattoo on her arm. If you have one, the best thing is to keep it covered.

Indonesia's tourist hotspot, the island of Bali, has introduced similar billboards in respect of Hinduism, urging tourists to dress well and neatly, and behave in an orderly way. A "Dos and Don'ts" card is now given to visitors on arrival, spelling out what is not acceptable in Balinese culture. Binge drinking and wild behavior can result in fines or deportation for those who overstep the mark.

Religious holidays, including Ramadan in Muslim countries, may have restrictions on food and drink. In many places, including non-Muslim countries, alcohol and meat are not usually available on religious holidays. Drinking, eating, or smoking in public on these days is culturally insensitive. Make sure you check what is acceptable or not.

How to interact with communities in a more meaningful way

The differences between yourself and peoples of other cultures are often regarded as stark — until you get to know them! And then you'll find the similarities are enormous, too.

When you travel, you're interacting and engaging with different cultures in myriad ways: food, music, dance, arts, and language are just some of them. Visiting galleries, temples, churches, museums, and attending performances will enrich your understanding of the lives of the people you are among.

Staying with a local family

TIP

If you want to really immerse yourself in the local community and culture, a good way of doing so is to stay with a family. As well as usually being cheaper than a hotel, this ensures that the money you spend is kept in the local community.

One way of doing this is through an organization like Home-stay (www.homestay.com), which has 63,000 rooms in more than 175 countries and operates on the philosophy that staying with a local is an important part of exploring a destination. Many Home-stay hosts expect stays of more than a week, giving you time to really get to know them.

Another option is to look for a company that incorporates homestays in their tours, although this is likely to only be a night or two.

G Adventures (www.gadventures.com) runs "local living" small group tours with seven- or eight-day itineraries in Ecuador, Italy and Croatia, with four to six nights with a local family. Meals are included — but expect to be asked to help with the cooking sometimes. G Adventures also includes homestays in other tours; I've had the terrific experience of staying with a Japanese family in the coastal city of Hagi on the island of Honshu, on a G Adventures' Back Roads of Japan tour, getting a rare glimpse into a century-old three-generation family home with tatami mat floors and bedrooms behind paper screen doors. Helping with the cooking, we learned to make the popular snack takoyaki under the watchful eye of our hostess, Toshiko-san and her 89-year-old mother Satoko-san. There was a lot of laughter, despite some language barriers.

Spending some time volunteering

If you plan to stay longer than a few days, consider spending some of your time volunteering with a local charity or organization that can benefit from your skills and bring you into meaningful contact with local people. There are many opportunities, including teaching English or working with wildlife researchers.

WARNING

Some aspects of volunteering can be controversial. Ensure you think about your ability to contribute in a meaningful and ethical way.

Make sure you do your research before signing up to be a volunteer. Look at the website of the organization you plan to volunteer with. Are they reputable, or a registered charity? Where is the money you are paying likely to end up? How much of that money will stay in the community rather than reverting to the organizer or foreign tour operator? How will the community you are volunteering in benefit from the presence of foreign tourists?

Look for organizations like Domino Volunteers (www.domino volunteers.com) in Colombia, which matches volunteers' skills to the needs of local charities. Volunteers stay with local host families and have opportunities to meet other volunteers and take part in community events. Projects might include teaching English, working in a care home for people who are aged, working in sports programs (surfing, soccer, scuba diving, or more), or promoting recycling programs. Foodies might prefer to help out on a sustainable food project. Placements range from one day to one month.

Attending a cultural festival or local event

Attending a cultural festival is another great way of connecting with a community, large or small. Timing your trip to coincide with a major national festival, where communities are celebrating wherever you happen to be, will bring you into contact with people in a relaxed, informal, and fun way.

If you want to boast of attending the world's largest festival, head to Carnival in Rio de Janeiro where you can expect to join a few million people as they party hard in the streets.

Anyone who has ever been in India during the Hindu festival of Holi, when people douse each other with colored powder, often using loaded water pistols and water balloons, will attest to the joy of celebrating with locals. Wear your oldest clothes on this day, and expect them to be ruined! South Asian communities worldwide, including in Australia and the United States, celebrate Holi, with the English city of Leicester said to have the largest Holi celebration outside India.

Thailand's Songkran Festival, held every April, is also a fun-filled water-soaked extravaganza over three days. It is also celebrated in Cambodia, Laos, and Myanmar.

Festivals of light are awesome. I spent time in Taiwan when the annual Pingxi Sky Lantern Festival, part of Chinese New Year celebrations, was on. In the small town of Shifeng, we joined locals and hordes of visitors — mostly Taiwanese — in decorating rice paper lanterns with messages of peace, hope, and love, and in darkness lit the candles inside them and sent them floating into the sky. As thousands of lanterns soared upwards, I realized that somewhere, they would descend . . . and that it probably wasn't the most environmentally friendly festival to take part in. However, I learned that most of the lanterns are biodegradable and there is a massive post-festival clean-up operation, which put my mind somewhat at rest. But it is a lesson to choose your festival wisely and do some research if you think there will be unwelcome after-effects for the local community.

Indigenous festivals should also be high on your list. These are often smaller than the massive world-famous festivals and can be infinitely more rewarding for the opportunity to talk to performers and learn more about their culture. One of the most spectacular I've been to is the annual Mount Hagen Show in the remote highlands of Papua New Guinea (www.papuanewguinea.travel). This *sing-sing* happens over two days in August and involves hundreds of performers from different parts of the country. It is best experienced through a tour operator as tickets and accommodations sell out early, travel in PNG is logistically difficult, and there is an element of danger for independent travelers. Being part of a tour will also give you behind-the-scenes access to see villagers and performers preparing for the show. Expect feathered headdresses, grass skirts, fully painted faces, and extravagant bone and shell ornaments, such as those worn by this performer I photographed (Figure 7-1).

Lee Mylne

FIGURE 7-1: The Mount Hagen Show in Papua New Guinea is one of the most spectacular in the South Pacific.

I double-dosed on sensory overload on that trip by also traveling up PNG's Sepik River by longboat to the small community of Ambunti for the Sepik Crocodile Festival, where more than 20 tribes gathered to celebrate the role that these revered reptiles play in their lives. In contrast to the Mount Hagen Show, attended by around 500 foreign tourists each year, there were few other

European faces in Ambunti. If you go, expect to see crocodiles of all kinds, including (small) live ones used as part of costumes.

The Gathering of Nations in Albuquerque, New Mexico, is North America's largest pow wow, with more than 3,000 Native American dancers and singers representing more than 500 tribes. It's a family-friendly event, which also includes market shopping and indigenous foods.

Australia's largest indigenous gathering is the Garma Festival, a four-day event held every August in remote northeast Arnhem Land in the Northern Territory. It showcases traditional *miny'tji* (art), *manikay* (song), *bunggul* (dance), and storytelling in a ceremonial site hosted by the Yolngu people. To help visitors, the festival website (yyf.com.au/garma-festival) outlines protocols and required conduct, including dress codes and photography and social media guidelines. In particular, it asks that old people be treated with the greatest respect because "they hold the knowledge and the power."

While large cultural festivals are exciting and often spectacular events, it's also worthwhile seeking out those smaller, local celebrations that will bring you greater connection with the people you are among.

One example is New Zealand's major cultural festival, Matariki, the Māori New Year, held in June/July when the Matariki star cluster appears. Events big and small are held all around the country, and wherever you are visiting is likely to have a community celebration. Matariki (also known as the Seven Sisters) is significant in Māori culture as a time of remembrance, celebration, and looking forward. A public holiday is observed to mark Matariki, with dates shifting annually to align with the lunar calendar.

Speaking the same language

Learning the local language, even if it is just a few basic words and phrases, is a surefire way to indicate respect for another country or culture. And it's not difficult. While you might not master it to conversational level, showing that you have made an effort will bring smiles to those you attempt to talk to, as they recognize that you have shown an interest in their culture. Sure, you might mispronounce words or confuse them with others that have a different meaning — but that very misstep might be the catalyst for ice-breaking giggles. Communication takes many forms.

While there are loads of translation apps available, which are undoubtedly useful for travelers, they do not provide the kind of connection with others that learning the language does.

TIP

Take time to learn basic words and phrases, such as, "hello," "my name is," "please," "thank you," and "no" as well as questions you might ask, such as, "How are you?" "How much is that?" "What is that?" "May I take a photo?" These phrases will get you far.

If you're planning to be in a country for a reasonable amount of time, consider taking a short course in conversational language before you go. You might go along to a class in your hometown, but if that's not a viable option, there are plenty available online and as apps or podcasts, where you can practice your pronunciation in private!

Duolingo (duolingo.com) is one of the most popular language apps, claiming more than 200 million active users. It's free and languages you can choose from include French, Spanish, German, Italian, Russian, Portuguese, Turkish, Dutch, Danish, Swedish, Ukrainian, Polish, Greek, Hungarian, Norwegian, Hebrew, Romanian, and Swahili. It's a great way to learn the basics of a language before your trip. And if you have more than rudimentary knowledge, there is an option to go a bit more in depth.

Tandem (www.tandem.net) is a free app that pairs you with a native speaker of the language you want to learn, with the idea that you teach each other. It's a casual approach that is likely to let you pick up popular slang terms as well. There are more than 150 languages to choose from and a community of more than a million members. You can communicate by text, audio, or video — whatever works for you.

If French is your preferred second language, check out Alliance Francaise language schools. There are 1,016 schools in 135 countries as well as locations throughout France. The United States has 110 branches in 45 states, including in New York, Chicago, Washington, San Francisco, San Diego, and Silicon Valley.

The effort you put in to learning even rudimentary conversation will be rewarded by the smiles you elicit when you put it into practice. See more about learning languages and language schools in Chapter 9.

Getting Snap-Happy

Photographs are among the tangible memories you'll take home after a fabulous trip. Digital cameras and mobile phones allow you to take hundreds — or thousands — of images to keep your memories alive. But some cultures regard photography with suspicion, and it is possible your seemingly harmless attempts to photograph people may be met with hostility or anger.

In most countries, it's not illegal to take photographs of people in public places or to post those images on social media. However, a polite and ethical traveler will always seek permission and explain the intention behind capturing the image.

In some places photography is banned completely. These include military zones, government buildings, or politically sensitive areas. Always obey "no photography" signs, no matter where they are, including in shops, galleries, or religious buildings. When in doubt, ask.

REMEMBER

Before photographing inside churches or temples, check that it is allowed. Make sure you turn off the sound and the flash on your camera, so you don't distract or upset worshippers.

Religious buildings are not the only sacred places that you need to be aware of. For many indigenous cultures, nature provides the sacred places, and photography is sometimes banned in these places. For example, Australia's monolith Uluru is sacred to the Anangu and while you can photograph it from a distance, there are some areas of "the Rock" where they ask that you do not take photographs of rock formations for cultural reasons.

TIP

To avoid any sticky situations, before heading off on your vacation abroad, do some research into your destination and find the answers to these questions:

>> Is it legal to photograph people without their permission?

>> Is it legal but culturally unacceptable?

>> Is it acceptable to photograph children without parental consent? The answer is no.

>> Are there any religious considerations that you need to be aware of?

>> Do you need any permits or licensed guides to access an area?

>> Is it okay to use a drone? What restrictions or privacy laws might apply?

REMEMBER

A no-photos rule is likely to be for a good reason. Photography can pose copyright infringement issues, particularly if artwork is involved. Flash photography has the potential to damage fragile or ancient works, and some venues ban all photography to minimize the risk of someone accidentally using flash.

Can I take your photo, please?

The number one rule when photographing people that you meet or see on your travels is to always ask for their permission before pointing your lens at them. Apart from anything else, it's polite and respectful to do so.

While some might argue that asking for permission takes the spontaneity from the moment and may result in a posed photograph, the right to privacy is more important that your desire to capture a private moment. Similarly, it is possible to use a long lens to stand back and photograph someone unobserved, but in doing so you are ignoring their right to give permission and missing a wonderful chance — if they agree — to learn more about them and their world.

You don't have to speak their language to ask permission. A little sign language will convey your request. Smile, point to your camera or phone, and ask, "Photo?" Most people will understand and either nod and smile agreement or hold up their hand or turn away from you to indicate "no." If they refuse, respect that and move on. Another opportunity will present itself.

Some people may ask for money to be photographed. Sometimes, they will ask before you take it and then you can decide if you want to pay; other times, they will demand money after you have snapped them, especially if you have not asked permission. This can lead to angry altercations, so always ask!

In general, it is not good to pay for photos. If you do, the transaction diminishes a genuine connection with the person you want to photograph. Setting a price also sets a precedent that may be adopted by other people in that community and becomes similar to begging. Future travelers may be hounded by locals — including children — demanding "photo, photo" and any genuine connection between people from different worlds disappears.

Having said that, there are times when payment for a photograph is valid. If you want to get the subject to pose, or to take a series of photos, it may be appropriate to offer payment for a mutually respectful transaction, where you negotiate the fee upfront and agree what you're paying for.

REMEMBER

While it's legal in most places to take and post photos of people for your personal use or social media, it is illegal to use someone's image for financial gain. This applies to professional Instagrammers, bloggers, and professional photographers who require written permission in the form of a model release (templates are easily found online and should be carried with you).

With agreement to be photographed, a door to engaging with people opens. Still, take some time; don't rush in and take a quick snap. Spend time with the person, making them at ease before you start to photograph them. Smile, express interest in what they are doing, and ask questions. Take photos of the surroundings without them in it before turning your camera on them.

Digital cameras and mobile phones with cameras have made it easy to show the image we have captured to the subject, and this often results in laughter and squeals of delight. There are still some places in the world where cameras are a novelty and still some people who have never seen a photograph of themselves.

If you are able to later send a print of the photograph to the person — either by post or by email — it is a lovely gesture that will make them remember your visit for a long time.

TIP

If you're traveling with a group, make sure not to crowd the person you want to photograph. If assent to being photographed has been given, still respect personal boundaries.

Photographing children

While we might never contemplate taking photographs of other people's children in our own country, most travelers are often enchanted by cute kids from other nationalities, particularly those who look different than ours.

While every country — and different states within countries — has different laws around photography in public places, photographing children can be particularly controversial, given concerns around the dissemination of images of children by pornography rings.

UNICEF offers guidelines to help press photographers minimize the impact of photographing and filming young people, and these can act as a guide to questioning the ethics around photographing children during your travels.

Most importantly, it's essential to have permission from the child and their parent or guardian. Think about how you'd feel about a stranger from a foreign country photographing your child. I actually had this happen to me, at the airport in my hometown, when my children were toddlers. An Asian family asked if they could be photographed with my little ones; I was taken aback, but I agreed and watched as my children stood awkwardly with a strange family and smiled in bewilderment for the camera. Later, I wondered how these people described the photo to their friends. Did they pretend they knew us? It's an odd feeling to think that perhaps, years later, that photo of my children is still in someone's family holiday snaps.

Whatever the law is, children have a right to privacy and dignity, just as adults do.

The serious issue of safety is one you must consider. If you're posting an image of a child on your social media accounts, is there the potential for that image to be used elsewhere without your knowledge or permission? Does this have more far-reaching effects on the child than you may have intended?

Another unintended outcome from tourists photographing children is that it can encourage them (or their parents) to beg for money in return. This form of income can then impact their school attendance and they may also be psychologically damaged by being photographed by tourists on a regular basis in order to provide money for their family.

Connecting with First Nations People

The United Nations estimates that indigenous peoples number between 270 to 500 million around the world, meaning almost any country you choose to visit will have an Indigenous population. Some will be the predominant part of the population, while others will be marginalized and almost invisible.

Many terms are used to describe the first peoples of lands that have been colonized — and it can be complicated. In most countries, there are many different groups within the indigenous population. For example, in Canada there are more than 50 different Indigenous Nations and in Australia there are more than 250 language groups within the Aboriginal and Torres Strait Islander nations.

In the United States, indigenous people are referred to as American Indian, Indian, Native American, or Native, and these are often used interchangeably. There are different terms for indigenous peoples in other regions. In the Arctic, the Inuit, Yup'ik, and Aleut peoples are culturally different from Indians. The Canadian Constitution recognizes three groups of Aboriginal peoples: Indians (usually described as First Nations), Inuit, and Métis, and the terms, First Nations, First Peoples, or Aboriginal are also used. In Mexico, Central America, and South America, the use of "Indian" can be offensive, and instead the preferred terms are the Spanish words *indígena* (Indigenous), *comunidad* (community), and *pueblo* (people). In Australia, many indigenous people prefer the term First Nations Australians. "Indigenous Australians" should only be used when speaking about Aboriginal *and* Torres Strait Islander people, who are culturally distinct. Many Aboriginal people prefer to be known by the name of their language group or "country" (lands).

In any country, when talking to individuals, the best approach is to ask them which term they prefer or use to describe themselves.

REMEMBER Indigenous tourism is growing worldwide as people become more aware of the deep knowledge and generational understanding of the land that First Nations people have. Indigenous values and lifestyles are deeply rooted in the land and as such contribute to promoting a more sustainable world. Making connections with First Nations people will enrich your travel experience in ways you cannot imagine before you leave home, as I found on a village cultural tour in Vanuatu (Figure 7-2).

Lee Mylne

FIGURE 7-2: Learning about traditional village life in Vanuatu.

REMEMBER

Expect things to be different when you are on a First Nations tour or attending an event. Things may move at a different pace. Be patient and leave behind your expectations of how things are learned or how things are explained. Listen carefully and when you have questions, ask them thoughtfully. Priorities of First Nations people may be very different to yours.

Why it's important to take a cultural tour

By culture, I do not mean — in this instance — a tour of an art gallery or museum or taking in a Broadway show. Yes, these are all important and wonderful things to do when we travel, but if you want to delve deeper into what makes a country tick you must look further.

Nothing defines a country and makes it unique as much as its First Nations culture. Going back in time with an indigenous guide will allow you to more fully understand the traditions and history of the first peoples of a country. Often, these histories are troubled and still unresolved. Speaking to guides, hearing their stories — often very personal — open up new understanding, if you choose to listen.

Taking an indigenous cultural tour can help support First Nations people economically and in their efforts to maintain their connection to their lands, but it also has a much deeper impact in fostering greater understanding on the part of visitors and greater pride among Indigenous people.

REMEMBER

If you have children, involving them in an indigenous activity such as making music or painting opens up a wonderful opportunity for appreciation of these cultures at an early age.

Tourism gives indigenous people a chance to share their culture, traditions, family structures, rituals and beliefs with others. Ask questions if you don't understand, and you will be met with respectful answers. Sometimes, knowledge cannot be shared with outsiders, so the answer you get may be vague or incomplete, but you have shown interest and that will be appreciated.

While in some countries you will need to seek out indigenous experiences, in others — such as Pacific island nations — most of the people you meet will be native to those places.

WARNING

Ensure you are aware of any restrictions regarding entry to First Nations lands.

Finding and choosing a cultural tour

The most important thing to consider when finding an indigenous tourism tour or experience is that it is owned, run, and led by First Nations people. This helps ensure not only that the information and insights you get are genuine and accurate, but that the financial benefit is also going to an indigenous community or group. It is important to understand the difference between these authentic experiences and other tourism businesses that are neither majority-owned nor operated by First Nations people but which offer "indigenous tourism experiences."

Tourism organizations like the American Indian Alaska Native Tourism Association (AIANTA) and Indigenous Tourism Association of Canada (ITAC) work with Indigenous peoples and can help you to find an experience that suits you.

AIANTA's Native America Travel website (nativeamerica. travel) can help you research authentic native experiences across 12 regions in the United States, including Hawaii and Alaska. You can search by destination or by experience, which might include road trips with a Native American theme, accommodation, shopping, history tours, outdoor adventures (think horse trekking, rafting, or birding), or festivals and arts events.

ITAC represents more than 20 Indigenous tourism organizations across Canada run by First Nation, Metis or Inuit peoples. The Original Original mark enables you to identify tourism businesses that have been vetted by ITAC and are at least 51 percent Indigenous-owned. To find and book Indigenous tourism destinations in Canada check out www.destinationIndigenous.ca.

A dedicated part of Tourism Australia's website (discover aboriginalexperiences.com) lists more than 160 authentic Aboriginal guided tourism experiences. Australia is home to the oldest living culture on Earth, dating back around 60,000 years and offers a huge range of activities and tours in a burgeoning Indigenous tourism industry. Visitors can take guided walks, including at the sacred monolith Uluru, taste "bush tucker'" foods, and discover ancient rock art. Aboriginal tourism experiences are available in every state of the country, in cities, rainforests, and in the vast Outback. It is even possible to do an Aboriginal tour of the Great Barrier Reef.

"Aussie Specialist" travel agents are trained to help you plan and book an Aboriginal-guided tour as part of a trip to Australia.

New Zealand's Māori culture and language is an integral part of daily life. From a cheery "kia ora" in the morning to simple words like kai (food) or whanau (family), you'll find Te Reo Māori words sprinkled through everyday conversation — and it won't take long to pick up on them! It's not hard to find a Māori cultural tour or performance anywhere in the country; you'll be hard pressed to avoid them. Tourism New Zealand (newzealand.com) has plenty of information on its website to help you choose one.

Polynesian countries of the Pacific are rich in Indigenous cultural experiences. The South Pacific Tourism Organisation (southpacificislands.travel) represents 20 island nations and has a strong focus on sustainable and cultural tourism. So if you have a hankering for palm trees and turquoise lagoons, if American Samoa, Fiji, New Caledonia, the Solomon Islands, Vanuatu, Tahiti, or even some islands you've never heard of are calling, check out the website for tour operators and to contact a South Pacific specialist travel agent who can help plan a cultural tour or experience.

Taking an indigenous cultural tour may change your entire perspective of a place — even one you thought you knew well. It's an enriching and exciting way to discover more about your own country or region, which is a good place to start.

Chapter **8**

Enjoying Ethical Animal Encounters

Wildlife encounters can often be the highlight of a trip. There is seldom anything more thrilling than seeing animals in their natural habitat and witnessing natural behavior in the wild. For many people, this is a life-changing experience or a lightbulb moment in understanding the importance of conservation of species and protection of habitat. Learning about other species and their importance to our world is one of the greatest things travel can teach us.

Encountering animals in their own habitat, done carefully and with regard to their safety (and your own), is an unforgettable experience. Whether you plan to swim with the whales in the Pacific Ocean, cuddle koalas in Australia, or trek to see mountain gorillas in Uganda, knowing what to look for — and what to avoid — is the key to doing your bit for the planet.

Introducing your children to ethical animal encounters, and in the process, teaching them about the importance of wildlife and wild places to the planet is one of the best gifts you can give them.

In this chapter, you discover ways you can enjoy animal encounters in a sustainable and ethical way — and how to avoid supporting tourism products and practices that harm them. There are many ways to enjoy nature, both while traveling and at home, that support efforts to protect and conserve, while still having an enriching experience.

FIND ONLINE

Check out www.dummies.com/go/sustainabletravelfd for links to all the web addresses mentioned in this chapter, as well as other helpful resources.

Choosing a Reputable Wildlife Tour

When planning your vacation, look for travel companies that clearly state and actively promote their animal welfare policies. If their website has no information on a Code of Conduct, contact them to ask what their stance is. Your questions may have the power to make them think harder about their responsibilities and may help ultimately stop the exploitation of wildlife.

Look for specifics, such as distances kept from the wildlife, rather than sweeping statements about caring for the environment. Find out if there's an opportunity to get involved in citizen science, conservation, or regeneration projects. What will you or your family learn from the tour? Does the company use First Nations guides?

Choose a company that specializes in small group tours, as these have less impact on the wildlife and habitats you are visiting. Avoid those who pack people into safari vehicles in order to maximize their profits; these tours are often stressful for the wildlife (and not very comfortable for you, either).

Good operators will keep a safe and respectful distance from the wildlife, approach slowly, and minimize the time they spend in each spot. They are also likely to partner with experts in the relevant field and have local guides. Naturalists, marine biologists, and expert guides will give you an enriching and educational tour and a deeper understanding of what you are seeing.

Pick a lesser visited region, as these will be the places where you get the most memorable encounters.

Ask if the tour operator supports a wildlife charity in the places that they visit. For example, in Dunedin/Otepoti, the "wildlife capital" of New Zealand, many tour operators follow a Wildlife Care Code and donate a percentage of their profits back into helping rare, protected, and endangered species, including New Zealand fur seals, northern royal albatross, yellow-eyed penguins, and blue penguins through conservation, habitat regeneration, and rehabilitation.

Many national tourist organizations run specialist training programs for travel agents, which ensure they are regularly updated on tour operators. Agents with specialist status can give informed advice about which tours are run under sustainable and ethical principles.

Travel companies play an important role in changing the demand for captive wildlife experiences — and in doing so, lessen the ability of those who exploit animals to profit from them. According to a 2022 poll by World Animal Protection, 84 percent of people believed that tour operators should not sell activities that cause wild animals to suffer and 70 percent said they would prefer to see animals in the wild than in captivity.

World Animal Protection reports on major travel companies that sell tickets to harmful experiences at captive wildlife attractions. Its website (www.worldanimalprotection.org) tells you which companies have heeded advice to improve their commitment to wildlife-friendly tourism and which have not.

WARNING

Tours that involve close interaction or handling of animals should be avoided, as should those where animals are trained to "entertain" tourists. Choose a tour company that takes you to see animals in their natural habitat; you don't need to touch wild animals to appreciate their beauty or their uniqueness.

Going on safari

Safari is the Swahili word for "journey" but in English it is used to describe game viewing, usually in Africa. On safari, with cameras poised, you can hope to capture images of the "big five" — lion, leopard, elephant, rhinoceros, and buffalo. If you also see hippopotamus, zebra, and giraffe, the experience is complete. There is truly nothing quite as exciting.

Safaris are — thankfully — no longer about game-hunting, as they once were, but firmly about conservation. Finding a safari company that operates responsibly and ethically will mean you are contributing in some way to conservation or social programs and giving back to the communities you visit.

TIP

Kenya, Tanzania, and South Africa are the most popular countries for safaris, but don't discount lesser known — but equally wonderful — destinations like Malawi.

My only African safari has been to Kenya with luxury travel company Abercrombie & Kent (A&K), taking in the Rift Valley and Masai Mara. It remains one of the most memorable trips of my life. I was confident that through the work of Abercrombie & Kent Philanthropy (AKP; www.abercrombiekent.com.au/philanthropy), the local people were supported by sustainable projects that help create jobs, giving them both a personal and financial interest in preserving the wonderful places in which they live. A&K Philanthropy has more than 40 projects in 24 countries, covering everything from scientists working in seabird habitats in Antarctica to supporting a women's co-op in Zambia that runs a bicycle repair shop, enabling the female mechanics to improve the education, health, and livelihoods of themselves and their families.

Choosing a company you're comfortable with

The range of companies offering African safaris is enormous. It's easy to be seduced by gorgeous websites brimming with wonderful images of lions, elephants, and hippos, but is it so easy to know if the safari will be run on ethical lines, with the welfare of the animals and the people who live in local communities at heart? Any good safari company should be committed to conserving wildlife and sustaining local communities. The following tips may help you to choose a company you feel comfortable with:

>> Is the tour company clear about its commitment to responsible travel? Ask for their policy if it's not on the website.

>> Does the safari camp you'll be staying in employ staff from the local community and pay them a fair wage?

>> Is the camp or tour working with wildlife conservation projects, such as monitoring populations or anti-poaching

charities, or with social projects to help local children or communities?

>> Look at reviews on TripAdvisor and other websites to see what other travelers are saying about the safari tour and accommodations.

>> Do the guides have proper credentials and are they well-trained? Are they paid wages or is tipping their main source of income?

In areas where tourism is the primary source of income, such as East Africa, hiring locally is extremely important. For some communities, the alternative to safari employment could be poaching. When local people are employed by safari companies, they learn how tourism and conservation can help support their families.

Costs and other considerations

REMEMBER

Make sure you find out whether your safari tour costs include local park management fees and conservation fees, or if you will need to pay extra for them.

There's no doubt that African safaris are expensive. It may be tempting to consider price when choosing your safari company, but remember that — as with everything — you get what you pay for. Many factors come into play in the price of a safari, including the simple fact that it is difficult and costly to provide all the services you expect in remote areas. Transport, camp accommodations, staff, guides, food, and other services are all expensive to provide, often at an expected level of luxury. In addition, there are conservation fees that go toward the future of these places that you want to see. Sustainable and ethical products and services are also often more expensive, including those materials used to build the safari camps you will stay in. Some camps are now moving to use electric safari jeeps, and these also cost more than those that guzzle gas. Well-trained and experienced guides should also expect to be well paid.

That doesn't mean that you can't find an affordable and ethical safari. All it takes is some effort on your part to do a little research. Look at what the high price tag gives you, and decide if you need all the five-star frills or whether you can have an equally wonderful experience with more basic accommodations. Do you need a camp with a swimming pool and high-end chefs? The high cost of the safari may be going into the accommodations rather than into the local community or conservation projects. That's not to say that luxury safaris are not conscious of their social responsibilities and not doing their bit for conservation; most of them are! But if your budget won't stretch to five-star, rest assured you can still find ethical safaris that are doing great work at prices that are affordable by providing basic or modest accommodations. Make sure you look at the times of year that may also cost less than peak seasons.

TIP

Asilia's Dunia Camp (www.asiliaafrica.com) in Tanzania's Serengeti National Park is the only camp in Africa that is run entirely by women. The Great Migration of wildebeest is within driving distance of the camp for most of the year.

If you are keen to visit a lesser-known safari park, check out those managed by the non-profit organization African Parks (www.africanparks.org), which works in 12 African nations to rehabilitate land and species, reintroduce poached-out animals, and establish or manage new tourism experiences, including camps and lodges. Twenty-two National Parks in Rwanda, Zambia, South Sudan, Mozambique, Chad, Angola, Zimbabwe, Congo, Benin, Democratic Republic of Congo (DRC), and Central African Republic (CAR) make up the network of parks open to visitors. Tourism dollars are channeled back into the work being done in the parks — and into the local communities. All "big five" animals can be sighted in Malawi's Majete Wildlife Reserve, while hippo-, elephant-, and crocodile-spotting cruises sail along Liwonde National Park's Shire River.

The 1,100-member South African Tourism Services Association (SATSA; www.satsa.co.za) has developed guidelines to position the country as an ethical tourism destination through — among other measures — banning unnatural contact with animals, such as elephant rides and lion cub petting, and recommending against animal performances, including those with elephants, primates, aquatic mammals, birds, and reptiles.

WARNING

Tourists who get involved in South Africa's lion cub petting industry are inadvertently supporting the supply of lions to the canned hunting and lion bone trade industries.

Alternative safari-style trips

Think laterally about safaris, too. You may be able to have a wonderful safari-style trip without heading to the plains of Africa. A safari tour to see Madagascar's endangered lemurs — found almost nowhere else in the world — may be an eye-opener to the plight of this primate. Yala, Sri Lanka's largest and oldest national park, is thought to be home to the world's largest density of leopards (check dates as the park closes during leopard breeding season, September/October).

There may not be big cats or elephants, but other types of "safaris" can take you to the habitats of bears, wolves, bison, or deer, particularly in North America or parts of Europe.

UK-based travel company Audley Travel (www.audleytravel. com) offers wolf-focused tours in British Columbia for groups limited to six people. The three-day experience sees participants traveling with two indigenous guides and camping in the traditional territory of Canada's Tlatlasikwala First Nation people, while looking for sea (or coastal) wolves by boat and on land. Smaller than grey wolves, with red-tinted coats, these wolves are only found between the coastlines and islands of south-western Alaska and Vancouver Island and have a diet of around 90 percent seafood.

Despite the name, desert safari tours in places like Dubai, Jordan, and Egypt are less about wildlife and more about activities like sandboarding, quad-bike rides on the dunes, and camel rides. While some of these are run as social enterprises to benefit Bedouin communities and offer an insight into these fascinating desert tribes, choose your tour company carefully. When looking for an eco-friendly desert camp, ask if it uses solar power, has air-conditioning (and how that is powered), employs local communities, and how its water is sourced for showers and toilets.

If you witness something during your safari that concerns you, be sure to bring it up with the company and leave a review online to alert other travelers.

Walking on the wild side

Hiking and trekking adventures that incorporate wildlife watching are a fantastic way to explore a new destination. Not only will you be limiting your impact on the planet by using only the power of your feet to travel, but you'll gain a whole new appreciation of the world around you.

Group excursions

While hiking and trekking can be done independently, group excursions run by reputable tour operators are a better option for many people. If your aim is to see wildlife on your adventure, the best choice is to go with experts who know the best places to find animals, know the safety issues that might arise, and who can take care of any necessary permits you might need.

For example, you cannot simply turn up in Rwanda, Uganda, or the Republic of the Congo (not to be confused with the Democratic Republic of the Congo or DRC) and hope to see the mountain gorillas independently. Any treks into remote or wilderness areas need to be carefully organized by a tour company and tourists must follow strict rules, including keeping your distance from gorillas, staying away if you have a cold or flu (even gorillas can catch them, as well as COVID-19), and wearing a mask while visiting gorillas. Visits to gorilla communities are tightly controlled to limit the number of tourists, to avoid disturbing the gorillas. Group sizes are limited (and to participants over 15 years old), as is the time spent observing the gorillas (one hour).

TIP

Gorilla trekking permits in Africa range from $400 to $1,500 (at time of printing). Remember to check if the cost is included in your tour package.

Gorilla trekking has proved to be a major conservation success story. There are now only about 900 mountain gorillas left on Earth and seeing them is a true privilege; there are no mountain gorillas in zoos, where they do not survive. The income from gorilla trekking tourism has transformed many poachers into conservationists, now earning their living from protecting these amazing creatures and valuing them. If the tour company offers you the services of a local porter for your trek, take it up; the small amount it costs will help provide a living for a local family and will encourage them to help protect the gorillas. Gorilla trekking tourism is now vital to the gorillas' survival.

TIP

Rwanda is the best place to see gorillas in Africa if you are short of time because of the proximity to Kigali International Airport.

In Rwanda, the critically endangered primates can be seen in Volcanoes National Park, where the legendary Dian Fossey (of *Gorillas in the Mist* fame) worked. As well as gorillas, you may see the rare golden monkey as well as many birds. Tourism ventures contribute 10 percent of revenue to community and conservation projects in the park.

In Uganda, Bwindi Impenetrable Forest National Park is the place to trek to the mountain gorillas, while Kibale Forest is the top spot for trekking to see chimpanzees. Mgahinga National Park is home to the golden monkeys on the slopes of the Virunga Mountains.

Congo's Odzala-Kokoua National Park is a sanctuary for the smaller Western Lowland gorillas. Access to gorillas is much easier here, without the need to trek for several hours as you do in Rwanda or Uganda. Congo also allows three-day treks, which the other two countries don't, and offers treks in search of forest elephants, buffalo, and chimpanzees.

TIP

Book as early as you can for gorilla trekking in Rwanda as tours have limited numbers and often sell out up to a year in advance.

Waking to the haunting sound of the song of the gibbon remains one of my own most memorable wildlife travel experiences. On a tour with The Gibbon Experience (www.gibbonexperience.org) in northern Laos, I trekked with local guides for three days in Nam Kan National Park. Our small group also "flew" by zipline through the jungle and slept in purpose-built treehouses high in the forest canopy. It's not for those afraid of heights, although I soon overcame my fears. The Laotian Black Crested gibbons were relatively elusive, although we saw them at a distance and heard them singing each morning. Founded by French national Jef Reumaux, The Gibbon Experience funds projects to give villagers an income that does not come from slash-and-burn farming, poaching, or logging.

In other parts of Asia, such as Indonesia and Malaysia, gibbons and other wildlife are being endangered by the loss of habitat, including to palm oil plantations. In Sumatra, plantations are destroying the habitats of orangutans and Sumatran tigers. Palm oil is found in almost half of all supermarket products, according to some estimates, but is not always labeled as such. Without even setting foot in another country, you can help these wild creatures by refusing to buy products that contain palm oil (sometimes disguised by being labeled "vegetable oil"). Palm oil itself is not inherently bad, but the destruction of rainforest to make way for plantations needs to be addressed. Either avoid buying products containing palm oil at all or ensure that any palm oil is 100 percent Segregated Certified Sustainable Palm Oil. Asian elephants are also at risk from habitat lost to palm oil plantations.

WARNING

A major threat to Eastern Lowland Gorillas, who live only in the Democratic Republic of Congo, is the mining of minerals such as coltan, a metallic ore used in mobile phones and other electronic devices. Mining destroys forest habitat and brings gorillas into closer contact with people, increasing the risk of disease and injury to the gorillas. Use your phone, or other device, for as long as possible and recycle it thoughtfully.

Walking on the not-quite-so-wild side

Not all wildlife treks require traveling to remote regions. Think outside the box and look for hiking adventures in North America, Europe, or Australia. Many tour companies offer multiday treks that give you the chance to see elusive animals along the way. For example, Much Better Adventures (www.muchbetteradventures. com) runs winter hiking and wolf tracking in Italy, wolf and moose tracking in Sweden, and tours to track wild bison, bears, and wolves in Romania's Tarcu Mountains.

Australia has some of the world's most unique species, including kangaroos, koalas, platypus, echidnas, quolls, quokkas, Tasmanian devils, wombats, and other lesser known marsupials. Some of them are more active at night, so consider a nocturnal walk as an alternative to day treks. Several reputable companies, including FNQ Nature Tours (www.fnqnaturetours. com.au) in Cairns and Premier Travel Tasmania (www. premiertraveltasmania.com), include these as part of their offerings. Often called "spotlighting tours" they can open up a new perspective on the life of these animals. However, if camping or looking for wildlife at night, remember that spotlights or white light can disturb them and potentially leave them temporarily blinded. Always use red-filtered spotlights and never use flash photography. Short nocturnal or day walks are a great way to see wildlife if you are short of time. On a day tour with FNQ Nature Tours in Queensland's Wet Tropics region, I spotted rare Lumholz's tree-kangaroos (yes, really!), Boyd's forest dragon (a type of lizard), and the always elusive platypus (for the first time in my life).

Encountering wildlife on your own hikes

Wildlife can also be a highlight of independent trekking, often as an unexpected bonus to a hike. Whether you are close to home, or traveling overseas, remember that if you are walking in unfamiliar or remote locations, you are the visitor and the animals you might encounter live there and should be treated with care and respect.

A few tips to remember if you chance upon some furry friends:

» Walk quietly and do not chase animals, forcing them to flee. An exception is in bear country where it is good to make a little noise so you don't surprise a bear.

» Always observe animals from a distance. If you encounter wildlife along a trail, give them space and do not approach — especially if it is a mother and her young.

» Never feed wild animals. Dependence on humans for food may affect animals' natural ability to hunt and forage and will endanger their health.

» When camping, store food in airtight containers and never leave food out at night. Be careful not to drop food scraps on the trail.

» Do not camp between animals and their water source. Camps should be 200 feet or more from water to minimize disturbance to wildlife and ensure they have access to drinking water.

» Be careful with washing and human waste disposal, so that water sources are not polluted, endangering animals who drink from them or live in them.

Whale-watching and other aquatic encounters

Gasps of wonder, surprise, and delight are common reactions for whale watchers, one of the most popular ways to connect with the aquatic world — mostly without getting wet. Around the world, whale watching tours can take you into the realm of these majestic giants of the deep.

While it seems a harmless activity — and one that engenders great joy for participants — it is essential to ensure that your tour does not harm the whales. Every country has its own rules around whale watching, so make sure that you are familiar with the local rules and that your tour operator adheres to them, including adhering to distance guidelines.

Responsible whale watching can educate us about the need to conserve the species and about the risks that still remain for them. These include entanglement with fishing lines and shark nets, pollution from toxic metals in the water, noise pollution, rising ocean temperatures, and ship strikes.

Most whale watching boats have experts aboard to talk about the importance of whales and to collect data. This is often where you can help; photos of whale flukes (the underside of the tail), like the one in Figure 8-1, can help scientists track movements.

Lee Mylne

FIGURE 8-1: A whale fluke pattern is as unique as a fingerprint.

Whale flukes are like fingerprints; each has a unique pattern of pigmentation, used to identify individuals. As the classic shot that every photographer likes to get is a whale's tail in the air as it dives under the water, these can be used by researchers, providing potentially useful scientific information. Sightings of individuals from year to year along a migration path can reveal valuable information about life histories, population size, migration timing, travel speeds, movement, and association patterns.

There are many species of whale — about 30 species live in Canadian waters alone — and tourist boats to see them have become big business around the world. But is our desire to see them actually harming the whales? Before booking your whale-watching tour, check out the relevant rules where you plan to go.

Most countries have strict guidelines and laws surrounding whale watching, with certification programs for tour operators. In the United States, most whale-watching tours follow the National Oceanic and Atmospheric Administration (NOAA) Marine Life Viewing Guidelines (which also cover other species including dolphins, porpoises, sea turtles, seals, sea lions, and corals). The International Whaling Commission has an online list of the guidelines followed in around 30 countries. While these vary according to the destination, they cover such things as minimum distances that boats may approach whales, the number of boats that are allowed to be around pods of whales, use of drones, what to do if you see an injured whale, and swimming with whales and dolphins.

WARNING

In some countries, whale meat is still on the menu. Although you can choose from many whale-watching tours in Iceland, be aware that this is one of the few places in the world where whales are still commercially hunted (along with Japan, South Korea, and Norway).

The World Cetacean Alliance, supported by World Animal Protection, has developed a global accreditation scheme which recognizes outstanding destinations that offer and celebrate responsible and sustainable whale and dolphin watching. These places are designated as Whale Heritage Sites.

Whale Heritage Site status provides tourists with an easy way to choose destinations where people can see whales and dolphins in their natural habitat and in an authentic and respectful way.

There are only four Whale Heritage Sites in the world: The Bluff, South Africa; Hervey Bay, Australia; Dana Point, California; and Tenerife-La Gomera in Spain.

Dana Point, California, is one of the best places to view the blue whale, has a variety of year-round whales and more dolphins per square mile than anywhere in the world.

Australia's Great Barrier Reef is the site of the only known predictable gathering of the dwarf minke whales in the world. First discovered in the 1980s, around 60 to 80 minke whales play in the waters off Queensland's northern ribbon reefs during the winter months (June and July). Under a Code of Practice developed for tourism vessels, encounters are carried out on the whales' terms and chasing whales is outlawed.

However, minke whales are curious, often seeking out dive boats, at times seeming to recognize divers and snorkelers, and following them to different dive sites.

Only seven licenses to conduct swims with dwarf minke whales are approved by the Great Barrier Reef Marine Park Authority, with only a few tour operators running liveaboard expeditions. Day and overnight trips are available to swim with these inquisitive whales.

Spotting whales from the shore

Of course, you don't have to be aboard a boat to see whales displaying their natural playfulness, breaching, tail-slapping, and so on . . . if you're on a coastline that overlooks a migratory path — particularly for humpbacks — it's often easy to spot them from the shore. Look for spouts and flukes!

In North America, The Whale Trail (www.thewhaletrail.org) lists 100 lookouts along the Pacific Coast from British Columbia to Southern California, where you are likely to spot whales, dolphins, porpoises, seals, sea lions, and otters. It also has a guide to the best times of year to see certain species.

Swimming with marine life

Fascination with marine mammals has led to new ways to get close to them, such as tours that promote swimming with whales and whale sharks. The South Pacific archipelago of Tonga is reputedly the world's best place for swimming with humpback whales, as they pause to rest on their annual migration from the Antarctic. Other places in the South Pacific where whale swims are allowed include Niue, French Polynesia, and Australia.

Swimming with humpback whales can potentially result in serious injury. Behaviour such as breaching and tail and fin slapping are important social behaviors — but getting in the way of a powerful 53-foot-long (16-meter-long) animal that weighs more than a small car is best avoided. Only swim with an experienced in-water guide on a tour with a reputable operator. If the whales are active, stay well clear, sticking to distance guidelines — or stay out of the water entirely.

Guidelines also apply to swimming with manta rays, which is popular in a number of places, including Hawaii, Australia, and the Maldives.

In a similar way to the identification of whales, images of manta rays' ventral surface (underbelly) can be submitted to the Manta Trust database to help research into migration patterns, population sizes, and movements.

The UK-based conservation charity Manta Trust (www. mantatrust.org) runs liveaboard and land-based dive and snorkel trips that allow visitors to get up close to manta rays, whale sharks and other marine species. Manta Expeditions operates in Indonesia, the Maldives, Mexico, Ecuador, Thailand, Myanmar, and the Azores.

In the Maldives, Manta Trust also partners with InterContinental Maldives Maamunagau Resort to run retreats based around swimming with manta rays. The resort is located within the UNESCO Biosphere Reserve Raa Atoll, home to a large population of reef manta rays, which feed in the Maamunagau Lagoon from December to April. As reef manta rays are listed as "vulnerable" and Oceanic manta rays as "endangered" on the IUCN Red List, the research in the Maldives helps to increase knowledge and understanding, which can be used to guide conservation measures around the world.

In French Polynesia, feeding of manta rays and sharks is banned, but swimming with whales, dolphins, sharks, and rays are all possible.

When in the ocean, make sure you are not wearing sunscreen that contains oxybenzone, octinoxate, or octocrylene, which are toxic to sea life. Some destinations, including the US Virgin Islands, have banned their use, but wherever you are, it is better to wear a rash suit and use only non-nano mineral sunscreen containing zinc oxide and titanium dioxide, the only sunscreen ingredients deemed safe and effective by the FDA.

WARNING

While this section has concentrated on swimming with marine life in the wild, avoid tours (such as those organized by cruise ships and some tour operators) that enable or encourage swimming with captive wildlife such as dolphins. See more on this later in the chapter.

Cuddling up to koalas

For many years, one of the top things on the list of international visitors to Australia was to cuddle a koala. These furry marsupials have a high cuteness factor and a photograph holding one was *de rigueur* for many Australians as well as visitors.

Australia's tourism industry, including the peak body Tourism Australia, promotes koala cuddling as an unforgettable experience, pointing out that measures are in place to protect the health and safety of the animals.

In reality, there are only a few recommended places you can get up close with a koala. Some Australian states have banned the practice of holding a koala, but it is still possible to hold one in Queensland, South Australia, and Western Australia. Some wildlife parks are now choosing to replace "cuddling" with the chance to stand beside a koala placed on a tree branch while you have a photo taken. Both of these experiences incur a fairly hefty fee.

TIP

There are no koalas in the Northern Territory.

In the wild, koalas are solitary animals. In captivity, they are usually kept in enclosures alongside several others. While they submit to handling, they have not entirely adapted to close contact with people and can sometimes become stressed. Wildlife parks rotate koalas for public display to try to limit the stress put on them.

WARNING

Even in captivity, koalas are wild animals. If you do decide to cuddle one, be aware that they have sharp claws (and are likely to cling to you), as shown in Figure 8-2, and have been known to urinate on unsuspecting visitors (including startled celebrities such as Harry Styles, Kelly Rowland, and Eva Longoria).

Lee Mylne

FIGURE 8-2: Koalas may look cute, but they have sharp claws.

The oldest and largest sanctuary is Lone Pine Koala Sanctuary, in Brisbane, Queensland, which is home to more than 130 koalas. An hour's drive south of Brisbane at Currumbin Wildlife Sanctuary on the Gold Coast, you can visit the excellent wildlife hospital which treats injured animals — including koalas — and releases them into the wild. An hour's drive north of Brisbane is Australia Zoo, founded by the late Steve Irwin (of *Crocodile Hunter* fame), which also offers koala cuddles. On Magnetic Island, off the Queensland coast near Townsville, you can hold one at Bungalow Bay Koala Village.

TIP

See koalas in the wild in Queensland's Magnetic Island National Park, where there is a population of around 800 koalas, introduced to the island in the 1930s. Take the Fort Walk for the best chance of seeing them.

There are plenty of wildlife attractions in and around Sydney where you can see koalas if you are not set on seeing them in the wild or holding them. One of the best is Featherdale Wildlife Park.

In South Australia, head to Cleland Wildlife Park in the Adelaide Hills or Gorge Wildlife Park, forty minutes' drive from Adelaide to hold koalas. On Kangaroo Island, you may see them in the wild and can get close up at Kangaroo Island Wildlife Park.

The only place in Western Australia that offers koala cuddles is Cohunu Koala Park, outside Perth, where there are around 25 koalas.

TIP

Other renowned spots for seeing koalas in the wild are on Raymond Island in Victoria and at White Hill Reserve, about 4 miles (7 km) from the Brisbane city center in Queensland. They are sometimes hard to spot, but a sure sign is people beneath the trees, gazing upwards!

Australian company Echidna Walkabout, which has been researching koalas for nearly thirty years, suggests the following Sustainable Wild Koala Watching Code:

>> Never touch the tree a koala is sitting in. This indicates predatory behaviour to the koala.

>> Maintain a distance of at least 33 feet (10 meters) from any wild koala.

>> Do not surround a koala's tree. Nervous koalas will move so the tree is between you and them; if they are surrounded, that is difficult to achieve.

>> Avoid excessive movement or noise around wild koalas. This can increase the koala's stress levels.

>> Do not try to get the animal's attention by making noises.

Echidna Walkabout (www.echidnawalkabout.com.au) also offers the chance for visitors to help with citizen science and tree planting to restore koala habitat in the state of Victoria.

Most of the wildlife parks in Australia also offer the chance to hold, pat, or feed a range of native animals, including kangaroos, wallabies, snakes, crocodiles, and more, under controlled conditions and for an additional cost.

Avoiding Unethical Animal Experiences

Have you ridden an elephant in Thailand? Patted a captive tiger cub? Cuddled a koala in Australia? Witnessed a bullfight in Spain or attended a rodeo in Colorado? Sure, it can be a thrill — and I confess I have done many of those things over the years. But I'm smarter — and better informed — now, and I won't be doing them again.

There's a growing list of animal encounters that we should avoid. Concerns over the conditions in which captive animals are kept and "trained" to do their keepers' bidding for our entertainment have made some animal encounters no longer palatable to many travelers. These animals, including elephants, big cats, primates, dolphins, seals, and many other species, live away from their natural habitats, often being subjected to abuse and made to perform for the entertainment of tourists.

Many people who love animals may actually contribute to the suffering of wild animals simply because they don't understand or see the cruelty that can be inflicted on performing or captive animals. But if you know what to look for, you can learn to make better informed, animal-friendly choices.

When I started traveling the world, few people — including me — gave any thought to how animals that were used for public entertainment were treated. I'm happy that times have changed.

The issue of animal cruelty and use of animals for the entertainment of tourists is a complex one, which is often the subject of heated and emotional debate. But there is a strong global movement against tourism experiences that exploit or potentially harm wild animals.

TIP

You can still experience the adrenaline-inducing sight of wild animals in their habitat by choosing the right tour operator or safari company, by thinking outside the box when deciding what nature-based holiday you might take, and by carefully considering the ethical implications of certain animal attractions.

The UK-based World Animal Protection (www.worldanimal protection.org.uk) estimates that there are up to 550,000 wild animals being used as tourist entertainment in wildlife attractions around the world. Every tourist who decides not to visit these attractions will help make a difference to the welfare of animals across the planet.

Some activities should be avoided at all costs. Others can open up a new world of discovery for you. In this section, I outline some of the traps and pitfalls of animal tourism and show you how to learn more about wildlife without endangering them. There are also some great ways to help save species and directly contribute to their welfare and continued survival. After all, who can contemplate a world where our grandchildren can't see an elephant or tiger, too?

REMEMBER

Think hard about activities that might also have an impact on unseen animals. If you decide to drink *kopi luwak*, that oh-so-expensive coffee made famous by Jack Nicholson and Morgan Freeman in *The Bucket List*, spare a thought for the civets who produce the raw material for it, often in cages in Indonesia. It's one case of out-of-sight, out-of-mind (and yes, guilty!).

Another aspect of the debate centers around zoos. Should we visit zoos, taking into consideration the good work they often do in conservation and breeding endangered animals? These are among the questions I address in this section, but it is up to you to decide how you approach each of these dilemmas.

Elephant encounters — the good and the bad

Elephant rides are offered to tourists in many places in Asia and are taken up enthusiastically by many. Thailand, India, Sri Lanka, and to a lesser extent Indonesia and Vietnam, are the places you are most likely to encounter elephant rides and other elephant entertainment.

While elephant rides and entertainment are no longer considered ethical, there are still places where you can see elephants without compromising your stance on such matters, including elephant hospitals and sanctuaries.

WARNING

Anywhere that elephants are in chains or living in small spaces is usually a place to avoid. It may be exciting to Western eyes to see elephants in a busy street in Bangkok or Colombo but the lives of these "domesticated" elephants are often characterized by cruelty, neglect, and exploitation.

In both Thailand and India, elephants are an integral part of the culture, being used for religious ceremonies, royal parades, festivals, and as working animals in industries such as logging. Some are well cared for, and domestication has been going on for centuries.

Thailand

The elephant is the national animal of Thailand, and they are considered sacred by Buddhists. But today most domesticated elephants in Thailand work in the tourism industry. According to the Tourism Authority of Thailand, more than 80 percent of all tourists who visit northern Thailand will visit an elephant camp or sanctuary. Interactions between tourists and elephants usually consist of riding, but, in recent years, there has been a move toward feeding, bathing, and accompanying elephants on foot on jungle treks, as rides have become less acceptable to international visitors.

However, there are also places that train elephants to do "circus tricks," including standing on their hind legs, kicking soccer balls, painting pictures on canvases (later to be sold), and even to play musical instruments.

TIP Before visiting any elephant attraction — even those called "sanctuaries" — make sure you research thoroughly their methods of operation, the conditions elephants are kept in, and the level of human interaction allowed. Have they been accredited by reputable animal welfare organizations or met any of the standards imposed by government bodies?

That said, some elephant sanctuaries do wonderful work in looking after tamed elephants, those who have worked in the logging industry, for example, and are not able to be released into the wild.

TIP If you are interested in the welfare of elephants in Thailand, a visit to the Lampang Elephant Hospital, pictured in Figure 8-3, is an eye-opener. Since 1994, this facility has treated thousands of sick and injured elephants — everything from shotgun or barbed wire injuries to those who have stepped on landmines near the Laos or Myanmar borders. I found it quite distressing, but it is a better place to visit than those that offer "shows" and rides, including the neighboring (but unconnected) Thai Elephant Conservation Center (which also has a hospital).

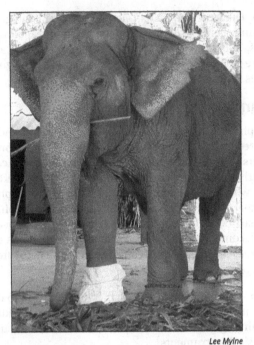

Lee Mylne

FIGURE 8-3: Patient at Lampang Elephant Hospital, Thailand.

There are several attractions in Thailand that are based on ethical standards of care. One of these, which I have stayed at, is the Elephant Hills Elephant Experience at Khao Sok National Park. Elephant Hills has a sister property, The Bush Camp in Chiang Mai, which overlooks the Ping River and offers accommodation in a tented camp powered by solar panels. Another highly regarded operation is Elephant Nature Park near Chiang Mai in northern Thailand. Both of these attractions have won multiple awards for responsible tourism and animal welfare. Neither of these attractions run elephant rides or allow visitors to bathe with the elephants, but they do give visitors the chance to wash and feed them.

India

As in Thailand, elephants in India were "domesticated" long before there was a tourism industry, being used for ceremonies, transport, construction, and logging. However, it is quite common now for these majestic beasts to be used for tourist rides.

A survey by the government-backed Project Elephant in 2000 found that 3,400 domesticated elephants were being used in forestry, temples, and by private owners, with around 200 of them housed in zoos or being used as circus animals. It is also not uncommon in India to see elephants working or begging in city streets, in conditions that are completely unsuitable for them.

WARNING

Most of the tourist elephants in India are found at the Amber Fort in Jaipur — a spectacular place to visit — where they are reputedly not well cared for. Think about this as you contemplate a ride.

While India does have some very strict elephant legislation in place, the laws are reportedly not enforced and largely ignored by elephant owners.

Sri Lanka

In Sri Lanka, domesticated elephants are used to give tourists rides, although this is less common than in places like Thailand and India. A major tourist attraction in Sri Lanka is the Pinnawala Elephant Orphanage, operated by the National Zoological Gardens. This puts it into the category more of "zoo" than "orphanage," although its original aim in the 1970s was to provide care for orphaned baby elephants found in the wild. Today, Pinnawala's 93 elephants make up the largest herd of captive elephants in the world as a result of a breeding program. However, recent reviews of this attraction — which I visited some years ago — are generally very poor and many major tour companies no longer include it on their itineraries because of poor conditions for the elephants.

TIP

Places to consider if you want to see elephants in Sri Lanka are Udawalawe National Park (home to the Elephant Transit Home), Minneriya National Park, Wasgamuwa National Park, and Yala National Park. While you can self-drive in these parks, safari tours of all parks are available and are a better option to maximize your chances of seeing wildlife.

Conflict between elephants and humans is a problem in some parts of Sri Lanka. In early 2023, Sri Lankan hotel group Uga Escapes opened the country's first Elephant Research Centre (ERC) in partnership with researcher Dr. Prithiviraj Fernando to try and resolve this conflict. The ERC is at one of Uga's five hotels, Ulagalla, near the ancient capital Anuradhapura, in Sri Lanka's north.

In 2020, 320 elephants and 70 people died in incidents relating to human-elephant conflict. At Ulagalla, trained guides and members of the local community are monitoring the elephants' habits and habitats in order to prevent local issues of human-elephant conflict. Guests can visit the research center, help track elephants, and visit the Minneriya Reservoir to see elephants congregating; from February to September up to 300 will gather. Nearby Nachchaduwa National Park is also frequented by elephants.

No easy answers

Elephants are iconic animals in Asia, and everyone has their own view about acceptable standards of care for elephants and of interactions with them. While I would never ride an elephant again, having been up close to them myself at sanctuaries that allow feeding and bathing, I understand the attraction of these activities.

But it's a complex issue and one that is a real example of the conflict between cultures. Western eyes may see captivity and cruelty, while Asian residents with generations of living alongside domesticated elephants see it differently. On a visit to Thailand in 2018 my hosts took me to a show which included — to my surprise — performing elephants (including baby elephants). The next day, on a day trip to a temple where elephant rides were being sold, I questioned my guide about her views on elephant tourism experiences. Her response was to ask: "Don't you ride horses in your country?" Her view was that the care and treatment of the animals was the relevant consideration, rather than their training for the entertainment of tourists.

Saying no to bullfighting and rodeos

Spanish culture has a long tradition of bullfighting and although many countries have already banned it, there are still places where bullfights and bull fiesta events are a tourism drawcard.

According to Humane Society International, about 180,000 bulls are killed each year in bullfights around the world, with many more injured in bull fiesta events. And it's a long, drawn-out, horrible death. I've been to one bullfight in my life, convinced reluctantly that it was something I should at least experience once. I left before the end, vowing never to attend another.

In Spain, bullfighting is legal but some cities have chosen to ban it. These include Calonge, Tossa de Mar, Vilamacolum and La Vajol. In South America, although bullfighting is banned in Argentina, it still takes place in Colombia, Venezuela, Peru, and Ecuador. France, Portugal, and Mexico also still allow it. In these countries, there are now places, such as Colombia's capital, Bogota, and five states of Mexico where bullfighting is banned. Mexico's Supreme Court has declared that bullfighting is not cultural heritage, and in June 2022 a suspension of bullfights at Mexico City's Plaza Mexico — the largest bullring in the world — became a permanent ban.

REMEMBER

Bullfighting is not the only practice that's cruel to bulls. Fiestas such as Spain's Running of the Bulls in Pamplona, El Toro Jubilo, where a bull is tormented with fire, and the Toro de la Vega, are other events that should be avoided.

Bullfighting events have also been traditional in other countries. In India, bull-taming contests known as Jallikattu were banned in 2014, leading to protests by supporters who claimed they are part of traditional local culture in the southern state of Tamil Nadu.

In South Korea, bull fighting of another kind is under fire. Annual bullfighting festivals — where two bulls are pitted against each other — are facing protests led by the Korean Animal Welfare Association.

The Association of British Travel Agents (ABTA) lists bullfighting and bull fiestas as "unacceptable practices" in its Animal Welfare Guidelines, which offer guidance to ABTA members and the wider tourism industry. Tourists can vote with their feet and their wallets by staying away from these events.

On a marginally lesser scale of cruelty, rodeos are also events that you should choose to avoid. While the animals are not intentionally killed, animal protection agencies are opposed to rodeos because of the potential for injury, suffering, and distress to bulls and horses. In some cases, animals have died or been so severely injured they need to be euthanized. Bronco and bull riding and events such as calf-roping and steer wrestling can result in serious injury to animals, as well as making them stressed, frightened, and anxious, even in the lead-up to the event.

In the United States, where rodeos are associated closely with Western and cowboy culture, there are no federal laws relating to rodeo animal welfare, and many states make rodeos exempt from animal cruelty laws. However, some states and cities are moving to protect rodeo animals — both horses and livestock — either through total bans or limits on certain events, such as horse tripping, or the use of electric prods.

In Canada, where the Calgary Stampede is one of the world's largest rodeos, attracting around 1.2 million visitors each year, there are few laws to protect the animals involved. In the 2019 Stampede, six horses died, including three in one chuckwagon race, with animal rights activists calling for the races — or the whole rodeo — to be canceled. According to the Vancouver Humane Society, there have been more than 100 animal deaths at the Calgary Stampede since 1986.

In Australia, rodeos are held in all states and territories except the Australian Capital Territory (ACT), the seat of the Federal Government, where they are banned. While some other states have codes of practice for the welfare of animals used in rodeos, the Royal Society for the Protection of Animals (RSPCA) in Australia believes these are "minimal requirements" and opposes rodeos.

New Zealand also has a rodeo culture which is under pressure from the court of public opinion. About 35 rodeos are held around the country each year under a Code of Welfare for rodeo animals, which many see as woefully inadequate. Animal rights campaigners are calling for a ban on all rodeos in New Zealand.

Beasts of burden

While we might balk at riding elephants, there are many other animals that are tamed and trained to carry tourists or their baggage.

In many parts of the world donkeys are beasts of burden and are often ill-treated. After witnessing this in Morocco, I visited a donkey refuge outside Marrakech to see the work being done to help working donkeys, who are often seen hauling carts of bricks and concrete for construction work. Jarjeer Mule and Donkey Refuge (www.jarjeer.org), run by retired English barrister Sue Machin, works in tandem with the Society for the Protection of Animals Abroad (SPANA), a British charity dedicated to the welfare of working animals. The refuge operates as an orphanage, retirement home, and care centre to around 50 animals.

If your tour uses pack animals such as donkeys, mules, llamas, camels, or horses, make sure they are being well-treated. This means not carrying loads that are too heavy; being given adequate food, water, and shelter; and not being mistreated. This also applies to dogsledding.

There's no doubt that there are some places where distances are great and terrain difficult for some visitors. Petra in Jordan is one of those and for many years camel and donkey rides have been offered. Jordan's Princess Alia Foundation (www. princessaliafoundation.org) was set up to promote better condition for the working animals of Petra but visitors are still reporting abuse of the donkeys and pestering by those selling rides is pretty relentless. Instead of buckling under pressure, if you are fit and able to walk, this is the best way of getting around Petra.

Camel rides are offered to tourists in a surprising number of places, including Middle Eastern and African countries and Australia. Is it worse than horse riding, or better than elephant riding? Camels have also been domesticated for centuries and were essential to the exploration of desert countries, including Australia.

While most experts say there is no evidence that riding camels hurts them, the real issue is whether they are well-treated. In many of the countries offering tourist rides, such as Morocco, Jordan, India and Egypt, there are no animal welfare laws, or if there are, they are not enforced. Take a close look at your intended ride and note if they look healthy and calm; if not, move on.

Avoid taking short camel rides with hawkers who operate outside major tourist attractions like the Great Pyramids in Cairo or Petra in Jordan. You will not see the conditions in which their animals are kept; it's better to book with a tour operator whose standards are clear.

What about zoos and aquariums?

Childhood memories of visits to the zoo linger and you may long to show your own children or grandchildren the amazing sights of exotic animals by taking them to the zoo, either at home or on your travels.

Critics of zoos say it is cruel to keep animals in captivity and that it removes their natural behavior and instincts. Supporters of zoos say they play an important role in conservation and protecting endangered species.

The World Association of Zoos and Aquariums estimates that more than 700 million people around the world visit zoos and aquariums every year. So how do we decide if zoos are good or bad?

Attitudes to keeping animals and marine life in zoos and aquariums have changed over the past couple of decades, with many major tour companies boycotting them and some countries introducing new policies around the display of captive animals. There have certainly been big changes for the better in the way animals are housed and cared for, with a trend toward more "natural" enclosures and better diets. Gone — for the most part — are the concrete cages that used to house so many animals.

There is an argument in support of zoos because of the conservation and breeding programs that many run and the work they do in saving endangered animals. But for many large species — such as lions, tigers, elephants, and marine mammals — captive breeding programs are never likely to result in their survival if released into the wild.

Some zoos have affiliations with conservation organizations that work against poaching or habitat loss, either through funding or research. The World Association of Zoos and Aquariums is concerned with the health of animals in zoos, while the focus of environmental efforts takes the form of research, captive breeding of rare animals, and conservation. Zoos are also often involved in genetic diversity programs for endangered species and provide "insurance" populations for them.

For example, aquariums around the world are involved in the STAR Project run by ReShark (www.reshark.org) to reintroduce zebra sharks to the waters of West Papua, Indonesia. In a world first, using genetic stock from aquariums around the world, zebra sharks have been bred, tagged, and released into protected marine areas where they are monitored. At the same time, local communities are educated about the ecological importance of sharks. ReShark is all about restoring sharks to their native habitat in order to balance ecosystems and maintain sharks as important predators in the food chain. More than 60 organizations, including a host of aquariums and the Association of Zoos & Aquariums, are involved in ReShark, which is dedicated to recovering threatened sharks and rays around the world.

WARNING

Some captive breeding programs do not contribute to conservation efforts. There are reportedly more captive tigers in Texas than there are in the wild (think Joe Exotic). Zoos or attractions operated by private individuals are less likely to be run on ethical lines than those run by governments or non-profit organizations, which are required to have accreditation, use reporting systems, and will prioritize animal welfare, education, and conservation.

Similarly, for many large animals, captivity can be bad for their physical and psychological health. Polar bears, for example, need a huge amount of territory to roam in, as do giraffes, bears, whales, dolphins, and other marine giants. Dolphins, orcas, and whales are particularly confined by small tanks, often separated from their mothers at a young age and are trained to perform in return for food.

Aquariums may be great for seeing sea horses, starfish, and small tropical fish but they are not the place for large species.

Zoos are important sources of education for children and can help to engender an interest in conservation. A good zoo will have a lot of information available about the animals — both near their enclosures and on the zoo website.

When deciding to visit a zoo, consider its track record in conservation and how it tries to educate visitors about issues that affect wildlife, such as palm oil plantations that destroy orangutan habitats. This education can help change everyday actions or purchases that can have an impact in the wider world.

TIP

The World Association of Zoos and Aquariums website (www. waza.org) has a searchable map to help you locate an accredited zoo in the destination you are visiting.

A number of countries, including Canada, Costa Rica, Bolivia, Chile, Brazil, Nicaragua, France, Norway, the UK, India, and the Belgian capital Brussels have introduced bans on the keeping of whales and dolphins in captivity, while Dutch travel association ANVR and South Africa's SATSA state that captive cetacean entertainment is unacceptable for their members. In Australia, the

New South Wales government has banned dolphin breeding and the importation of dolphins to the state. Some other individual cities and states have also banned or restricted dolphin and whale captivity.

Look for an open-range zoo, which gives animals more space to roam in habitats that simulate their native territory. These zoos sometimes allow visitors to self-drive through them or offer safari-style bus tours for viewing the animals.

When deciding to visit a zoo, consider these issues:

>> Is the zoo accredited by an organization such as the World Association of Zoos and Aquariums (www.waza.org)? WAZA has more than 400 members around the world.

>> Are the animal enclosures designed to encourage natural behaviors and to provide the space that large animals need? Is there any sign of swaying, pacing, or head-bobbing by the animals?

>> Are the baby animals kept with their mothers? Are their public appearances regulated?

>> Are you allowed to touch the animals? Good zoos will regulate the contact between animals and visitors.

>> Are scientists and veterinarians on the staff? What research projects are they working on?

>> Is there plenty of educational information about the animals and their wild habitats?

What More Can You Do?

By the time you have read this far, I hope you have a better understanding of some of the issues raised by the desire to see other species, either in the wild or in captivity. They are many and sometimes complex, but thinking about our actions and their impact on animals is the first step in making the world a better place for all species, human and animal, and reducing potential conflict.

Perhaps all this information has left you feeling a little confused and helpless. I hope not; there are steps — big and small — that everyone can take to ensure that the desire to travel and to see the wild world in all its glorious diversity does not adversely impact animals or their environments.

Taking time to have your say

When you are planning your holiday — or if you return after seeing something you're not happy with — take time to tell the travel professional you've dealt with. That might be your travel agent, booking agency, tour company, or hotel. By taking a moment to write an email or send a tweet, you can tell companies who are still selling captive wildlife entertainment that you will not book with them again until new policies are put in place.

Write a review on TripAdvisor and report any mistreatment of animals to an animal welfare organization. Tell your friends. Use social media to spread the word.

This might seem a fruitless exercise, but numbers count and if everyone did this, pressure would be brought to bear on these companies. So you will have made a small but meaningful impact to help improve the lives of wild animals around the world.

Looking for other options

If you want to contribute to animal welfare as part of your travels, look for alternatives that will truly benefit them. Choose activities that are supported by local animal welfare organizations and communities.

Do some research before taking part in any wildlife experience and don't be afraid to ask questions of your travel agent, tour operator, or the attraction you are intending to visit. Having a good understanding of the conditions in which animals live will help you decided whether to go ahead and book your visit — or not.

If you can hold or ride an animal or if the "show" is akin to a circus, it's likely that you should decide to avoid the attraction.

How to be an animal-friendly tourist

Being aware of the many issues surrounding the use of animals in tourism is the first step in helping ensure the welfare of animals.

All animals — whether captive or in the wild — should be able to live healthy and protected lives. As a tourist, your encounter with animals can take many forms, and it's up to you to decide whether it is acceptable to you. These tips may help you make good decisions.

>> Visit national parks to view wild animals in their natural habitats.

>> Stay away from nests and dens to avoid putting stress on the animals, especially those who may have young.

>> Understand that when an animal changes behavior because of human presence, it means you are too close.

>> If traveling locally, leave your pets at home!

>> Be calm and quiet. Noise can stress wildlife.

>> Observe animals from a safe distance, whether on land or in the water. Use binoculars, scopes, or a telephoto lens for a closer view. Watch from hides, blinds, or viewpoints that provide minimal interference to the animals.

>> Do not feed or interact with wild animals. Human food is not good for them, and they can become dependent on people as a food source, which can lead to aggression.

>> Be wary of tours that visit animal shelters or "sanctuaries." Do your research and ensure that the facilities are well-run and have the core aim to provide short-term rehabilitation for injured, abandoned, or abused animals or to provide lifelong care for those who cannot be rehabilitated or released into the wild.

>> If you see an animal in distress, report it. Note the details (where, when, and what), take photos or video as proof if you can, and report it to your guide, tour company, local tourist office, and local animal protection organizations.

>> Don't feed "stray" domestic animals, such as the numerous cats that roam Moroccan cities or the dogs in many Asian countries. Sometimes these animals may be free roaming but cared for by a community. Keep your distance to avoid transmittable diseases such as rabies and seek urgent medical advice if you are bitten or scratched.

>> Avoid elephant rides. Bull hooks are often used for training and control of elephants, which begins at an early age and

can involve "breaking" techniques including isolation from their mothers, beatings, and being chained up in small spaces.

>> In Africa, avoid lion cub handling, walking with lions, and photo opportunities with lions. These activities are created by captive breeding to provide a continual supply of cubs, who are taken from their mothers soon after birth. Once they are too big for handling, they are forced into photos or lion walks with tourists. Others are sent to hunting camps to be shot by trophy hunters.

>> Avoid animal circuses, dancing bears, dog or cockerel fights, bullfights, and any festival that causes suffering to animals.

>> Don't visit aquariums or marine parks where large mammals like dolphins or whales are captive in small tanks. While some may be rescued after injury, others are taken from their family groups and exploited for your entertainment.

>> Don't buy souvenirs made from animal products, including ivory (banned in many countries), fur, feathers, shells, seahorses, rhino horn, or turtle shells. Steer clear of "traditional" medicines or remedies derived from endangered or threatened species, such as tiger bone or shark fin.

>> Don't eat at restaurants that include shark fins, turtle eggs, birds' nests, or whale meat on the menu.

Chapter **9**

Escapes That Are Easy on the Earth

A s modern life gets busier and faster, the chance to slow down and reconnect with nature is becoming increasingly valued. Leaving behind digital devices and exploring the wonders of the great outdoors has never been more important. In recent years, when travel was not easy or always accessible, many of us — myself included — reflected on new ways to travel that wouldn't make as much impact on the planet.

Whether it is putting your toes in the sand, hiking through ancient forests, bending low to discover tiny flowers and fungi, diving to see coral reef, or looking up into the night sky, there is a nature-based experience waiting for anyone of any ability or age. Aside from animal encounters, the natural world has much to offer travelers of all kinds and all ages.

Exploring nature is free and available to anyone, a sensory exploration of the world around you. Delighting in everything that Earth can offer may just deliver the most memorable and deeply enriching experiences of your traveling life. Seeking out escapes in which you travel lightly on the planet will reward you in ways you may never have expected.

In this chapter, I make suggestions of nature-based adventures that you can undertake either alone, with companions, or as a family. They do not cost the earth, nor are they hard to source.

This chapter provides numerous online resources. Find links to all of them and more at www.dummies.com/go/sustainabletravelfd.

FIND ONLINE

Choosing a Nature-Based Adventure

While getting up close and personal with animals that we have only seen from a distance — or through books and film — is a dream for most people, there are countless other ways to enjoy the natural world.

Immersing yourself in nature doesn't necessarily mean roughing it. Nature-based tourism encompasses almost anything you can do in the outdoors — and that includes five-star "glamping" and many experiences that don't require high levels of fitness or a deep knowledge of biology. Nature-based tourism is about enjoying natural and undeveloped areas while still caring for and ensuring no damage is done to them. It's the perfect way to reconnect with the simpler things in life, take the opportunity for a digital detox, and recharge your internal batteries. Being active, spending time with family, and perhaps learning something new are all among the benefits of nature tourism. While nature-based tourism is not wedded to eco-tourism, it's a close cousin.

Nature-based tourism is a growing trend, with a huge variety of activities available that can enhance your understanding of the diversity of the planet; improve your own well-being, fitness, and mental and physical health; help with conservation efforts; and help you learn about different species. The following suggestions are just a few of them. Some are easy to organize independently, some can be done without traveling far from home — wherever you live — and others may be best achieved with the help of tour companies.

In choosing a nature-based experience, you're making a decision that will be likely to reduce your impact on the environment by minimizing your travel footprint, as ethical and sustainable nature-based travel has a lower environmental impact than many other forms of tourism.

Whether you consciously wear the mantle of eco-tourist or not, by seeking to minimize your carbon footprint by planning carefully and wisely, you're helping to protect the planet for others. By choosing an authentic and educational tour company that works with local communities, you're also giving back to those who welcome you to learn about their lives and the place they live.

Away with the Birds

I confess: I'm a birdwatcher. I love the infinite colors and variety of birds. They're sometimes weird and always wonderful, and I love to photograph them. I don't take it as seriously as a true birder, twitcher, or chaser, some of whom will travel long distances just for the sight of a rare bird, but I do get enormous pleasure from any sighting of feathered friends, even in my own backyard.

Birdwatching tours are available in almost any country in the world that takes your fancy, but often you don't even have to leave your own in order to see some spectacular avian sights.

From penguins at the poles, to flightless kiwi and kakapo in New Zealand or macaws and hummingbirds in Costa Rica, there are birds everywhere to brag about when you come home.

REMEMBER

Don't feed wild birds. And don't buy souvenirs that are bird products, such as feathers or eggs.

Kitting yourself out for birdwatching doesn't need to be expensive or complicated. Invest in a good pair of binoculars and a field guide (or the relevant app for your destination) and — if you want a visual record — a decent long lens for your camera. A notebook for jotting down anything you may need to remember (time, location, and so on) is also handy.

So, whether you're sitting on your balcony in sunny Spain or in the depths of the Amazon jungle, you only have to look up to see birds going about their business. If you're a complete beginner, start honing your birdwatching skills at home before you sign up for more exotic species.

Birdwatching tours are typically small — 4 to 12 people — in order to get the best experience. Some companies offer boat-based tours as well as land tours, and guides are almost always experienced and passionate birders themselves.

TIP

Look for an app that lists species of bird in your intended destination. Most of them also allow you to record details of sightings, such as date and location.

Wanderlust Magazine named Costa Rica as the world's best birdwatching destination in 2022, particularly the Wilson Botanical Gardens and Curi-Chancha Reserve. Other countries in its list of top places for birders were South Georgia, for its huge numbers of king penguins, Peru's Colca Canyon, Kruger National Park in South Africa, Iceland for puffins, and Yellowstone National Park in the US. North Norfolk in the UK was recommended for its marshes and dunes, including Titchwell Marsh and Cley Marshes. Kenya's Rift Valley is home to more than four million flamingos, and Papua New Guinea has some species of bird-of-paradise that are found nowhere else in the world.

TIP

eBird.org is a website and app developed by the Cornell Laboratory of Ornithology in New York which helps track declining populations — so you can be a citizen scientist as well. In Australia, BirdLife Australia's app and website is birdsdata. birdlife.org.au. A great site for budding birders in North America is www.audubon.org, which has a free field guide to more than 800 species of birds.

If you want to time your birdwatching trip to coincide with an event that will bring other birders together, check out the range of birding festivals that celebrate these extraordinary creatures.

Research can reveal some unexpected places for birdwatching. Instead of going to the most obvious places, look for those that might fly under the radar (so to speak). For example, Chattanooga, Tennessee (www.visitchattanooga.com) has a wide range of protected habitats for year-round birdwatching. The Tennessee Riverwalk is a 13-mile walkway where the great blue heron is often spotted. Belted kingfishers, wood ducks, fishcrows, broadwing hawks, and more can be found in Audubon Acres along the creek and hardwood forest. Nesting ospreys, warblers, owls, and woodpeckers are spotted on Maclellan Island, which is only accessible by water and offers a different perspective on wildlife in the middle of the city.

REMEMBER

Nesting season is a time when many birds are particularly sensitive to intrusion. Keep your distance and stay quiet and hidden, if possible, and never handle a nest or chick. Most birdwatching organizations won't accept photographs of nests with eggs or chicks and have strict guidelines regarding the photography of fledglings.

Kissimee, Florida, may be popular for its theme parks, but birders know it as the home of the largest population of nesting bald eagles in the contiguous 48 states. The Great Florida Birding Trail covers 800 miles and is a re-entry location for the nearly extinct whooping crane. Kissimmee Prairie Preserve State Park also offers excellent seasonal birding, with the chance to see the burrowing owl, grasshopper sparrow, or crested caracara, among others.

In South America, BirdsChile (birdschile.com) runs naturalist-led small group birding and wildlife tours, mostly in Patagonia, following a strict code of ethics and sustainable travel principles. Colombian tour company Manakin Nature Tours (www.manakinnaturetours.com) runs tours to see the harpy eagle, listed as vulnerable to extinction. Manakin works closely with local communities who provide homestay accommodation and meals to birdwatchers. At the start of 2022, there had been less than 100 recorded sightings of harpy eagles, among the world's largest eagles, on eBird.org.

WARNING

Plastic pollution in our waterways can be harmful to seabirds, but the most lethal item is a balloon. Research has found that seabirds are up to 32 times more likely to die when they swallow balloons than any form of hard plastic. Say no to balloons!

It's important that your enthusiasm for birds doesn't result in unintentional harm to them. Always keep an appropriate distance from birds and never harass, pursue, or flush them out in order to get a good photo or a clearer look at them.

Diving Deep

Oceans cover around 70 percent of Earth's surface. If that seems amazing, just think about how vast it seems when you're swimming in it, or on a small boat without much else around. And under the surface of the ocean is another world, just waiting to be explored. If you've ever snorkeled or donned scuba gear to dive, you'll know what I mean.

Diving and snorkeling form a huge part of the tourism industry and provide a wonderful way to see things you've never dreamed of. But just as the rest of our planet is under pressure, the oceans are in need of care.

If you plan to go diving, it's important to travel with a dive operator that values the environment it works in and treats it with respect. Many reputable operators work within guidelines to ensure that oceans, coral reefs, and marine life are protected, conserved, and rehabilitated. Look at organizations such as Green Fins (www.greenfins.net), which promotes standards for marine tourism and lists 700 member companies — dive and snorkeling centers and liveaboards — that adhere to a Code of Conduct.

If you're looking for a dive holiday, you'll be choosing between a resort-based vacation, where you go out diving each day, or a live-aboard package, where you stay on the dive boat for several days. The latter may also include night dives. For most dive vacations, you will need to be certified by an internationally accepted dive instruction program, although some will include "introductory" dives or the possibility of becoming certified during your vacation.

The most popular certification program is run by PADI (the Professional Association of Diving Instructors), the world's largest ocean exploration and diver organization. PADI operates in 186 countries and with a global network of more than 6,600 dive centers and resorts running dive courses. Other well-regarded certification courses are run by SSI (Scuba Schools International), NAUI (National Association of Underwater Instructors, in the US), SDI (Scuba Diving International), and BSAC (British Sub-Aqua Club). PADI and its UK-based partner organization, The Reef-World Foundation (reef-world.org), now offer PADI Eco Center accreditation to those who demonstrate continued commitment to ocean conservation. One of the criteria is membership of Green Fins.

Sadly, there are others who have only profits in mind, resulting in damage and overcrowding. Many dive sites have been damaged by unrestrained visitation and operators who don't care. Do your research before signing up for your tour and check out diver feedback on review sites.

The regeneration of some places — which had been victims of over-tourism but gained respite during COVID lockdowns — showed too clearly how they had been loved to death. Thailand's Maya Bay on Phi Phi Leh Island in the Andaman Sea is a good example. It starred in the 2000 Leonardo DiCaprio movie *The Beach* and was inundated with up to 5,000 tourists a day as a result. Speedboats bringing visitors had a devastating impact on the coral reef and marine life. When the bay reopened in 2022 after being closed for four years it had regained its health and strict controls on boat traffic, visitor numbers, and length of stay were imposed.

TIP

Scuba Diving magazine (www.scubadiving.com) surveyed its readers in 2023 to rate the top dive destinations in the world. Overall, in the Caribbean and Atlantic, Mexico and St. Lucia came out on top; in the Pacific and Indian oceans, Thailand and Indonesia pipped Hawaii at the post. In the United States and Canada, Florida Keys was voted #1, followed by Washington and Florida.

Whenever you are lucky enough to enter the ocean, especially if you are diving on a natural wonder such as Australia's Great Barrier Reef or Ningaloo Reef, in Pacific islands like the Maldives or the Solomon Islands, or in the Caribbean or Red Sea, there are ways in which you can ensure you are acting to preserve these incredible places for others to enjoy.

When choosing a dive company, check out the website for reassurance that they are operating under sustainable guidelines — or ask that question before booking. Look for opportunities to join citizen science programs where divers can help monitor the health of coral reefs or marine life, or join tours that encourage sustainable tourism, engage local communities, or enable you to learn about First Nations' connections to the sea. Most good reef tour companies have on-board marine biologists so that even as a first-time snorkeler, you will get to learn about what you will see when you hit the water.

If you're diving from a private vessel or from the shore, make sure you know about any marine areas that are protected by law and that you don't disturb any underwater heritage sites.

A few ways that you can dive or snorkel sustainably:

>> Wear reef-safe sunscreen. Choose one that doesn't contain harmful chemicals including oxybenzone, benzophenone-1, benzophenone-8, OD-PABA, 4-methyl benzylidene camphor, 3-benzylidene camphor, nano-titanium dioxide, nano-zinc oxide, octinoxate, or octocrylene.

>> Dive locally. Reduce your carbon footprint by diving close to home and support local businesses.

>> Look for dive or snorkel tours that operate with small groups and visit lesser known locations that won't be crowded by other boats and/or divers.

>> Explore shore diving. There are many places where you don't need a boat but can simply wade into the water to begin your dive or snorkel.

>> In the water, watch your buoyancy control, and avoid the need to kick out, potentially damaging coral or marine life.

>> Don't touch anything in the ocean, including coral, plants, or marine life of any kind. Do not try to make contact with larger animals such as manta rays or turtles in order to get an underwater selfie.

>> Consider carrying a mesh bag (trshbg.com is a good option) with you on every dive to collect trash you might see either in the water or on the seabed. Carry a dive knife to cut free any fishing line you see tangled around objects in the water that could endanger marine animals.

>> Don't collect souvenirs, including shells.

Being Botanical

If tip-toeing through the tulips or getting down to ground level to photograph tiny colorful fungi is your idea of communing with nature, there are myriad places to release your inner flower child.

Timing is everything when chasing the best blooms. Spring and summer in either hemisphere will bring out the best that Nature can offer in floral displays.

REMEMBER

Resist the temptation to pick flowers, even in the wild where there are plenty (and no one to see), or to collect seeds. Instead, take a photo or draw a sketch; if everyone picked a few flowers, the effect would be devastating. Picking flowers prevents the development of seeds that produce next year's plants and flowers. Collecting seeds to take home can unintentionally result in non-native species potentially becoming invasive species in a new location. Take home the memories instead.

A few ideas to get you started in your quest for flora:

>> California's **Antelope Valley Poppy Reserve** is ablaze with the native poppy that is the official state flower and 7 miles of walking trails open up this incredible spectacle. Pick a sunny day, as the flowers will close up in poor weather. See it in March and April.

>> Japan is famed for its **cherry blossom season** (March/April in Tokyo and Kyoto, but as late as May in the northern cities such as Sapporo), but it's also a very busy time to visit, with huge crowds turning out to see the best places. Equally lovely, but less crowded, is plum blossom season, which begins in mid-February. Another option for cherry blossoms is Washington DC's Tidal Basin, which holds an annual National Cherry Blossom Festival in March/April.

>> **Tulips** may not be wildflowers, but in the Netherlands they are iconic. The central and northwest areas are the best places to photograph fields of tulips. In Lisse, the 80-acre Keukenhof Gardens displays seven million colorful tulips. Go in April and May.

>> The **lavender fields** of Provence, France, can be explored from June to August by following the lavender trail through the regions of Luberon, Mont-Ventoux, Sault, and Valreas. Stop off at the Musee de la Lavande in Gordes.

>> Western Australia claims to have **the biggest wildflower collection on Earth,** with more than 12,000 species bursting into bloom across the state each season. Because of the vast size of the state, wildflower season has a six-month window, starting in June and moving across different areas. In the state capital, Perth, the September showing is easily seen in the inner-city Kings Park/Kaarta Koomba, home to more than 3,000 wildflower species.

>> **Jacaranda** season in parts of South Africa and Australia will have you in a haze of purple from September to November. A native of Brazil, the jacaranda has taken well to other southern climes. The best places to see them in full bloom are in Pretoria in South Africa, Brisbane (Queensland), and Grafton (New South Wales) in Australia.

>> In New Zealand's South Island, the sight of waving **fields of lupins** (you may know them as "lupines") has stopped many passing summer road-trippers in their tracks (me included) from late November to January. Lupins are actually considered a weed in New Zealand (as an invasive import from North America), but their shades of pink and purple make a wonderful contrast to the turquoise lakes of the Mackenzie Country, including Lake Tekapo.

TIP

Citizen scientists can take digital photos of flowers, grasses, and herbs that are not usually seen and upload them to apps for identification by experts. iNaturalist (www.iNaturalist.org), a joint venture by the California Academy of Sciences and the National Geographic Society, is a world leader. iNaturalist Australia (inaturalist.ala.org.au) is run by the Atlas of Living Australia.

Hiking and Trekking Adventures

Hiking and trekking are among the most sustainable ways to travel, at least once you are in your destination. Anyone with a reasonable level of fitness can do it, and your carbon footprint is low once your feet become your mode of travel.

Whether you decide to tackle a challenging long-distance, multiday (or months) trek, or to go for a day walk, hiking has many rewards and the benefits of getting into fresh air and nature will stay with you for a long time. If you are short of time or want to build up your fitness for a long walk, start with shorter walk. Some long-distance walks can be tackled in stages, and most have websites that will detail how to access certain parts of the trail and how to manage the logistics of independent one-way trekking.

Getting started with shorter walks

One-day (or shorter) walks are also available without heading to the wilderness. Consider an urban hike in your own backyard or when visiting a city. San Francisco's 16.5-mile (26.5-km) **Crosstown Trail** (www.crosstowntrail.org) winds through city streets, dirt paths, and walkways and can be explored using an app, a map, or following signs along the way, taking in the Golden Gate Park and revealing places you might never otherwise stumble upon. Similarly, Boston's **Emerald Necklace** greenway (www.emeraldnecklace.org) is a mix of urban and natural landscapes, covering 1,100 acres and stretching 7 miles (11 km), to link seven parks and green spaces.

Local walking groups often welcome visitors; check social media or websites to find out what's available. For example, in the UK, walking charity The Ramblers offers free "well-being walks" for members, with newcomers or visitors given three free walks. The group runs 50,000 group walks across Britain every year, an excellent option for travelers wanting to explore off-the-beaten track places and to get to know the locals.

REMEMBER

Stick to tracks and trails wherever possible, to avoid trampling plants, delicate mosses, insects, and bugs that are important to the environment. Avoid the temptation to shortcut trail switchbacks by leaving the trail.

Longing for more distance and adventure

If you're looking for serious adventure on long-distance or wilderness treks, wherever you go in the world there will be a hike to suit you. Some great walks to consider when planning your hiking adventure include:

>> Sightings of bears and wolves are not uncommon for hikers on the **Pacific Northwest Trail** (www.pnt.org), which runs 1,200 miles (1,931 km) from the Rocky Mountains of Montana to Cape Alava, Washington, on the shores of the Pacific Ocean. Less well-known than the Appalachian or Pacific Crest trails, it can be tackled in ten sections and crosses some of North America's wildest public landscapes.

>> If you're an experienced hiker, Canada's **Great Divide Trail** (www.greatdividetrail.com) may be the challenge you're looking for. Described as "one of the most spectacular and challenging" long-distance trails in the world, the trail traverses the continental divide between Alberta and British Columbia, covering 684 miles (1,100 km), with some parts of the trail unmarked.

>> If you're looking for a *very* long-distance walk where you can choose your own path, look no further than **Land's End to John O'Groats** (www.landsendjohnogroats.info) in the UK. The beauty of this trek is that there is no definitive way of doing it; choose from a multitude of possible routes between England's southern-most point, Land's End in Cornwall, and John O'Groats at the northern tip of Scotland. The most direct route will cover around 1,100 miles (1,770 km) and take two to three months, depending on your pace and number of rest days.

>> Scotland's **West Highland Way** (www.westhighlandway.org) winds for 96 miles (154 km) between Milngavie, north of Glasgow, and Fort William in the Highlands. Start with the less difficult sections at the southern end of the route (at Milngavie) and expect to walk between 9 and 15 miles (14.5 and 24 km) each day. You'll find plenty of places to stay along the way at campgrounds, hostels, bunkhouses, pubs, B&Bs, and hotels.

>> One of the most famous walks in Europe is the **Camino de Santiago** (the Way of St James), a network of ancient pilgrim routes that come together at Santiago de Compostela in northwest Spain. The most popular route stretches for nearly 500 miles (780 km) from St. John-Pied-du-Port, near Biarritz in northern France to Santiago de Compostela. Pilgrims of all kinds have been walking this trail since the ninth century, and today it is traversed by around 350,000 people each year.

>> A long-distance trail that actively promotes responsible tourism is the **Via Dinarica** (viadinarica.com) in eastern Europe. Spanning about 783 miles (1,260 km) through the Dinaric Alps and Sharr Mountain Range across eight Western Balkans countries, from Albania to Slovenia. As well as providing a hiking adventure, the trail is designed to open up the cultures and traditions of communities along the route.

It is broken into 120 stages, so don't feel you need to do it all! Guided tours of some sections are available. In Western Europe, **Via Alpina** (via-alpina.org) is a network of five walking trails across eight countries, with 342 day-stages along its 3,106 miles (5,000 km).

» Egypt may not be the first place you think of when contemplating a hiking trip, but the new 106-mile (171-km) **Red Sea Mountain Trail,** managed and led by members of nomadic Bedouin tribes, has opened up new opportunities for Middle East trekking. The challenging 10-day adventure is a community tourism project supporting local communities. Expect to see Nubian ibex and desert-dwelling lizards. A sister trail is the 342-mile (550-km) **Sinai Trail,** a circuit through Egypt's Sinai Peninsula.

» South America's iconic **Inca Trail** in Peru, begins from the Sacred Valley and ends at Machu Picchu. There are many other Inca footpaths in Peru and the Andes but there is only one "official" Inca Trail that leads directly into Machu Picchu National Park. All other hikes end in the village of Aguas Calientes, from where shuttles take tourists to Machu Picchu. You cannot tackle the Inca Trail independently; access is controlled by licensed tour operators who employ Peruvian tour guides to accompany hikers. Many reputable travel companies, including World Expeditions, Intrepid Travel, and G Adventures run group treks.

» Book early for New Zealand's most famous walk, the **Milford Track,** which can be undertaken independently or in a guided group. Over five days, you hike (New Zealanders call it "tramping") through the heart of the South Island's Fiordland National Park to spectacular Milford Sound. Guided walkers stay at private lodges, while those who go it alone stay in Department of Conservation huts. Independent hikers must use a booking system which is open only from October to April/May. The easiest way is to book with a guiding company (fiordland.org.nz). On the North Island, the 12-mile (19.4-km) **Tongariro Alpine Crossing** (tongarirocrossing.com) has the reputation of being one of the world's best one-day walks — but it is not an easy one, with unpredictable mountain weather being a major concern. In peak season (December to February), up to 3,500 people each day make the trek up the volcanic Mt. Tongariro, across the saddle and down the other side. Planning and booking is essential; always make sure someone knows of your plans.

>> Australia has many multi-day walks. One of my favorites is the **Overland Track** in Tasmania, which covers 40 miles (65 km) over six days. Independent walkers should have experience, but the other option is — like me — to join a guided group, pictured near Cradle Mountain in Figure 9-1. This ensures everything is taken care of, including accommodation and meals along the track. The spectacular landscape varies from eucalypt forests to glacial valleys, rainforest and golden moors, against the backdrop of the Cradle Mountain-Lake St Clair National Park. **Australian Walking Holidays** (australianwalkingholidays.com.au) has guided walks in every state and territory and commits to a thoughtful travel charter based on sustainability principles. **Great Walks of Australia** (greatwalksofaustralia.com.au) is a collection of 12 of Australia's best multiday guided walks, including the **Larapinta Trail** in the Northern Territory, Queensland's **Scenic Rim Trail**, and the **Margaret River Cape to Cape Walk** in Western Australia.

Lee Mylne

FIGURE 9-1: Walking the Overland Track, Tasmania.

>> Japan's ancient pilgrimage trails provide some wonderful opportunities for self-guided walks. The **Kumano Kodo** trail across the Kii Peninsula is one of only two World Heritage listed walks (the other is the Camino de Santiago in France and Spain). The five-day **Nakasendo Way** takes you through forests, mountains, small towns, and countryside, with the chance to stop off at onsens (bath houses) and stay in local guesthouses. A number of tour companies offer packages that will book your accommodation and transfer baggage for you.

Taking sustainability on the trail

So now you have some ideas about where to go, it's important to remember that sustainable hiking or trekking is not only about your carbon footprint (or lack thereof). Your actions along a trail will also have an impact on the planet, so planning and preparation — especially for long walks and camping in wilderness areas — are essential.

Ensure you are able to carry out all your waste and rubbish, leaving nothing behind. Litter is not only an eyesore, but it can also be dangerous to wildlife. Inspect your campsite and rest areas for trash or spilled foods and make sure you take it all with you. Plastic bags, fishing line, and even organic matter like apple cores or orange peel, should be properly disposed of. If you see something left by earlier visitors, take that, too! Encourage children to take part in the clean-up, teaching them the importance of leaving a place as pristine as you found it and explaining why you need to do it.

Think about issues such as how you will dispose of human waste, toilet paper, and tampons. The best option is to store them in plastic bags and carry them out of wilderness areas with you; another option is to ensure waste and toilet paper is well buried where animals cannot dig them up (tampons should be carried out, as they do not decompose easily). Toilet paper should never be burned, as this can result in wildfires.

Remember to be considerate of other hikers along the trail. If you are resting, leave enough space for others to pass, and travel quietly. Other trekkers and the wildlife and birds will appreciate the silence, and you are more likely to see animals if you do not scare them off.

While it might be tempting to take a souvenir in the form of a beautiful natural object — a shell, rock, feather, driftwood, or even fallen antlers — leave them behind. In some places, such as national parks and other protected lands, it is illegal to remove natural objects.

Leave No Trace (lnt.org) is a useful website that has lots of advice about how to tread lightly on the great outdoors while hiking and camping.

Dark Sky Places

Anyone who's ever camped out or stayed in remote places far from the bright lights of cities or large towns knows the magic of looking up into the night sky. There's no sight more awesome than the Milky Way blazing across the inky sky.

Now, we can find the best places to see the stars in dark sky reserves, parks, and sanctuaries, places where the quality of the starry nights is protected. The International Dark-Sky Association (IDA), the recognized world authority on light pollution and how to combat it, assesses these places based on their exceptional quality of starry nights and nocturnal environment and protects them for their scientific, natural, educational, cultural, and heritage value as well as for public enjoyment.

There are dark sky (www.darksky.org) places all over the world: 115 dark sky parks, most of them in the USA, 20 dark sky reserves, and 16 dark sky sanctuaries, a category for some of the most remote places on the planet.

Big Bend National Park in Texas is the world's largest dark sky park, with more than 1,290 square miles (3,342 square km) protected. Big Bend is one of the best places in North America for stargazing and has the darkest skies of any national park in the lower 48 states.

For the highest concentration of dark sky places in the world, head to Utah. Bryce Canyon National Park has year-round ranger-led programs and an annual Astronomy Festival in June. Many state parks, including Dead Horse Point, Antelope Island, and Kodachrome Basin, have dark sky park status.

The world's largest dark sky reserve is more than 1,686 square miles (4,367 square km) of New Zealand's South Island, covering Aoraki/Mount Cook National Park and the Mackenzie Basin region. Each June and July, New Zealand celebrates Matariki, the Maori lunar new year, when the Matariki star cluster appears. Events are held all around the country, offering a great opportunity to learn about this star cluster and its significance in Maori culture. A public holiday is observed to mark Matariki (dates shift annually to align with the lunar calendar).

Sanctuary status is also held by New Zealand's Great Barrier Island, off Auckland, and Stewart Island/Rakiura, at the southern tip of the country. Another sanctuary I've visited is Pitcairn Island, which claims the title of the most remote place in the world, far out in the Pacific Ocean.

For me, the Australian outback is the place where the star-studded skies have had the most impact, where you can trace the constellations and marvel at the infinite expanse of it. The Jump-Up Dark Sky Sanctuary in far western Queensland, near the Outback town of Winton, is home to the Gondwana Starts Observatory, part of the Australian Age of Dinosaurs attraction.

Australia has only one Dark Sky Park, Warrumbungle National Park in central New South Wales, which in 2019 became the southern hemisphere's first. I mention this in part because nearby is Warrumbungle Observatory, owned by a man with a wonderfully appropriate name, Peter Starr!

Africa has only one Dark Sky Reserve, in NamibRand Nature Reserve (namibrand.com). The reserve is home to the Namib Desert Environmental Trust Centre, which runs an environmental education center in the coastal town of Swakopmund.

In 2020, the tiny Pacific Ocean island of Niue (niueisland. com) became the world's first dark sky nation. Niue is among the least visited countries in the world, with flights once a week from Auckland, New Zealand, with Air New Zealand. Like most Polynesian nations, Niue has a long tradition of navigating by the stars and traditional life was regulated by the moon and the stars. Visitors to Niue can take guided astro-tours.

If this section has put your head among the stars, while you plan your dark sky adventure, get some practice by heading into your own backyard after the sun has set. It may not be as dazzling as a dark sky place, but there's still something wonderful about looking up into the vast universe in which our planet spins and realizing how insignificant our troubles are.

Sailing on the Wind

Using the power of the wind and the sea to sail the ocean waves can be one of the most relaxing ways to get away from it all, leaving terrestrial worries behind. I'm not an experienced sailor, but one of the most relaxing vacations I've ever had was aboard a yacht sailing off Australia's tropical Queensland coast for two weeks. I was afraid I might become bored — to drive the same distance along the coast would have taken five hours — but those thoughts soon vanished as the appeal of a cruisey sailing holiday soon kicked in. With experienced sailors taking care of the tricky parts, I turned my attention to the sea and found a dreamy reconnection with nature. Dolphins, manta rays, turtles, and seabirds delivered moments of joy and excitement, there were rainbows and sunsets and scudding clouds, and occasional kayaking trips to islands and beaches to stretch our legs on the sand.

While sailing sounds idyllic and is a better choice than a motorboat in terms of emissions, the proximity to the sea also means you see the issues that oceans face, including plastic and other forms of pollution. If you are chartering a yacht for a holiday — and the options are many — you'll need to think about how you can follow sustainable principles in dealing with your waste and lessening any impact you might have on marine life.

Before you embark on a holiday charter, remember these tips for an eco-friendly vacation on the seas:

>> Switch off the engine and use sail power whenever you can.

>> Don't throw anything overboard, or leave plastic wrappers, hats, or other items where they can be blown overboard. Save it and dispose of it at the marina.

» Keep plastic to a minimum, especially single-use items and straws. Take reusable cups and bottles, or use paper or biodegradable plates, cutlery, and cups.

» Know the local rules for discharging grey or dark water. Never empty your tank next to the beach or in shallow water.

» Be careful where you drop the anchor, so you do not damage coral reefs or marine life. Anchor in sand or mud instead.

» Use the oars on the dingy rather than the engine. Even small engines cause pollution. And think of the workout you'll get by rowing ashore. Better still, take a kayak on board!

» Be sure to respect protected marine areas. Throughout the world, there are areas where sailing is prohibited or limited to protect fragile ecosystems.

Where to go for your sailing holiday? The Caribbean offers fantastic sailing, as do the Mediterranean countries like Türkiye (Turkey), Greece, Italy, and Croatia. All are renowned for their sailing and many tour operators run group sailing trips and charters. In Europe sailing is usually from May to September, although the Turkish season extends a month or two longer. If you're thinking about sailing in Türkiye, consider taking a cruise on a traditional wooden gulet, a motorsailer that might carry around 20 passengers plus crew. Similarly in Egypt, feluccas are simple wooden sailing boats that ply the waterways – they are particularly popular for Nile cruises – carrying up to ten passengers and providing a serene experience (but be warned, there are no toilets aboard).

Rubicon 3 Adventure (www.rubicon3adventure.com) is a UK-based sailing company that invites people to hop on and off the yacht at certain points on its journey. No sailing experience is required for some trips and the course of the passage is made up as you go along, depending on the wind, the weather and the group you are sailing with. The custom-built 60-foot (18-m) expedition yachts accommodate eight people, including the skipper and crew — and many guests are over-50s. You may be sailing in the Caribbean, across the Atlantic, in the Baltic Sea, or off the coast of Scandinavia, England, or Scotland.

Australia's Whitsunday region has 74 islands off the coast of Queensland, on the Great Barrier Reef, where Airlie Beach and Hamilton Island are the centers for all sailing trips and charters. In Australia, chartering your own yacht (without a skipper) is known as *bareboating*. The best time of year to sail in the Whitsundays is between July and October, but the weather is warm and comfortable year-round. However, this season also coincides with the humpback whale migration along the coastline, so be watchful for these giants of the sea.

TIP

Download the Eye on the Reef app from Australia's Great Barrier Reef Marine Park Authority to help monitor the health and life of the reef. Taking part in this citizen science effort is as easy as posting your underwater images and videos!

If you're an experienced sailor, there are often opportunities to crew on yacht deliveries from one port (or country) to another. Find a Crew (www.findacrew.com) is a global online network that connects boats and crew in more than 200 countries.

Tall ship sailing adventures are also a great way to get on the water. While many tall ship organizations offer sail training programs largely for students, they also usually run day sails or longer voyages that anyone can sign up for. You don't need to be an experienced sailor but will be expected to help out and "learn the ropes" as you go. For sailing in the United States, check out Tall Ships America (www.tallshipsamerica.org) or for Australia or New Zealand, www.tallships.org.au/get-on-board. In the UK, the Tall Ships Youth Trust (www.tallships.org) offers sailing for anyone from age 12 to 80, with some voyages venturing as far as Portugal and the Canary Islands. Before you sign up with a sailing company, check its sustainability policy or credentials.

Freewheeling on Two Wheels

What's not to love about jumping on a bike and pedaling your way through your holiday? Freewheeling through the countryside or cycling along city streets . . . there's no better way to reduce your carbon footprint and to get into the real world, where you're in touch with the locals in a way that traveling by car or bus can never achieve.

If you are an intrepid and experienced cyclist, you may want to go it alone or take part in a hard-core multiday or weeks-long ride, but there are plenty of options for those who are occasional bike riders or prefer the convenience of a tour where everything — including punctures! — is taken care of for you. Specialist cycling tours are a safe and easy way of exploring by bike, with the advantage of having bike and all gear provided, an itinerary that includes your accommodation along the way, and a support team.

TIP

If you're new to cycling or it's been years since you hoisted yourself into a saddle, prepare for your cycling holiday by getting some practice before you leave home! Head out on the weekends and explore your local area so you're fit for a longer ride.

Perhaps you're not ready for more than a few hours, or a day, riding. Many major cities around the world now operate bike share schemes that enable you to hire two wheels for a short time to explore. Hundreds of cities across the United States and around the world also have dedicated bike lanes or paths to take the stress out of dodging traffic and making it easy to incorporate pedal power into any style of holiday. Some schemes also have electric bikes or scooters available. These are great options for families as they are safe for young riders who may not be able to ride alongside vehicle traffic.

In the US, Portland and Minneapolis both have great reputations as cycle-friendly cities. Portland has an extensive 400-mile (644-km) network of protected bikeways, 100 miles (161 km) of greenways and multi-use paths. For even more cycling fun, time your visit for the **Pedalpalooza Bike Festival** (June to August) or the World Naked Bike Ride.

TIP

Portland, Oregon, hosts the largest event of the annual **World Naked Bike Ride** (worldnakedbikeride.org), drawing up to 10,000 people. This worldwide protest against dependency on oil and fossil fuels has been held every summer since 2004. Founded in Canada, it is now celebrated in more than 74 cities across 17 countries. Streets are closed to cars and thousands hit the streets. Dress code: As bare as you dare.

Minneapolis, Minnesota, is rated as one of the best biking cities in the United States. It has 98 miles (157 km) of bike lanes, 101 miles (162 km) of off-street bikeways and trails, and 16 miles (25 km) of on-street protected bikeways.

When choosing to make cycling part of your holiday, consider places where cycling is an integral part of life. Vietnam, China, or the Netherlands — which has the highest number of bicycles per person in the world — spring to mind. Whether on a multiday or single day cycling trip, you will be able to get to places a car cannot go and gives you something in common with the locals.

Almost anywhere you choose for your vacation will have cycling tours available. A guided cycling day tour in Thailand — despite the humidity and some wobbly moments across narrow bridges — revealed a side of Bangkok I would never have seen otherwise. Riding a bike gave me an escape from the heaving traffic of the city and revealed hidden neighborhoods, small temples (such as the one in Figure 9-2), river estuaries, and more green space than I had imagined. My tour was with **Grasshopper Adventures** (grasshopperadventures.com), but there are other reputable companies all across Asia that offer similar tours, including nighttime bike tours.

TIP

Check out the reviews for your cycling tour to make sure that the bike and gear provided will be up to standard.

The Colombian capital Bogotá has become famous for the *ciclovía*, a weekly event on Sundays which sees over 60 miles (96 km) of the city's streets closed to cars on Sundays and public holidays, enabling people to explore by bike or on foot. Rent a bike and join the locals. Bogotá's cycling network, which covers more than 372 miles (600 km) of streets, is the most extensive in South America and one of the largest in the world. By 2024, the city aims to have added 174 miles (280 km) of bike lanes and to have encouraged residents to be making half of all their daily trips by bike or alternative transport, such as scooters.

TIP

Worried you aren't fit enough? Electric bikes are the answer for those who aren't match-fit for a cycling holiday, and most cycling tour companies offer them as an option.

Lee Mylne

FIGURE 9-2: A bike tour of the Bangkok's less-crowded places.

European countries are among the most cycle-friendly in the world. Apart from the Netherlands, those that rate cycling as part of their normal day's travel are Denmark, Germany, Sweden, and Norway, where bikeways will get you almost anywhere.

For cyclists looking for long-distance challenges, over days, weeks or months, Europe also offers some great options. The **Trans Dinarica** is cross-border cycling route of 2,090 miles (3,364 km) in Eastern Europe, to be completed in 2024. At the time of writing, it connects Slovenia, Croatia, and Bosnia and Herzegovina but will ultimately traverse eight countries (the others are Montenegro, Albania, Kosovo, Serbia, and Macedonia) enabling cyclists to pedal through many UNESCO heritage sites, villages, and national parks.

Rail trails, disused railway tracks that have been repurposed as cycling routes, are also great for off-the-beaten track cycling adventures. The advantage is that, because trains generally can't tackle hills, they are mostly on flat terrain. The **Adventure Cycling Association** (adventurecycling.org) in the United States has plenty of information about cycle tours, including a route network map that also pinpoints bike-friendly campgrounds, inns, shops, and services along the routes. The **US Bicycle Route System** links 19,425 miles (more than 31,000 km) of routes in 34 states and Washington, DC. The organization also runs guided cycling tours for all levels of experience and fitness.

For super-athletic and experienced riders, mountain bike holidays are another way to experience the great outdoors beyond paved roads and traffic. As always, if you're on unfamiliar terrain, it's best to head out with local experts on a guided or group tour. Some great destinations to look at for inspiration include Canada, Iceland, New Zealand, and Australia.

Chapter **10**
Making a Difference by Volunteering

olunteering while traveling has long been a popular way for people of all ages to experience life in another culture, while feeling they're helping improve conditions for other people, animals, or the environment. Volunteering can take you out of your comfort zone and give you a sense of satisfaction and achievement that a normal holiday may not. The opportunities cover a broad scope, from working in animal sanctuaries or helping empower women in developing countries to being citizen scientists or coaching football or surfing. Whether you're 18 or 80, traveling solo or as a family, or can work for one day or three months, there is a volunteer project for you.

In this chapter I take you through some of the opportunities available, consider some pitfalls that may arise in your volunteering journey, and look at some common concerns about voluntourism.

**FIND
ONLINE**

All the web addresses mentioned in this chapter, along with other helpful online resources, are linked for your convenience at www. dummies.com/go/sustainabletravelfd.

Introducing Voluntourism

Voluntourism is a term coined to describe the common practice of volunteering your time or labor while traveling. If done responsibly, it can be a fantastic way to travel and to make a difference to the lives of others or the natural world. According to some studies, around 900,000 Americans volunteer abroad each year. Another suggests that 2.5 million UK residents take part in gap year development projects. In monetary terms, **Save the Children** estimated in 2017 that the voluntourism industry was worth $2.6 billion a year.

Most volunteers find their placements through agencies that offer a wide range of experiences across the globe. Voluntourism is a two-way street; as well as volunteering your time and energy, you're likely to find it an enriching and rewarding experience that you'll be talking about for years to come. However, it's wise to think your plan through carefully and consider all angles before jumping in to volunteer. As a responsible traveler, it's important for you to be mindful of the aspects of voluntourism that might not be immediately obvious.

REMEMBER

Bear in mind that you may not be able to change the world in one day or one week, but any small contributions you make to changing a life — whether it's a family in Africa or a turtle hatchling on a beach in Australia — will be worthwhile. As climate change and environmental issues dominate the news, every person's actions can help in some small way.

Volunteering also gives you the chance to work alongside other like-minded people of all ages, from all walks of life and many different countries. Ask your chosen volunteer organization who a "typical" volunteer would be on your project to get a sense of the people you might be working with.

Combining travel with volunteering

Volunteer programs exist all over the world. Narrowing down your search will depend on what time you have available, how far you want to travel, what kind of voluntary work you want to do, and your budget. It may be possible to just spend one day of your vacation helping out on a community project such as beach-cleaning or tree-planting, or you can commit weeks or even months to immersing yourself in another culture and volunteering at the same time. Working alongside locals is a sure way of learning more about the place you are volunteering in.

Take time to look at the most popular types of programs available to evaluate what appeals to you and where you want to travel to. Consider your travel budget, as most voluntourism programs require you to pay (more on that later in this chapter).

TIP

Are you looking not so much for a volunteering holiday, but rather to volunteer *on* holiday? There's a big difference! Many five-star resorts now offer the chance for guests to spend a day on local environmental projects that don't require continuity or any particular skills — but which help chip away at a task like cleaning plastic litter from a beach or planting trees. It's a fun way to meet other travelers and the locals and see a side of the destination you won't glimpse from the pool.

But if you're after something longer term and immersive, start by doing serious research. First, ask yourself these questions:

>> Why do I want to volunteer? Am I doing it for the right reasons?

>> Will the work I do, or contribution I make, actually make a positive change for the environment or the people in this community?

>> What will be the outcome of my volunteer work?

>> What skills can I pass on to help my host community to be self-sufficient?

>> Can I volunteer at home instead?

Are you looking for a vacation where you can be in the great outdoors and volunteer at the same time? Many programs offer options with conservation projects. **Conservation Volunteers International Program** (www.conservationvip.org) trips are focused on sustainable projects such as planting trees (in Scotland), maintaining trails which protect fragile landscapes (Patagonia, Alaska, Yosemite, Virgin Islands), protecting wildlife (Galapagos and Costa Rica), preserving cultural sites (Machu Picchu and the US Virgin Islands), removing invasive species (Machu Picchu), and picking up trash and filtering beach sand to remove microplastics (Galapagos). Conservation VIP also encourages volunteers to offset the carbon emissions from their travel by donating to **Trees for Life.**

Make sure your travel insurance covers everything you will be doing as a volunteer. It also needs to cover emergency medical evacuation and repatriation, particularly if your host country's healthcare facilities are not sophisticated. Consider the time you'll be away and get special insurance cover if you need it.

If you want to encourage your children to explore the world and make a meaningful contribution as well, consider a family volunteering trip. **Responsible Travel** (www.responsibletravel.com) offers more than 30 family volunteer holidays in Tanzania, India, Borneo, Greece, Costa Rica, Thailand, Sri Lanka, South Africa, the Maldives, Peru, Nepal, Cambodia, and Romania. Expect the whole family to be active participants in the work, which is usually concerned with animal welfare or wildlife and marine conservation. Some examples include monitoring sea turtle nests in Costa Rica, helping walk rescued dogs in Thailand, working in a bear sanctuary in Romania, or helping with elephant research in Sri Lanka. You and your children will be working alongside scientists, conservationists, and other volunteers.

Some aspects of volunteering, such as working with children, can be controversial, and some volunteer opportunities may be concerned more about profit than helping others. Ensure you think about your ability to contribute in a meaningful and ethical way.

Near or far? Deciding whether to volunteer at home or abroad

You don't have to go abroad to volunteer. Within your own country will be many opportunities that you can take up and still be making a difference. Many of the organizations that have opportunities abroad will also have projects in your own country that you can apply for. The advantage of volunteering in your own country is that you won't have any issues with cultural misunderstandings or language and will have a fair idea of what to expect in terms of accommodation and food! In addition, by staying close to home you'll be reducing your travel miles and carbon footprint.

Most of these volunteer opportunities are likely to be with environmental, wildlife, or community projects. Community placements might involve working in homeless shelters, food banks, donation warehouses, schools, or community centers. Typically, you might work three to five hours a day, Monday to Friday, and usually need to commit to a stay of between one and twelve weeks. The rest of the time is yours to explore the city you're in.

TIP

Check out reviews from volunteers about the project you're keen to work on. This will give you a clear idea of some of the realities you might face, even in a relatively familiar environment.

Many companies have begun introducing corporate volunteer days, where you're given paid time off to undertake volunteer work. Ask if your company does this and who it partners with to facilitate this. If your work involves international travel, it may be possible to combine a work trip with a vacation during which you can also volunteer. Extending your work trip to include traveling time can help save on airfare costs, fits with a slow travel philosophy, and may improve your connection with local business contacts.

Paying to volunteer

It may seem odd that you're asked to pay for the privilege of volunteering, but almost all voluntourism programs require you to pay a fee — and sometimes it's a considerable one. While your fee will generally cover your accommodation, meals, and transport on the ground, you'll also have to pay your own airfare to get to your destination.

So before you decide where to go, make sure that your budget will stretch. Having a clear idea of what the fee covers will help you to budget for your trip. As well as your airfare, you need to allow for extra expenses while you're in your destination. How long are you planning to stay? What expenses will you need to cover yourself, and will you want to buy souvenirs?

Why does it cost so much to be a volunteer? The simple fact is that it costs money to host and run volunteer programs. As well as covering the cost of hosting you, your money will also be helping to pay for administration costs and the salaries of the organizer's local staff members. Volunteers are transient, so organizations need paid staff members to ensure continuity of their programs. Most fees also include a direct donation to the project itself.

To help you better understand your role and the local practices of the country you're volunteering in, some organizations hold an orientation and cultural awareness course for new volunteers. Some will also provide language training. The fees paid by volunteers helps the program providers hire and train leaders for these courses.

Staff will also be the people you'll turn to in an emergency, and who will have the ability to take charge and sort things out. It may be a personal issue for you, such as a visa problem or needing a doctor who speaks English. Maybe you've been robbed or scammed. Whatever it is, these are the people you'll need. In the event of a major emergency, such as a natural disaster, which means you'll need to be evacuated, the staff will be the ones ensuring you're safe. They'll also be keeping in touch with your family or next of kin if you are seriously ill.

Some programs also include excursions for their volunteers, visiting local places of interest, sometimes over a few days, and this adds to the experience of seeing the country and getting to know the staff and volunteers in a different setting.

REMEMBER

It's entirely reasonable for you to ask about where and how your fees will be used. How much of the money you pay will stay in the local community, rather than going to the organizer or a foreign tour operator? A responsible volunteer program will be transparent about how they spend their volunteer fees, by publishing their financial information online (perhaps in an annual report). If you request this information and they're unwilling to provide it, answer questions, or to explain anything, be wary.

TIP

The good news is that there are still some ways that you can volunteer your time without having a big budget. Following are two well-established organizations that offer opportunities to exchange your time and labor for room and board. Both require a membership fee to sign on to their websites, which act as a contact point for connecting with potential hosts.

>> **WWOOF** (www.woof.net): World Wide Opportunities on Organic Farms (WWOOF) is a great choice for anyone who wants to work on an organic farm or learn about growing food sustainably (see more in Chapter 4). The WWOOF membership fee ranges from $40 in the United States

to $55 in Canada and 10 to 35 euros in Europe (pay in the country you want to volunteer in).

>> **Workaway** (www.workaway.info): Workaway's fee is $49 for a single person or $59 for two, with opportunities to work on sustainable projects including permaculture in Italy, animal care in Portugal, working on a sheep farm in Western Australia, in an eco-sanctuary in New Zealand, or an organic vineyard in France.

How to Choose Your Volunteering Experience

The choices available for you to volunteer can be overwhelming. So many countries, so many projects . . . it can be hard to know where to start. There's everything from working with animals or teaching English to building houses, planting trees, or helping scientists with data collection — the list goes on. Browse any volunteer website and there is sure to be something — or somewhere — that catches your eye.

A good place to start with your decision-making is to think about the skills you can bring to the work, your own interests — both in the destination and in the work — and the kind of living conditions you'll be happy with. Think about how hands-on you want to be — you don't need to be out in the field to be an effective volunteer. Some projects need help with marketing, website building, administration, and other indoor tasks. If remote and fairly basic living conditions aren't for you, keep looking! City-based volunteering is also an option, with school and community work providing an urban experience.

How long do you have for your trip away? The duration of your volunteering vacation will also be a factor in your choice. While staying for several weeks will enable you to build relationships within a local community, not everyone has that kind of time, and some projects will welcome you for a couple of days or a week.

REMEMBER

The most important thing is to do some thorough research into the volunteer organization you're considering traveling with and the project you'll be volunteering for.

Deciding where to go

Perhaps you've always wanted to go to Africa and see the animals that make up the big five. Or you're a keen diver and think volunteering on Australia's Great Barrier Reef would be the ideal combination of holiday and giving back. Having an interest in a destination will certainly help in making a decision about where to go, but the possibilities for volunteering are endless. So unless your heart is set on a particular place, be flexible in your thinking.

Find out as much as you can about the place you'll be volunteering. Be prepared for cultural clashes. Do you understand the culture of the place you'll be volunteering in? Are you happy to conform to dress codes or other rules that might be required during your stay?

TIP

When you've decided where to go, make sure you have all the correct vaccinations. Visit your doctor or health clinic at least eight weeks before you travel as some require a course of shots over a period of weeks. If you plan to work with wildlife or will be in a remote area, inform your doctor as this might require more than the standard vaccinations (such as rabies).

REMEMBER

While many volunteer projects are in developing countries, remember that you don't need to go across the world in order to make a difference. Think beyond the lure of the exotic location and consider the logistics involved — how easy is your destination to get to, and what is the cost likely to be? Weigh up what's important to you and whether your budget can easily cope with your choice.

Looking closer to home can not only be less expensive, but it can help lower your carbon footprint, as can choosing a project in a city, reducing the need for extensive travel once you're in your destination country. Wildlife and habitat conservation projects may involve a long-haul flight followed by a lot of road travel (or a domestic flight) to your placement. For volunteers who are planning to spend a long time working on a project — rather than just a short break — it's worth looking at more remote destinations. Go somewhere that you've never been or are unlikely to get back to again, somewhere off-the-beaten-track. The longer you spend at your destination, the more cost-effective and carbon-friendly your flights will be.

Find out about the climate at the time of year you're traveling. Even in places like Africa, it can be very cold on winter nights, and many places have distinct wet and dry seasons. Make sure you pack appropriate clothes for the climate, but remember that if you're working outdoors you will need to protect yourself from the sun; pack long-sleeved shirts, a hat with a brim (not a baseball cap), and sunscreen.

TIP

Check online traveler review sites for the organization you're thinking of signing up with. Most reviews are honest, and they're also a good source of tips about specific projects.

Picking a volunteer activity

The diversity of volunteer projects is almost as broad as the countries you'll find them in. Most fall into three categories — wildlife, conservation, and community projects. Within those areas, you're certain to find something that appeals, but don't be tempted by the desire to do something completely different. The value that your volunteer work will bring in many cases will be all about the skills you already have. While it might be your dream to work with orphaned orangutans in Borneo, the reality might be that your skills lie elsewhere, and you'd be a more effective volunteer in a community project in Colombia working in a senior care home or teaching teenagers to surf. For the chance to work alongside local people and learn from them, about their culture, their country, and their way of life, look for projects that offer training and where you can pass on skills.

Consider the following ideas when you're pondering which volunteering style is for you.

Community projects

These can be either social projects, working in schools or clinics, or building the physical buildings needed by a community. If you're a builder or engineer, you're perfect for construction projects. A few years ago, I was one of 16 international volunteers in a Community Project Travel group with adventure travel company **World Expeditions** (www.worldexpeditions.com), combining the chance to trek and see village life in Peru with the opportunity to support a community in a practical way. After a three-day trek through the remote Urubamba mountains, our traveling party joined the villagers from the isolated village of Quelqanqa in the

Cusco region to build a stone bridge and install a water pipeline to bring clean water to village houses, shown in my picture in Figure 10-1. As most of us had never done this kind of work before, it was overseen by a local qualified engineer to ensure it was carried out with the villagers' safety in mind — and this is an important aspect of volunteering when the labor force is not skilled. This is still one of the most memorable travel experiences of my life, despite the hard and dirty work involved.

Lee Mylne

FIGURE 10-1: Volunteers help build a bridge in Peru.

For social projects, look for organizations like **Domino Volunteers** (www.dominovolunteers.com) in Colombia, which matches volunteers' skills to the needs of local charities. Volunteers stay with host families and take part in community events. Your volunteer work might include teaching English, working in a senior care home, working in sports programs (surfing, soccer, scuba diving), promoting recycling programs, or helping out on a sustainable food project.

WARNING

Any volunteer work with children, such as teaching English or caring for children, should only be undertaken through an organization that has clear rules in place for screening volunteers. Background checks should be required — if not, be wary and ask more questions about how the children are protected.

Responsible Travel (www.responsibletravel.com) has strict guidelines for any trip that involves volunteering with children, including in youth centers, residential facilities, trafficking shelters, or women and children violence refuges.

Wildlife projects

Working with wildlife is often the dream volunteer role. Washing elephants and playing with orphaned orangutans or monkeys feature high on many volunteers' wish lists. The reality of wildlife projects is often very different — for good reason. On most wildlife projects, you're likely to be at a distance from the animals, as you track, monitor, or observe, helping to collect valuable data on their habits and movements. Other tasks might include more mundane tasks, such as helping with administration, cleaning enclosures or turtle tanks, or preparing food for rescued animals. Don't expect that you'll be up-close-and-personal.

There's a good reason for that. Some animals — such as orangutans — are vulnerable to human disease. If there's any chance of working closely with them, you may be asked to quarantine for a period of time beforehand (in this case, you'll need to be committing to a long period of time as a volunteer and to undertaking training). Limited contact with people also increases the chance of successful reintroduction to the wild.

If you have research and surveying skills or are an expert in data management, you'll be highly valued for animal conservation projects. If you're a vet student or someone with experience in caring for animals, projects such as caring for abandoned or orphaned animals in cities may appeal to you. Not every animal welfare project involves heading for the jungle or the savannah.

On many projects, you'll be working alongside conservation experts as a citizen scientist, and that can be very rewarding. The **European Nature Trust** (theeuropeannaturetrust.com/travel) has wildlife experiences like this, such as tracking lynx in Spain's Andalucia region or wolves in the Apennines in Italy. All trips include a donation to the local projects to support their work in restoring habitats, monitoring populations, anti-poaching initiatives, and dealing with human-wildlife conflict. Each itinerary also includes plenty of chances to explore the local area.

TIP

Before packing, buy t-shirts and other work clothes at a charity shop. Much of the work you might be doing — feeding animals, planting trees — will involve getting wet or dirty; not only are you recycling, but you won't ruin your best clothes! Anything you don't need when you leave can be donated to the next intake of volunteers.

Environmental projects

Aside from working directly with wildlife, many environmental projects are also designed to benefit the natural world. **Earth Watch** (www.earthwatch.org) is another science-based organization that offers the chance to join researchers around the world. You might be monitoring the health of bee populations in Utah or birdlife in Cuba, helping protect penguins in South Africa, or tracking sharks and rays in Florida.

Marine conservation projects are available around the world. **The Barbados Sea Turtle Project** (www.barbadosseaturtles.org), run by the University of West Indies, accepts volunteers from May to November each year, usually for two to four months. On Australia's **Great Barrier Reef**, just part of which is seen in Figure 10-2, there's a multitude of citizen science and volunteer opportunities, from a day's work at a turtle rehabilitation center on **Fitzroy Island** (www.cairnsturtlerehab.org.au) to undertaking a "Marine Biologist for a Day" reef monitoring program (www.passions.com.au).

Environmental projects can also include tree planting, beach clean-ups, weed eradication programs, and more. Hawaii's **Kanu Pledge** (www.kanuhawaii.org) asks visitors to help protect the islands of Hawaii and to sign on to a choice of hundreds of volunteer programs, many of which require only a one-time commitment and are nature-based.

Medical and public health

If you have a medical or healthcare background, you can be of enormous help in developing countries. Volunteer placements might be with a health clinic or educating local residents on proper sanitation. Sometimes, while you're traveling independently, these skills can also be put to good use without being an official volunteer. On a visit to a remote Pacific island a few years ago, another tourist I befriended on the journey revealed he was a dentist. When we got to the island — which had a well-equipped dental clinic for the population of around 50 people, but no resident dentist — word quickly spread and he was asked if he would look at a woman with a dental emergency. After agreeing, he opened the clinic to everyone and spent most of his week's holiday there; the reward was a huge outpouring of gratitude. Be open to helping out if you can!

Lee Mylne

FIGURE 10-2: Australia's Great Barrier Reef.

Evaluating a voluntourism operator

There are many tour operators and organizations advertising volunteer opportunities for travelers. How do you choose one that operates sustainably, effectively, and ethically?

WARNING

Make sure you do your research before signing up to be a volunteer. You need to be wary about "community washing," a version of greenwashing in eco-tourism, which relates to activities that are supposed to benefit the local communities but in fact do not.

When you've narrowed down your choice to a destination and a project you feel would be good for you, it's time to do some serious research into the organization running it. Look at the website to find out if it's a registered charity or a company with a good reputation. Most groups will provide a mission statement that you can use to get an idea of what its aims and methods of operation are. Read any other material they have, such as brochures and newsletters, carefully.

If you have other questions, email or call them. They should be able to tell you what they are in need of, what they require of volunteers, where your fees will be spent, and how the community you are volunteering in will benefit from the presence of foreign volunteers. Also ask about training and safety procedures they have in place for volunteers, both while working on the project (if that's relevant) and in general. If you're volunteering in a remote area without emergency services or in a city with a high crime rate, do they have in-country support services in place for volunteers in trouble? Check what the procedures are if you're sick, injured, or have to leave the placement urgently.

Ask if they can put you in touch with former volunteers; reputable organizations will usually be happy to do this. Ask other volunteers what they achieved during their time in the community and if they believe it was worthwhile. Satisfactory answers to these questions will reassure you that your voluntary work and the fee you pay are doing the good you hope for and will protect you from a bad experience.

REMEMBER

It's important that any project for which you volunteer is meeting a need identified by the local community and that locals are involved in it. Your expertise and that of other volunteers should be helping to bolster and strengthen the local community and be of genuine and ongoing benefit, even after you leave.

Addressing Common Concerns

The popularity of voluntourism in the past decade or so has also raised concerns around the ethics of some aspects of it. You're right to think about the issues often raised around the value of volunteering as a tourist and about what kind of volunteer efforts are the most ethical. As placements have become more inclusive, however — with fewer skills and less commitment required from volunteers — so criticism of voluntourism has grown.

Common types of voluntourism include teaching English in schools and orphanages and building schools or houses. As outlined earlier in this chapter, the main issue with these — and indeed with many types of volunteering — is the lack of skills and experience of the volunteers. Even for qualified teachers, there is a lack of continuity in the learning process because of the short length of stay. Some volunteers may also be taking jobs away from local skilled workers who need it to support their families. While I'm not trying to dissuade you from volunteering, these are among the concerns you need to think about before you decide where and how you'll spend your time as a volunteer.

Am I really helping?

Volunteers can truly make a difference. But before you commit to a volunteer program with the best intentions in the world, ask some questions to ensure that your efforts are of tangible benefit to the community you are working in.

Finding out about the community you're going to help and how the project has been developed is a good start. Will you be working alongside locals, helping to train them towards self-sufficiency, or creating something that will be embraced by them long after the volunteers have left? Crucially, is your presence taking a job away from a local?

Are you well qualified for the task at hand? If what you're doing as a volunteer is not something you'd be qualified to do back home, then are you the right person for the job? Has the volunteer organization offered you enough training? If you're going to be teaching English but have never taught a class before, think carefully about taking on the role or at least take a Teaching English as a Foreign Language (TEFL) course. The more qualified you are, the better the experience will be for you and the people you're trying to help.

While there's a feel-good factor to working with wildlife rehabilitation, it's worth considering if there are other ways in which you could contribute that would give greater long-term benefits to their environment. For example, would reforestation projects help restore their habitat, or is there a community project that would reduce the incentive for logging or poaching?

If you're considering a short-term stint in voluntourism, think about the kind of work that will still be effective and meaningful. A two-week holiday might be enough to make a contribution to an animal welfare or environmental project, but social programs generally need a longer commitment. Children generally don't benefit from having a teacher for two weeks who then disappears; they need continuity.

If you can't stay for as long as you'd like, remember that volunteering can continue long after you've returned home to your normal life. You can become a regular donor, fundraise in your home country, or promote the organization you traveled with to friends and family who might also be interested in combining their holiday with a chance to volunteer.

TIP

Before you leave home, ask the volunteer organization about items the community needs that you could bring with you. Does the local school need books or pens? Does the health clinic need bandages, disinfectant wipes, or surgical gloves? Packing a suitcase with these practical items can make a huge contribution to the community.

Avoiding orphanages

Orphanage tourism, common in some developing countries, may seem like a good thing at first glance. Well-intentioned tourists visit an orphanage, meet the children, perhaps watch a performance of some kind — music or dance — and give a donation to help with the running costs. Others volunteer their time for a few days, weeks, or months to help out. Surely that's a good thing to do? Unfortunately, everything is not always what it seems.

For a start, the children are often not orphans. According to **ChildSafe** (www.thinkchildsafe.org), an organization based in Cambodia, 80 percent of the eight million children living in orphanages across the world are not orphans. ChildSafe likens orphanage visits to zoos, rightly arguing that these children have a right to privacy, and says it is better to support organizations which provide vocational training, income-generating activities, and social services for young people and their families. Orphanages are sometimes commercial businesses that break up families and exploit children for profit.

In some countries, the removal of children from their families to live in orphanages is considered modern slavery, and while orphanages no longer exist in the US, UK, or Australia, they are still operating in Africa, Asia, South America, and some parts of eastern Europe.

ChildSafe does accept volunteers to work in Phnom Penh, but this work doesn't involve directly working with children. The organization believes this is a job for local experts who speak the language and understand the culture, not travelers who are passing through.

Another organization with information about the pros and cons of supporting orphanages is ReThink Orphanages (www. rethinkorphanages.org), which makes suggestions on other ways you can help young people.

WARNING

When you give children money, food, or gifts, you're encouraging them to beg. This becomes a source of their family's income and prevents them from going to school.

REMEMBER

Avoid organizations or tours that run or promote orphanage volunteering, visits, or day trips. When you're traveling, support ethical local businesses and social enterprises, which pay their workers fairly and offer a benefit to the community.

Chapter **11**

Learning on the Move

Travel is intrinsically educational. You cannot travel without learning something new every day about this fascinating world you live in. Travel will stretch your mind and expand your belief in the possibilities that lie ahead. You'll gain knowledge and experience without even trying — but perhaps sometimes you want to make an effort and set your mind to learning something new while still traveling. As the late Anthony Bourdain said: "Travel is not reward for working, it's education for living."

In this chapter, I introduce you to some of those transformative possibilities, from expanding your knowledge of a new language or understanding of a different culture, to improving your prowess at your chosen sport. Go live and learn!

FIND ONLINE

For links to all the web addresses provided in this chapter, as well as additional resources, check out www.dummies.com/go/ sustainabletravelfd.

Getting an Education While You Travel

Whether it's a short or long course, signing up to learn a new skill will greatly enrich your travel experience — and your life! While undertaking a course of some kind, you might be limited to one place for a period of time, but you will have a much deeper connection to that place — and the people who live in it — than if you'd just passed through for a day or two, ticking off the sights and moving on to the next town. It's a form of slow travel that has many benefits, including the ability to truly get to know the place you're in, talk to the locals — perhaps in their own language — and explore the surrounding countryside, taking time to get under its skin in a way that's not possible on a short visit.

REMEMBER

Educational travel is travel with a purpose. Your purpose may be different to those of your classmates, but having a common focus will bring you together with other likeminded travelers.

Do you want to learn a new language, take up a sport, or explore the cultural heritage of places you've only read about? The opportunities are vast, and the destinations you can visit and linger in while you learn are myriad. At any age, you will develop knowledge and skills by taking classes, meeting new people, and immersing yourself in culture, landscape, and history. Whether you join a group tour or go it alone, you'll be challenged, your curiosity will be piqued, and your hunger for learning is likely to increase.

Language Schools

While learning a few basic words and phrases may get you by if you're just passing through a country, and is certain to be appreciated by locals, if you want to become fluent, signing up to a language school is the answer. Whether you want to learn German, Hindi, Arabic, Japanese, Mandarin, Turkish, or Urdu — you'll find a language school to help you.

If you're planning to be in a country for a reasonable amount of time, it might be worthwhile spending the first week or two enrolled in a language school. This kind of full-immersion can really boost any fluency or knowledge you already have and set you up for greater interaction with the locals. You'll find yourself among students of all ages and nationalities with different levels of language ability.

Spanish is the second-most widely spoken language globally in terms of native speakers (474 million) and is spoken by more than 548 million people. According to online language school **Berlitz** (www.berlitz.com), there are 21 Spanish-speaking countries in the world, with many more that have large Spanish-speaking populations. Mexico has the largest population of Spanish speakers in the world, followed by Colombia and Argentina, with Spain coming in fourth place.

If you want to learn Spanish in Spain, the choices are overwhelming, but you should look for a program that is accredited by the **Instituto Cervantes** (www.cervantes.es) or is a member of the **Federation of Associations of Spanish Schools for Foreigners** (www.fedele.org/en). If Mexico seems a little easier, there are as many choices! One school to consider is **Instituto Cultural Oaxaca** (www.icomexico.com), which offers a range of programs year round, including for children, and includes an *intercambio* or language exchange with a local who is studying English.

Recognized as the world's leading French language teaching organization, **Alliance Francaise** (www.af-france.fr/en) has more than 800 schools in 133 countries — but there's nowhere better to learn French than in France, where there are 30 schools. You can learn everything from conversational language to grammar and choose from two- or four-week courses.

There are Italian language schools all over Italy. One of the best is **Il Sasso** (www.ilsasso.com), in Montepulciano, in the heart of Tuscany (about midway between Rome and Florence). Certified and recognized by the Italian Ministry of Education, it has been running for more than 30 years and is open all year round. Classes run in the morning, with afternoons free to take extra one-on-one classes (for an additional fee), to explore on your own, or to join other students on optional activities such as cooking classes.

TIP

Many language schools will also help you organize accommodation for the duration of your stay, often with the option of a homestay so you can more fully immerse yourself in the language.

Road Scholar

Boston-based not-for-profit Road Scholar (www.roadscholar.org) claims to be the world's largest creator of experiential learning opportunities. Road Scholar offers around 5,500 "learning adventures" in 150 countries and in all 50 states of the US, with more than 100,000 people signing up each year.

As a not-for-profit organization, Road Scholar keeps costs low and even provides scholarships that help offset costs so that financial constraints don't prevent people taking part.

Among its tour offerings are 133 trips that visit national parks in the US, discovering colorful and ancient landscapes, paddling rivers and lakes, and wildlife watching. Cultural offerings include everything from the jazz bars of New Orleans and theatres of New York to the Biblical landmarks of Israel, Jordan, and Egypt, the architecture of Prague, or UNESCO World Heritage sites like Mont-Saint-Michel in northern France, pictured in Figure 11-1. Guides are experts in their field.

Lee Mylne

FIGURE 11-1: The abbey of Mont-Saint-Michel in France.

Road Scholar also hits the mark in the sustainability stakes, offsetting carbon emissions by investing in projects such as rainforest preservation in Brazil, methane recapture in Florida, wind farms in India, and reforestation in Kenya. It patronizes hotels that have sustainability certification and restaurants that serve locally sourced foods, and it uses locally owned and operated services wherever possible. Guides are trained to advise on cultural sensitivities including respecting dress codes and rules around photography.

Although aimed at older travelers, Road Scholar also promotes intergenerational travel, with tours designed for travelers and their grandchildren, and three generations.

Photography Tours and Workshops

Photographs — or digital images — provide the memories of your trip long after it is over. For that reason, it's important to make them the best quality they can be, reflecting what you saw on your travels. Learning from the experts is an ideal way to improve your photography skills and learn to see what's in front of you in a different way, with a photographer's eye, rather than a tourist's view.

Photography tours come in all shapes and sizes, from African safaris to those that focus on architecture (not just the famous landmarks), portraiture, landscapes (mountains, deserts, rolling farmland, rocky escarpments), and festivals. Others might focus on underwater photography or a particular seasonal event like whale watching. There are numerous tours to capture the Northern Lights — that most elusive of phenomena.

Think carefully before signing up for a photography tour to ensure that the photographer leading it has the same values as you do. Ask them about their philosophy in regard to the impact that photography can have on people, in particular, and what their guidelines are around wildlife and the environment (more on this in Chapter 5). Avoid tours that will take you to the busiest over-Instagrammed places.

When choosing a tour, decide whether you want plenty of instruction — a workshop-style tour — or just some guidance if you ask for it and the chance to be taken to some great spots for the best angles. Make sure that the group size isn't too large. Anything more than around eight people and you might not get the kind of personalized attention that you expect. Ask about the pace of the trip — will there be early starts every day, and how many locations will you be visiting? Seeing the full detailed itinerary will help you decide if it's the style of trip for you. Think slow: One or two locations may be more relaxed and give you more time to really discover the destination and connect with the people and places you're photographing.

REMEMBER

Always ask permission before photographing people — and respect their answer! Don't be tempted to sneak a photo of someone who's asked you not to snap them, and don't photograph children without their parent's permission. Instead, take some time to talk to your subject, perhaps buy a sample of their wares, or ask them a question. The photos you make will be all the better for it.

Approach wildlife with care. Don't cause an animal to change its behavior, and absolutely don't try for a selfie! A photo of an animal behaving naturally is always a better one.

Think about the time of year that you plan to travel. Do you want blue skies for your images, or are you happy to turn your lens to anything the weather gods dish up, creating moody or dripping shots wherever you may be?

Finally, what do you plan to do with your images when you come home? If you plan to share them with others, how will you do that? Consider how you will present them to your audience, likely on social media. If you photograph a sensitive site that may attract the Instagram crowd, consider not mentioning where it's located. Tell the story of how you took the image, how far away you were from the subject (particularly important for wildlife shots), and what lens size you used. Don't pretend that captive animals were in the wild. You're able to give lessons to others through your honesty, leading by example.

Art and Cultural Tours

It's not possible to travel without having cultural encounters of some kind. Even unconsciously, almost every travel experience is a cultural one. But sometimes we want to go further in expanding our knowledge of the arts and culture and take a deeper dive into those areas.

If you want to unleash your talents in art and craft, consider signing up for **Vacation with an Artist** (vawaa.com), which offers one-on-one masterclasses in more than 25 countries. These "mini-apprenticeships" will see you working with an artist to learn their craft, which could be anything from tile and ceramic art in Istanbul to making shadow puppets in Malaysia, bookbinding in Portugal, bamboo crafts in Kathmandu, or desert-inspired pottery in California's Yucca Valley.

You'll spend around four hours a day in the artist's personal studio, usually over three to five days, with the rest of your time free to explore the location you're in. The fee does not include airfares, accommodations, or meals — just the lessons, use of the artists tools, materials, and supplies, and your finished work to take home.

If painting is more your style of art, UK travel company **Azenart** (www.azenartholidays.com) runs small group plein-air painting holidays led by accomplished tutors. Seven-day courses are held across France, Italy, Greece, Spain, Portugal, and India, with all tutoring in English. All materials are provided, and there is a range of tours, including botanical, portrait, and landscape painting. This is a great option for solo travelers — most of your traveling companions will be as well — as all the accommodations are single rooms (with no single supplements).

If you've ever visited Buenos Aires and swooned at the sight of locals dancing the tango, it might be time to learn the steps yourself. As well as intensive tango lessons, the courses at **Mente Argentina** (www.menteargentina.com) offer the chance to learn about Argentinian wines, take a cooking class, or train as a bartender or DJ over 2 to 12 weeks. The cost of the course also includes accommodation in Buenos Aires, including homestays, shared and private apartments, and shared student rooms.

If immersing yourself in a destination means developing a deeper connection and knowledge of its history, search out tours like **Black Cultural Heritage Tours** (www.experienceblackculture.com), which reveals aspects of African American, Caribbean, and Afro-Cuban history in South Florida through music, food, art, dance, and storytelling. Tours support Black-owned small businesses through single or multiday visits and also visit local museums and cultural neighborhoods.

First Nations tours are an important way of connecting with the history and culture of the country you are visiting (see more in

Chapter 5). Talking to an Indigenous guide will allow you to more fully understand the traditions and history of a country's first peoples.

With the burgeoning of First Nations tourism around the world, finding tours is not difficult. AIANTA's **Native America Travel** website (nativeamerica.travel) can help you research authentic native experiences across 12 regions in the United States, including Hawaii and Alaska. **Destination Indigenous** (www.destinationindigenous.ca) will help you find tours, cultural centers, museums, and heritage sites that will broaden your knowledge of the First Nations peoples of Canada. **Visit Natives** (www.visitnatives.com) is a tour operator working with Indigenous communities in Norway and Tanzania.

A dedicated part of **Tourism Australia**'s website (discover aboriginalexperiences.com) lists more than 160 authentic Aboriginal guided tourism experiences in every state of the country, in cities, rainforests, and in the Outback. **Tourism New Zealand** (newzealand.com) has plenty of information on its website to help you choose one from the myriad Māori cultural experiences available. The **South Pacific Tourism Organisation** (southpacificislands.travel) represents 20 island nations and has a strong focus on sustainable and cultural tourism.

Getting Sporty

If you have always wanted to learn a sport, or to improve your prowess, there are myriad places that you can do that around the world. Most will be in destinations that lend themselves to a particular sport — or where it is a passion for the locals!

Golf

Golf is one of the world's most popular sports, with the National Golf Foundation estimating that about 119 million people around the world regularly play. In 2022, the NGF says 41.1 million Americans swung a golf club either on a golf course or at a driving range or similar facility. However, golf courses are notoriously huge users of water to keep those links green, and they often use chemicals to keep pests and weeds away. Add to that the carbon footprint that many players create by traveling to play in or watch tournaments, and it's not always a pretty picture. However, many golf courses are now conscious of their impact on the planet and are taking steps to mitigate it.

Teeing off at the world's oldest and most famous golf course, St Andrews Links in Scotland (www.standrews.com), is a dream for many golfers. If you want to improve your swing, the **St Andrews Academy** at the "home of golf" might be just the place to do it — but it comes at a price! From individual 30-minute lessons with PGA-qualified coaches to three- or five-day golf schools, golfers who want to improve their game will find something to suit.

You'll also be pleased to know that the St. Andrews Link Trust is connected to several local sustainability projects, including coastal erosion, beach cleans, and restoring dunes. Greenkeepers are also responsible for a successful kestrel breeding project to increase the numbers of birds that live on the links.

The US's top golf course, **Pebble Beach Links** (www.pebblebeach.com) on California's stunning Monterey Peninsula, has an equally renowned golf academy. You can sign up for your own private instruction or join a group program designed for all levels of ability, from "learn to play" onwards. Pebble Beach Company has introduced several sustainability measures, including a water conservation program (both on the golf courses and in its resort guest rooms). The company funds a $67 million wastewater reclamation project, which provides recycled water as the only source of irrigation for its seven golf courses, including Pebble Beach Links. High-tech irrigation systems monitor the greens and control the watering schedule based on soil needs and weather conditions. Pebble Beach Links also has a recovery program to retrieve errant golf balls that end up in the waters or beaches of Monterey Bay. These and other sustainability initiatives are detailed at www.pebblebeach.com/green-initiatives.

From luxury resorts in the Middle East to indoor facilities in Europe, there are golf academies and schools all over the world. Most staff are PGA-qualified pros. Golf tuition holidays are a great way to improve your golf, and groups are usually limited to four amateurs for each golf pro. A useful comparison website and directory is www.golfschool.com.

Make sure you check out a golf course's sustainability credentials or initiatives before you book your tee time.

REMEMBER

Sailing

Whether you've never been on a yacht, or you just want to learn a bit more, sailing courses are available just about anywhere in the world where there's a marina. Some courses will give you internationally recognized qualifications, while others will just show you the basic ropes. If you have ambitions to find a crew position on a yacht or want to charter for your next sailing holiday, having a certificate will be an advantage.

TIP

Sailing clubs in your chosen destination are also likely to offer regular classes — usually only a half day or a few hours — to introduce you to the basics of sailing.

Dreaming of the Greek islands? The **Aegean Sailing School** (www.aegeansailingschool.com) runs a Competent Crew course over five days that will prepare you to be a crew member on a yacht, with intermediate and advanced courses in skippering and yacht mastering if you're dreams are bigger.

Sailing schools are also available in Australia's Whitsunday region, where sailing is a way of life. The **Whitsunday Sailing School** (www.whitsundaysailingschool.com.au) offers the chance to combine your holiday with a sailing course. You live aboard the yacht and sail around the Whitsunday Islands (there are 74 of them) while learning your new skills. The cost includes tuition, course notes, logbook, all meals, and accommodation on board. An introductory course takes three days, and at the end you'll be able to work as a crew member on a sailing vessel, with an International Certificate of Competence (ICC) for those who want to charter yachts in Europe. See more on sailing adventures in Chapter 9.

Surfing

Wherever the waves are up, you'll find a surfing lesson being given. In an hour, good surfing teachers can have you on your feet and tackling modest waves. But to become skilled, you need some practice, and that's where a good surf school comes in. There are surfing schools everywhere from Hawaii to Portugal, Tahiti, and even on the south coast of England.

Let's start with the birthplace of surfing. The legendary Duke Kahanamoku was surely the first surfing instructor in the world, and Honolulu's **Waikiki Beach** is still a hot tip for hanging ten.

If you're looking for somewhere a little less crowded to test your skills, head to **Ewa Beach** or **Diamond Head Beach.**

TIP

If the weather is colder than you expected, ask your surf school about renting a wetsuit. Two hours (the normal lesson time) is a long time to be shivering.

Kima Surf (www.kimasurf.com) has surf camps/resorts in Bali and Sri Lanka, offering twice daily surf lessons, board hire, yoga and fitness classes, social activities and excursions, and full daily board. There are four camps, two in Bali and two in Sri Lanka. As part of their commitment to sustainability and the environment, Kima Surf organizes regular beach clean-ups and banned single use plastic packaging and plastic drink bottles from its kitchens and restaurants long before it became law in 2018.

Visitors to Australia shouldn't miss Sydney's **Bondi Beach,** where there are surf schools aplenty. One of the best is **Let's Go Surfing** (www.letsgosurfing.com.au), which offers daily group and private lessons, including family and female-only lessons, as well as a six-week surf course (one hour each week). Further north, Queensland's **Gold Coast,** where I took the photo in Figure 11-2, has plenty of options for wannabe surfers. There's a reason why the main beach there is called **Surfers Paradise!** Actually, the Gold Coast is a 26-mile (42-km) stretch of adjoining beaches, and one of the best for learning to surf is Currumbin Beach. **Currumbin Alley Surf School** (www.currumbinalleysurfschool.com.au) offers lessons year-round (it's warm enough!) for all ages and abilities.

Yoga

If mindfulness is what you're seeking, consider a yoga course. Mindfulness is a key part of making decisions on how to travel sustainably, but it's something many people grapple with. Practicing yoga can help you develop the skills to achieve mindfulness. As India is the birthplace of yoga, anywhere you go there are opportunities to take part in classes or courses in English. One of the world's most famous yoga centers is **The Yoga Institute** (www.theyogainstitute.org) in Mumbai, India. It teaches classical yoga, with a range of courses, from the popular twenty-one-day Better Living course to a seven-day Healthy Living course, or you can attend a one-hour regular class most days (there are also special classes for men and women). The institute also welcomes volunteers who can commit time to working in its social initiatives, including the Annam Brahma program that distributes free meals to the needy.

Lee Mylne

FIGURE 11-2: Surfing on Australia's Gold Coast.

Claiming the title of "yoga capital of the world" is the small town of **Rishikesh** in northern India, made famous in the 1960s by a visit by The Beatles, where you can practice yoga at luxury resorts. If you are interested in becoming a yoga teacher, the **Himalaya Yoga Valley** (www.yogagoaindia.com) is a leader in the field, with teacher training courses that run for around three weeks, as well as shorter workshops and retreats. Based in the coastal resort town of Goa, it's a great place to combine a holiday with learning. The school's ethos is based on the Hindu concept of *seva* (selfless service), believing that yoga should not only aid the wellness of the individual but also of the community. It supports Welfare for Animals Goa, International Animal Rescue, and several charities in Ireland (where it also has a yoga center).

To find yoga centers in other parts of the world, search the **Yoga Alliance** directory, www.yogaalliance.org (there are 95 registered yoga schools in Bali, Indonesia, alone).

REMEMBER

When choosing a yoga retreat or school, ask about their commitment to sustainable practices.

Chapter **12**

From Sustainable to Regenerative Tourism

B y reading this book, you have already made your commitment to, or interest in, sustainable travel clear. Travel has changed over the past decade, as the impact it has on our planet and everything that lives on it has become evident. The COVID-19 pandemic closed international and state borders and gave us even more reason to question the way we travel — how far, how often and by what mode of transport. Global warming, climate change, and carbon emissions are now household words and all of them directly affect our travel plans.

In this chapter, I look toward the future and at what comes next for travel and for those who want to travel sustainably, responsibly, and ethically. In Chapter 1, I showed you why you should care about sustainable travel and what it really means. Looking forward, the next shift for conscious travelers is regenerative travel.

FIND ONLINE

Head to www.dummies.com/go/sustainabletravelfd for links to all the web addresses provided in this chapter, along with other helpful resources.

Where To after Sustainability?

In 2015, the United Nations World Tourism Organization (UNWTO) released the 2030 Agenda for Sustainable Development and the **Sustainable Development Goals** (SDGs). Sustainable tourism has the potential to have an impact on many of those 17 goals — including wildlife, culture, carbon-neutral accreditation — either directly or through providing the income for communities to work toward achieving them.

Sustainable tourism operators — whether airlines, accommodation providers, hospitality, or tour operators — are increasingly aligning their sustainability policies and actions with specific SDGs (www.sdgs.un.org/goals). One way to assess the sincerity of an operator when it comes to sustainability is to check their stated commitment to the goals.

The **Glasgow Declaration on Climate Action in Tourism** (www.unwto.org/the-glasgow-declaration-on-climate-action-in-tourism) urges travel businesses and organizations around the world, collectively responsible for an estimated 8 percent of global carbon emissions, to support a worldwide commitment to halve those emissions by 2030 and reach net zero as soon as possible before 2050.

As businesses aim for that pinnacle of sustainability, "net zero" is a phrase on everyone's lips (and websites). But what does it actually mean? And is it possible for travelers to also be net zero, that is, reducing our emissions as much as we can and neutralizing the rest by contributing to off-setting programs such as wind farms or tree planting. While you're not likely to achieve climate positive status as an individual, as a traveler you can support companies and destinations that are.

Already, as you've seen in examples I've used in the pages of this book, tourism businesses across the world are taking huge steps to transform their businesses to meet sustainability goals. By supporting businesses who do this, by asking questions of those who don't (yet), and by spreading the word about the importance of making sustainable choices you are also making a difference. Every traveler can contribute to the solution. It's a collective effort.

But the term *sustainable tourism* is undergoing a shift, as its meaning and what it encapsulates evolves. While most travelers are conscious of their impact on the environment, sustainable travel is much more than that, just as sustainable tourism development is more than controlling and managing the industry's negative impact on the environment. It is about realizing tourism's potential in impacting local communities economically and socially and raising awareness about environmental conservation.

In 2022, the UNWTO launched its first **World Tourism Day Report**, under the theme "Rethinking Tourism," setting out its ambitions and hopes for a transformed tourism industry in the wake of the COVID-19 pandemic. The report saw the pause in global travel during the pandemic as a chance to "kickstart the emergence of a more ethical type of tourism." It also noted that if tourism was to realize its full potential to drive sustainable and inclusive development while also fulfilling its climate action responsibilities, it could not continue along the same pre-pandemic path and that it was "vitally important" to rethink and transform the tourism sector.

Another new movement that is springing up under the umbrella of sustainable travel is **community conscious travel,** where the protection of residents of popular destinations is paramount. Over-tourism is a word we all know and dread. Unmanageable numbers of visitors to popular destinations are ruining normal life for those who live there — and travelers are not enjoying it either. Queues, fully booked restaurants, packed public transport, log-jammed laneways, and airspace bristling with selfie-sticks are taking away the very wonder of being there.

"Untourist" is a word I came across in the 1990s when I contributed research to a guide book with that theme. Now the word is back again, meaning travelers who are completely independent, exploring on their own and shunning commercial tours while looking for the hidden secrets of a destination that only the locals know. That there are now guide books and anti-tourism tours based on this premise seems ironic.

Leaving a Place Better Than You Found It: Regenerative Tourism

The new term on tourism's lips is *regenerative tourism*. Put simply, this means leaving a place better than you found it by contributing to it in some way. Embracing regenerative tourism is part of being a sustainable traveler, but it takes your actions a step further. It's about making sure that what we enjoy today as travelers will be there for the next generations to enjoy, too. When we hear about endangered species or plundered rainforests, it becomes even more imperative to ensure that's the case.

While sustainable tourism seeks to lessen the harm done by the global demand for travel, regenerative tourism aims to have a positive impact for everyone — hosts, local communities and hosts, wildlife, the environment, and travelers. But to achieve that, you need to redefine your idea of going on holiday or a life of traveling. You need to commit to being a proactive, conscious, and intentional traveler.

REMEMBER

Regenerative travel can take many forms, but the idea is that you, the traveler, will go home with a greater sense of the lives of others, having made a lasting and meaningful connection with the places and communities you've visited — and even made friends — by taking part in projects that improve their lives. It's about recognizing that traveling is not all about your own agenda. In turn, those communities are less likely to have a negative view of tourists and to recognize the benefits tourism can bring.

Early leaders in regenerative travel

Starting from the ground up, regenerative travel also means local communities must be involved in any new tourism developments or ventures, ensuring they bring value and maintain cultural heritage and traditions for future generations as well as protecting or enhancing the environment in which they live. While the meaning of regenerative tourism is still being fully shaped, some tourism business operators are taking their own steps toward achieving their understanding of it.

The World Travel and Tourism Council (www.wttc.org) holds up **New Zealand** (www.newzealand.com) as an example of a destination where regenerative tourism works. It starts with the Tiaki

Promise (www.tiakinewzealand.com), a pledge that Tourism New Zealand asks all visitors to take to care for the nation's people, culture, land, sea, and nature. Many other destinations have similar pledges, asking you to consciously acknowledge their expectations of you as a visitor (see more on this in Chapter 2). The New Zealand government has taken the lead in announcing a move to transform its tourism industry into a regenerative model, based on the simple premise that regenerative tourism ensures that tourism gives back more to people and places than it takes and must actively enrich communities and help protect and restore the environment.

First Nations cultures and values play an important role in defining a regenerative path for tourism, and this can be clearly seen when you read the tourism pledges many destinations are asking visitors to take. The New Zealand model is an excellent example of this, being based on the Maori principles of *manaakitanga* (respect, kindness, and hospitality), *turangawaewae* (sharing of knowledge) and *kaitiakitanga* (guardianship).

Several New Zealand regional tourism organizations have stated their commitment to regenerative tourism. **Tourism Bay of Plenty** (www.bayofplentynz.com) on the North Island runs sustainability program for tourism operators to "motivate and maximize individual steps towards regeneration." **Queenstown Lakes** (www.queenstownnz.co.nz) in the South Island requires operators to put people and places at its center to promote a viable and regenerative tourism future. New Zealand's tourism industry has long been practicing regenerative tourism, often through Maori-owned and operated businesses (www.maoritourism.co.nz) where visitors are treated as *whanau* (family). Some examples include Bay of Plenty's **Kohutapu Lodge and Tribal Tours** (www.kohutapulodge.co.nz), **Kapiti Island Nature Tours** (www.kaptitiisland.com) near Wellington (see Figure 12-1) and **Footprints Waipoua** (www.footprintswaipoua.co.nz) in Northland.

Seattle-based travel agency **Global Family Travels** (www.globalfamilytravels.com) operates under the mission statement "Learn, Serve, and Immerse," partnering with nonprofits to develop tourism experiences that support education, conservation, cultural preservation, and economic growth, and which foster cross-cultural understanding. As well as "community adventures" in Seattle, it offers a range of tours around the world. In Canada's **Bay of Fundy**, visitors take part in a shoreline tree planting with the **Atlantic Coastal Action Program** (www. acapsj.org) or a beach clean-up with the **UNESCO Fundy Biosphere Region** (www.en.unesco.org/biosphere/eu-na/fundy), and immerse themselves in the region by meeting the locals, eating the food, and discovering the natural beauty of the area.

Lee Mylne

FIGURE 12-1: Kapiti Island Nature Reserve, New Zealand.

Global Family Travels also runs a series of regenerative travel tours to Peru's **Sacred Valley,** where in Andean culture Pachamama (Mother Earth) provides sustenance and life to all living things. As well as the Inca ruins of Machu Picchu, seen in Figure 12-2, and Ollantaytambo, tours visit communities where their presence helps support traditional practices such as weaving; takes visitors to where they can learn about the ancient Andean practice of *chalay* or bartering; and takes them to the Potato Park, dedicated to the conservation of the heritage of six Indigenous communities and to the growing of Peru's 1,300 varieties of potato.

Lee Mylne

FIGURE 12-2: Weaving demonstration at Ollantaytambo, Peru.

Community-based tourism is another aspect of regenerative travel, where communities are taking tourism into their own hands and ensuring economic benefits stay with them. In this way, travelers can gain an authentic and immersive insight into a community's heritage, culture, and natural experiences. One example is the remote **Rewa Eco-lodge** (www.rewaecolodge.com), in Guyana, a small country in the north-eastern part of South America, bordering Venezuela, Brazil and Suriname. The solar-powered eco-lodge was built and is run by local villagers, providing employment and helping protect the natural environment and biodiversity. Among its activities is catch-and-release fishing for the world's largest and rarest freshwater game fish, arapaima, in the Rupununi River, which is part of a project to study and monitor the population's migration and breeding patterns. Every fish is measured and tagged before release.

In Indonesia, Bali-based **Astungkara Way** (www.astungkaraway. com) is an organization that defies easy labels but is showing the way by creating alternatives to mass tourism that support regenerative agriculture and local culture. A desire to connect travelers with rural communities — rice and lemongrass farmers and their families — has led to the development of tourism experiences that give visitors insight into the challenges and priorities of Balinese people.

Walking the Astungkara Trails means slowing down, connecting with nature and seeing a simple, sustainable lifestyle in action. The ten-day coast to coast regenerative trail takes visitors on an 84-mile (135-km) trek across the island (south to north) through rice paddies, villages, and bamboo forest, and past temples and waterfalls. Accommodation is hosted by regenerative rice farming families who share knowledge and culture through activities including foraging, cooking, meditation, and morning stretching. Two- and five-day walks are also available. The aim of the project is to create a sustainable and chemical-free farm landscape in Bali and to preserve traditional rice farming methods. Tourism income is helping to make this possible.

Being a nature-positive traveler

Many of these examples are what is also sometimes termed "nature positive," the concept that it's not enough to limit the damage you do to the natural environment — you need to also ensure that your presence has a positive impact on it. The World Travel and Tourism Council's Nature Positive Travel & Tourism report urges the travel and tourism industry to become "guardians of nature" and "nature positive" by 2030 through recovery and regeneration.

For travelers, this could be as simple as choosing your tour wisely, taking time to join a tree planting or beach-cleaning project, or visiting a place that is not crowded with other tourists. It could mean simply planning your vacation so it enhances life for the people who live in your chosen destination and using your love of travel as a force for good.

TIP

The WTTC suggests the following tips for being a nature-positive traveler:

>> **Leave nothing behind.** One simple way of doing this is to minimize your use of single-use plastics (bring your own water bottle, shopping bag, and coffee cup).

>> **Think local.** Support local communities by buying fresh food at markets or a handcrafted souvenir from the person who made it.

>> **Keep it clean.** Many coastal communities around the world have regular beach clean-ups and it's easy to join in. Take your own trash with you and pick up trash if you see it in a national park or on a beach — or anywhere, really!

>> **Choose animal encounters carefully.** Check if the animals are well-cared for, the tour or attraction is ethically run, and if they help or support animal conservation projects.

>> **Choose accommodations and other travel providers mindfully.** Are they committed to responsible, sustainable, and regenerative travel? Are they locally owned and operated?

Chapter **13**

Ten Ways to Travel Sustainably

Making the decision to travel sustainably is easy. Making sure that all the smaller decisions you make add up to achieving that goal is easy, too — it's just a matter of keeping a few things at the forefront of your vacation planning. Wherever you plan to travel to, there are sustainable options to help you along the way. These are some of them.

Offset Your Carbon Footprint

When you blithely board your plane, high on the euphoria of the upcoming vacation time, it's easy to dismiss the thought of the carbon footprint you are leaving behind. Frequent travelers like me create appalling carbon emissions. Avoiding flying entirely is not possible for most people, but mitigating your emissions by choosing more carbon-efficient routes and planes and off-setting your travel miles are the best ways to limit the damage being done.

The first step is to tick the box to offset your emissions when you book your flight. Most airlines now have this facility and it's easy. Those few extra dollars you pay will contribute to a project that helps reduce emissions (such as tree-planting) and/or provides benefits to a community (such as providing environmental education).

Even if you are not flying, use online tools to calculate the carbon emissions of your trip — whether it's by road, rail, or sea — and pay to offset them. If your airline, transport operator or tour company doesn't offer that option, seek out environmental projects that you can support independently.

If you do need to fly — and of course, that's often unavoidable — pack lightly by limiting your baggage to essentials (carry-on only if possible), as this means less weight on the plane and reduces fuel usage. Take reusable items like water bottles and tote bags. Choose destinations where even the airports are switching to renewable energy sources and taking other measures to reduce their carbon emissions.

Travel at Ground Level

Ditch air travel in favour of trains, buses, or road trips. Trains are the most sustainable form of travel (after walking or cycling) and an overnight train has the added benefit of saving you the cost of a hotel room. Train travel is so on-trend now that the Swedes have a word for it — *tagskryt* or "pride in taking the train" — that you can use to boast about your eco-cred in taking the train instead of the plane. While there's a plethora of luxury — and very expensive — train journeys around the world (some of them covered in Chapter 2), there are also regular trains that will take you to the same destinations for a fraction of the price.

If you're road-tripping to or at your destination, consider renting an electric vehicle (EV), which will cut emissions drastically and save you heaps on fuel costs.

Choose Sustainable Accommodations

Look for hotels or other accommodation that have earned certification for their commitment to sustainability. While you're staying, remember to conserve energy by turning off lights and air conditioning and reusing your towels. Put up the do-not-disturb sign to keep the cleaning staff out.

Before you book, look online for the property's sustainability policy and ask questions about the accommodation's sustainability practices. The more potential guests who do this, the more likely the hotel is to take notice and lift its game. Look for alternatives to big hotels, such as homestays, home-swaps, hostels, or even couch-surfing. Staying at locally owned accommodations (as opposed to big international chains) helps ensure your dollars stay in the community.

Find out if they use solar-powered electricity, natural and sustainable materials in their building process, have a commitment to social responsibility, or take measures to reduce their own carbon footprint. Are the furnishings or artwork made by local crafts workers? What waste reduction and disposal measures do they use? Do they recycle, plant trees, or educate their employees about conservation? Where does the food for the restaurant come from?

Jump Aboard Public Transport

Walk, cycle, or use public transport wherever you can. Opt for destinations where local governments have taken tangible and visible steps to providing residents and visitors with clean transport. If you fly, take the train or a bus from the airport, starting as you mean to go on. Trains, trams, buses, and ferries can usually get you anywhere you want to go — and you might even strike up conversations with local commuters along the way. Trains and buses also usually deposit you in the heart of a city, without the need for extra travel that most airports require. Look for local bike share schemes and hit the cycling trails and paths.

Major cities have extensive public transport networks, but even using local buses in smaller destinations can provide memorable experiences as you board with locals going about their daily business.

Take the Road Less Traveled

Stay away from crowds and avoid contributing to over-tourism. If you want to see one of the big-ticket attractions (Eiffel Tower, Statue of Liberty, Pyramids of Giza), plan to travel in the off-season when the crowds will be thinner, wait times shorter, and prices cheaper. You might also avoid sticky summer heat by traveling in autumn or winter.

Look for alternatives to your first, more famous choice. There is bound to be a secret, quieter spot not far away, that will give you a similar experience that might be more affordable, less crowded, and more welcoming.

Nature-based travel is increasing in popularity for good reason. Take the family camping and rediscover the joys of the outdoors; just make sure you leave the environment as you found it.

Connect with Cultures

Cultural connection can be one of the richest rewards of travel. Seeing how other people live and appreciating the differences between your lives is a wonderful learning experience. Take some language lessons before you go, even if just to master the basic phrases. It shows you're interested in the local culture and even if you get it wrong, you're sure to get a smile just for trying.

Learning about and connecting with First Nations cultures will open up new perspectives on your destination. Taking an indigenous cultural tour helps support First Nations communities economically and also fosters greater understanding on the part of visitors and greater pride among Indigenous people.

Remember to be respectful of other cultures' traditional and laws. Not only is it good manners, but it may save you from tense encounters with locals and potentially with the law. Find out about tipping, dress codes, and what might be considered offensive or insulting.

Slow Down

Have you ever returned from a vacation feeling like you need . . . a vacation? All that rushing about, ticking sights off your list, can take a toll. Embrace the concept of slow travel and you'll return home feeling restored and refreshed, as you should. Slow travel doesn't need to mean a long journey over a period of time; it's also about the mindset you take with you. On a given trip, visit fewer places (minimizing transport emissions) and be more mindful of the details — you might surprise yourself at how you begin to appreciate features you'd never otherwise notice.

Slow travel also means greater connection with the places you are visiting, whether it's a nature-based vacation or discovering a new culture or community. It can also mean staying closer to home, exploring places you may have overlooked in the rush to get away. Your own backyard can have unexpected treasures and you will keep your carbon emissions low.

Support Sustainable and Ethical Travel Companies

Spending your hard-earned holiday dollars isn't something to be done lightly. By supporting travel companies that have transparent goals of their own when it comes to sustainability, you are helping their efforts go further. Do your research before booking tours, hotels, flights, or other transport, and check out any credentials that each company you use claims to have. Look for eco-certification that tells you the company's values align with your own.

If you can, choose a travel provider that's a signatory to the United Nations World Tourism Organisation's Glasgow Declaration on Climate Action in Tourism (www.unwto.org/the-glasgow-declaration-on-climate-action-in-tourism). These companies have pledged to halve their carbon emissions by 2030 and to reach Net Zero before 2050.

Be an Animal-Friendly Traveler

Encounters with other species is one of the most thrilling — and sometimes emotional — experiences you can have while traveling. There's a reason that wildlife rates so highly on our travel agendas, but the excitement is sometimes tempered by the sad knowledge that not all human encounters impact positively on animals. To be an animal-friendly traveler, you must be mindful not to support enterprises that exploit or harm animals in any way.

Shun any attraction or destination that is based on activities that are cruel to animals. This includes elephant-riding, bullfights, rodeos, trained dolphins, captive bears, lion-patting, or any other number of tourism attractions or activities which are sadly still too common around the world. Instead, chose experiences that will have a positive impact, through supporting conservation or protection efforts. Choose a reputable wildlife tour operator with clear animal welfare policies, who hire local guides and partner with experts in the field. Pick a less-visited region for a more memorable encounter or look for safari-style tours closer to home to see native wildlife.

Dispose of waste — particularly plastic — properly. Not only is litter unsightly, but your discarded rubbish can end up in the ocean and be fatal for marine creatures. When camping, be careful not to leave food scraps around and camp away from water sources.

Buy from Local Businesses

Whether it is eating out, buying fresh food (or patronizing local supermarkets), or choosing souvenirs to take home, buying from small businesses will help support the local economy and make visitors more welcome. Be old-fashioned: Buy postcards to send the folks back home! It all adds up to spending your money in the place that is welcoming you.

Look for items made from natural materials, such as organic cotton, hemp, or bamboo and for things that have been handmade by locals. Check labels to see where that "authentic" souvenir has been made. Buy from fair-trade stores, direct from the makers or artists, and look for certificates of authenticity.

Chapter **14**

Ten Places to Go and Still Travel Sustainably

Deciding on your next dream destination should be as easy as consulting that mental bucket list you have been building over the years, but with sustainability in mind the issues become a little more complex. By the time you've reached the end of this book, hopefully things are a little clearer and the decision to travel to a place that's embracing sustainable, responsible, ethical tourism is one you feel equipped to make. Is your top-of-the-list destination doing the right thing by the people who call it home? Can you visit that desirable destination and still tread softly on the planet?

Many places are taking huge strides forward in welcoming visitors while maintaining a low impact on the environment and helping local communities to benefit from sharing their lives with others. In this chapter, I put forward ten places to consider for your next vacation based on their commitment to sustainable tourism practices and their communities. It's heartening to see many destinations taking a serious approach to sustainability issues, helped by thoughtful travelers who support those efforts.

Everyone will have their bucket list destinations (mine is the Galapagos), but increasingly people are wanting to take the roads less traveled, shunning places that are suffering from overtourism or those where the presence of tourists may be detrimental to those who call it home. I'm sure you will find, as I have over a lifetime of travel, that the most memorable and rewarding travel experiences are those that are not in any guide book or must-do list. They are often the most challenging and sometimes not without angst — but they are definitely the ones that I am still talking about years later.

So, look at places that will take you away from crowds and Instagrammers jostling for position. The world is vast and glorious and full of warm and welcoming people who are not jaded by hordes. If you really can't bypass some of the major tourist hotspots (of *course* you want to see the Colosseum in Rome at least once in your life), book to go during offseason. The monuments will still be there, but the crowds will be thinner.

Costa Rica

Costa Rica is the poster child for sustainability, regularly making it onto lists of countries that rate highly in the sustainability stakes. That also, of course, makes it a hugely popular destination for many people, but I think it's still worth including on this list. With three UNESCO World Heritage sites — La Amistard Reserve and National Park, Area de Conservacion Guanacaste, and Cocos Island National Park — it is home to 28 national parks, covering more than 25 percent of the country, and a host of exotic species. The slogan "Pura Vida" (Pure Life) sums up Costa Rica's approach to tourism, with an emphasis on natural wonders: hot springs and geysers, rainforests, birdlife (850 species, including colourful macaws and parrots), and stunning beaches.

Costa Rica's environmental credentials are exemplary, with more than 98 percent of its energy from renewables. A National Decarbonization Plan to tackle transport, energy, waste, and land use was launched in 2019, aiming to achieve net zero emissions by 2050. If you visit, there are plenty of eco-conscious places to stay!

Aotearoa/New Zealand

Aotearoa/New Zealand's reputation for nature-based activities, clean air, and breathtaking natural beauty is backed up by its leading stance on sustainable tourism. Head to Kaikoura on the South Island to watch whales year-round, hike in ancient forests of towering trees, or explore the geo-thermal regions of the central North Island around Rotorua and Lake Taupo, where you'll see spouting geysers, soak in thermal baths, and know that this source of energy accounts for more than a fifth of the nation's power resources. While Queenstown might be New Zealand's adventure capital, consider some of the less-visited regions at the extremes of the country, such as Northland or Stewart Island, where you might be lucky enough to see (or hear) kiwi in the wild. Almost one-third of New Zealand is preserved as national parks, reserves, or heritage sites.

Borneo

Orangutans. Need I say more? They are the biggest drawcard for visitors to Borneo, but it's important to remember that there's so much more to this island (the third largest in the world). Orangutan habitat is being decimated by palm oil plantations that are taking over the rainforests of Borneo, so it's important to ensure that whatever you buy (at home and while traveling) does not contain palm oil. This problem is not limited to Borneo, and you'll find more about it in Chapter 6.

Borneo's biodiversity and rare species need preserving and tourism has an important role to play in this. Visiting sanctuaries that support the care of injured or orphaned orangutans can help: Find them at Semenggoh, Matang, and Sepilok. Your visit also helps demonstrate that wildlife tourism is a viable alternative to palm oil propagation. Other wildlife that need help include pygmy elephants and proboscis monkeys.

Borneo is shared between three countries — Indonesia, Brunei, and Malaysia. Most of the orangutan rescue centers and guided tours are in the Malaysian states of Sarawak and Sabah. Batang Ai in Sarawak is one of the few places to see orangutans in the wild; look for a tour that has local indigenous Iban people as guides.

Off the north coast of Borneo is Malaysia's biggest marine park, Tun Mustapha Park (TMP), which protects a vast coral reef and fifty islands. Sustainable management plans are ensuring fish stocks can recover and damaged reefs rebuild. Take a dive or snorkel tour to see green turtles, dugong (manatees), and fabulous coral.

Bhutan

The tiny Buddhist kingdom of Bhutan, high in the Himalayan mountains, is the world's only carbon-negative country — but be warned, if it's on your bucket list the experience will come at a considerable cost. In 2023, Bhutan (www.bhutan.travel) introduced a new Sustainable Development Fee, meaning all visitors to the country (except children under six years old) will pay an entry fee of $200 per day as part of their visa application. Children under 12 pay half price. This is an effort to limit the impact that increasing numbers of tourists inevitably brings, to preserve its natural assets and to protect its culture.

The good news is that your tourist dollars go back to the people of Bhutan through the employment of local guides or homestays. In fact, staying for longer is a good idea because the fee reduces if you stay five nights or more. If you visit before August 2027 — and pay in US dollars — the fee will be reduced to $100 per person per night. Other revisions may be made over the course of time, so check the website for details.

Ecotourism is a mainstay of Bhutan's tourism offering, with wildlife sanctuaries, birdwatching, festivals, and homestays key elements of it. Expect to see red pandas, exotic birds and butterflies, and golden langurs. The Royal Society for the Protection of Nature (www.rspnbhutan.org), a citizen-based conservation NGO, works with the government of Bhutan to ensure its forests and stunning glacial valleys are preserved and protected.

Rwanda

The stars of Rwanda's tourism industry are the endangered mountain gorillas. Tragically, years of poaching and habitat destruction have taken their toll on the gorilla population, and protection of their greatest tourism asset is top of the list for the Rwandan government's conservation efforts (www.visitrwanda. com). Encounters with gorillas are carefully managed, with expert trackers and guides leading small groups of tourists. Sign up with a reputable tour company to trek in Volcanoes National Park, where 12 gorilla troops (family groups) live. There are now only around 1,000 mountain gorillas in the wild, but the population is slowly increasing because of efforts by government, communities, and NGOs. Paid permits are required — and are expensive — but underwrite management costs and help limit the impact of visitors on the gorillas' daily lives.

Rwanda's gorilla-based tourism strategy also directly benefits the communities that live near the national parks in both economic and other ways. It not only generates jobs and income for those directly involved in gorilla tourism, but benefits the wider community, including people involved in cultural tourism, agriculture, and other joint ventures, as well as providing money for schools and healthcare.

Finland

As well as consistently topping the World Happiness Report (www. worldhappiness.report), Finland has an enviable record in the sustainability stakes. Around 80 percent of the country is covered in forest, and Visit Finland's Sustainable Travel Finland program helps guide sustainable choices for destinations and tourism companies. Visit Finland (www.visitfinland.com) and 60 Finnish tourism operators have signed the Glasgow Declaration on Climate Action in tourism, aiming to be carbon neutral by 2035. From Helsinki to Lapland, the commitment is real. Where to go? I highly recommend Finnish Lapland, where you might be lucky enough — at the right time of year and in the right weather conditions — to see the incredible aurora borealis (northern lights), as well as experience Sámi culture.

Slovenia

Bordering Italy, Austria, Croatia, and Hungary, and renowned for its breathtaking scenery, Slovenia (www.slovenia.info) is one of Europe's most underrated destinations. As far back as 2016, the capital Ljubljana, was voted the European Green Capital. Making guilt-free choices to get around the city is easy: Trains are electric, there is a bike-borrowing scheme, a large no-car zone in the city center, and a system of free electric buggies called *kavalirs* (gentle helpers) that you can hail if you need help getting around it. Beyond the city, more than a third of the country is forested conservation land, and Slovenia is home to four UNESCO Biosphere Reserves. Hiking, caving, river safaris, and cycling are all sustainable options when discovering Slovenia. Look for the **Slovenia Green** label on tours and products.

Argentina

Since 2010, Rewilding Argentina (www.rewildingargentina.org) has worked to expand and create national parks, with 2.47 million acres (1 million hectares) of land and more than 38,600 square miles (100,000 square kilometres) of ocean now protected. Rewilding Argentina's work builds on that of The Conservation Land Trust, launched in 1997 by Doug Tompkins, founder of the adventure clothing company North Face. Among its success stories is the **Iberá Wetlands,** South America's second-largest wetland ecosystem, where you can see tapirs, giant anteaters, giant otters, and — if you are lucky — the elusive jaguars, reintroduced in 2021.

Rewilding Argentina boosts fragile wildlife populations while helping indigenous communities build a nature-based tourism economy. Along the coastal "Blue Route" in Patagonia's Chubut Province, you can see penguins, whales, dolphins, elephant seals, sea birds, guanacos, and armadillos.

Greece

Who doesn't love a Greek island? If your idea of a beach idyll is just that, why not head to the island of **Paros,** which aims to be the Mediterranean's first plastic-free island by 2025. With a resident population of around 15,000, Paros is visited by up to 600,000 tourists during the holiday season. This has a huge environmental impact, but sustainable tourism is top of mind for the locals. Blue recycling bins are found all over the island, and you can find tourism operators, hotels, and business that have signed up to Clean Blue Paros (www.commonseas.com/countries/clean-blue-paros; there are about 100 of them so far). You can refill your water bottle at one of the refill stations around the island, and if your timing is right, take part in a beach clean-up project (held four times a year). While this project is in its infancy, the target items are those that are easy to shun: plastic straws, coffee cups, water bottles, and shopping bags.

Scotland

Wilderness is never far away in Scotland (www.visitscotland.com), from its beautiful islands to the Cairngorm mountains. The European Nature Trust (www.theeuropeannaturetrust.com) has conserved 23,000 acres of the Scottish Highlands at Alladale Wilderness Reserve (www.alladale.com), where tree planting and conservation projects are helping bring back Scottish wildcats and red squirrels from the brink of extinction. Activities at Alladale, which is north of Inverness, include hiking in old-growth Caledonian forest, mountain-biking (e-bikes are available for rent), birdwatching, and wild swimming in the lochs and rivers. Scotland's UNESCO Trail links 13 places across the country, from cities to islands and everything in between. To find eco-friendly accommodation and tours, look for the Scotland-founded Green Tourism certification logo, held by 2,500 businesses, including whiskey distilleries, restaurants, castles, museums, campsites, and more.

Index

A

Abercrombie & Kent Philanthropy (AKP), 122

Aboriginal tourism (Australia), 117, 202

accommodations
asking about sustainability, 78–79
eco-friendly, 73–74
homestays, 71–73, 104–105
Indigenous-owned, 74–75
luxury hotels, 75–77
overview, 69–71, 219

Aegean Sailing School (Greece), 204

Africa
dark sky places in, 169
gorilla trekking in, 126–127
safaris in, 121–124

African Parks, 124

air travel. See flying

Alladale Wilderness Reserve (Scotland), 229

Alliance Francaise, 109, 197

American Indian Alaska Native Tourism Association (AIANTA), 116–117, 202

Amsterdam, Netherlands, 51

Amtrak, 45, 46

animal encounters. See wildlife

Antelope Valley Poppy Reserve (USA), 161

anti-tourism, 209

Aotearoa. See New Zealand

aquariums, 145–148, 151

aquatic wildlife encounters, 129–134

Argentina, 228

art tours, 200–202

Arthur Hotel Group, 77

arts and crafts markets, 89

Asia
elephant encounters in, 139–142
medicines harming animals in, 98–99
Songkran Festival, 106
train travel in, 47–49
wildlife trekking in, 127–128

Asilia Dunia Camp (Tanzania), 124

Astungkara Way (Bali, Indonesia), 213–214

Audley Travel, 125

Aurora Expeditions, 40–41

Australia
dark sky places in, 169
flower-based tourism in, 161–162
hiking and trekking adventures in, 128
Indigenous cultural tours in, 117, 202
Indigenous festivals in, 108
Indigenous peoples in, 114
Indigenous-owned lodging in, 75
koala cuddling, 134–136
learning to sail in, 204
learning to surf in, 205, 206
long-distance treks in, 166
marine conservation projects in, 188
rodeos in, 144
sailing in, 172
sustainable tourism pledges in, 24–25
train travel in, 46–47
whale watching in, 132

Azenart, 201

B

B Corp certification, 31

Back Roads of Japan tour (G Adventures), 72, 105

Bali, Indonesia, 104, 205, 213–214

Barbados Sea Turtle Project, 188
bargaining for souvenirs, 92–94
bear bile farming, 98–99
beasts of burden, 144–145
beche de mer, 84
Berlin, Germany, 51
Bhutan, 226
bicycle travel, 14, 52–54, 172–176
Big Bend National Park (USA), 168
biodynamic food, 80
bird's nest soup, 84
birdwatching, 155–157
black bear products, 98–99
Black Cultural Heritage Tours, 201
Blue Train (South Africa), 47
Bogotá, Colombia, 174
Book Different, 28
Boracay island, Philippines, 26
Borneo, 225–226
botanical tourism, 160–162
Buddhism, 103
budget family travel, 32–33
bullfighting, 142–144
Byway, 28

C

Calanais Standing Stones (Scotland), 21
Caledonian Sleeper (UK), 45
Calgary Stampede (Canada), 144
camel rides, 145
Camino de Santiago trek (Europe), 164
Canada
    Indigenous arts and crafts in, 90
    Indigenous cultural tours in, 116, 117,
        202
    Indigenous peoples in, 114
    long-distance treks in, 164
    regenerative tourism in, 211–212
    rodeos in, 144
    sustainable tourism pledges in, 24

train travel in, 46
    wolf-focused tours in, 125
Cape Town Declaration on Responsible
    Tourism in Destinations, 6–7
captive animals
    beasts of burden, 144–145
    breeding programs, 146, 147
    bullfighting and rodeos, 142–144
    elephant encounters, 138–142
    unethical experiences, avoiding,
        137–138
    zoos and aquariums, 145–148
car travel, sustainable, 49–50, 218
carbon footprint, 9–10, 38–40
carbon offsets, 12–13, 30, 39, 217–218
cargo ship travel, 41–42
carry-on luggage, 65, 68
charities, wildlife, 121
Chattanooga, Tennessee (USA), 156
cherry blossom season, 161
children
    photographing, 112–113
    sustainable travel with, 32–34
    volunteering with, 180, 186–187
ChildSafe, 192, 193
Chilean Sea Bass, 85
China, 50, 51
CITES (Convention on International
    Trade in Endangered Species of
    Wildlife Fauna and Flora), 95
civets, 84, 138
climate change, 8–10
close to home destinations, choosing,
    18–19
clothing
    choosing when traveling light, 66
    respecting local laws and
        customs, 103
    as souvenirs, 99
    sustainable travel, 59–62
    for volunteering, 185, 188
coastal (sea) wolf-focused tours, 125

Colombia, 105, 157, 174, 186

communities. *See* local community

community conscious travel, 209

community projects, volunteering on, 185–187, 191–192

community washing, 189

community-based tourism, 213

Congo, 127

conservation programs, 146–147, 187–188, 191–192

Conservation Volunteers International Program, 179–180

Convention on International Trade in Endangered Species of Wildlife Fauna and Flora (CITES), 95

Copenhagen, Denmark, 51

coral souvenirs, 97

Costa Rica, 224

counting food miles, 81

COVID-19 pandemic, 8–9

credentials, travel provider, 30–31

crocodile farming, 97

cruises, 38, 39–42

Cuba, 72

cultural festivals, 106–108

cultural sensitivities

  connecting with First Nations people, 114–118

  local language, learning, 108–109

  meaningful interaction with communities, 104–108

  overview, 101

  photography, 110–113

  respecting local laws and customs, 102–109

cultural tours, 115–118, 200–202

cultures

  connecting with, 220

  travel provider policies on, 29

customs, respecting local, 102–109, 220

cutlery, reusable, 63

cycling, 14, 52–54, 172–176

Czech Republic, 51

D

Dana Point, California (USA), 131–132

dark sky places, 168–170

Democratic Republic of Congo, 128

desert safari tours, 125

destinations, sustainable

  Argentina, 228

  Bhutan, 226

  Borneo, 225–226

  Costa Rica, 224

  Finland, 227

  Greece, 228–229

  New Zealand, 225

  overview, 223–224

  Rwanda, 226–227

  Scotland, 229

  Slovenia, 227–228

  tips for choosing, 18–22

dining

  counting food miles, 81

  eating like a local, 82–83

  foodprint, reducing, 81–82

  knowing what not to eat, 84–85

  overview, 69, 79–80

  seafood, 80–81

diving, 27, 157–160

dolphin captivity, 147–148, 151

dolphin meat, 84

domesticated animals. *See* captive animals

Domino Volunteers (Colombia), 105, 186

donkeys, 144–145

Duolingo, 109

dwarf minke whales, 132

E

Earth Watch, 188

Eastern & Oriental Express, 48

Eastern Lowland Gorillas, 128

eating. *See* dining

Echidna Walkabout, 135

eco-friendly accommodations, 73–74

eco-tourism, 8. *See also* sustainable travel

Ecuador, 75

educational travel. *See* learning while traveling

Egypt, 165

electric bikes, 174

electric vehicle (EV) travel, 49–50

electronics, packing, 66

elephant encounters, 138–142, 150–151

Elephant Hills Elephant Experience (Thailand), 140

Elephant Nature Park (Thailand), 140

environmental impact
  of travel, 8–10
  travel provider policies on, 29
  when going off the beaten track, 54–55

environmental projects, volunteering on, 188, 191–192

ethical animal encounters. *See* wildlife

ethical tourism, 8. *See also* sustainable travel

Europe
  cycling in, 175
  Fairbnb in, 70
  hiking and trekking adventures in, 128
  long-distance treks in, 164–165
  sailing in, 171
  train travel in, 43–45

European Nature Trust, 187

EV (electric vehicle) travel, 49–50

expedition cruises, 40–41

F

Fairbnb, 70

fake souvenirs, 90–92

families, staying with local, 104–105

family travel, 32–34, 180

feminine hygiene products, 65

festivals, cultural, 106–108

Finland, 24, 44–45, 227

First Nations peoples
  accommodations owned by, 74–75
  buying souvenirs from, 89–90, 91–92
  connecting with, 114–118, 220
  cuisine of, trying, 83
  cultural tours, 116–117, 201–202
  festivals, attending, 106–107
  regenerative tourism, 211

Flight Free Pledge, 26

flowers, tourism focused on, 160–162

flying
  carbon offsets, 12–13, 217–218
  flight-shaming (*flygskam*), 9
  sustainably, 38–39

FNQ Nature Tours, 128

foie gras, 85

food containers, reusable, 63

food markets, eating at, 82–83

food miles, counting, 81

foodprint, reducing, 81–82

foot travel, 14. *See also* trekking

Footprints program (World Nomads), 30

France, 43, 161

freighter travel, 41–42

French language schools, 109, 197

furs, 96–97

G

G Adventures, 71–72, 105

galleries, buying souvenirs at, 89, 92

garbage. *See* waste

Garma Festival (Australia), 108

Gathering of Nations (USA), 108

Germany, 51

Gibbon Experience (Laos), 127

Glasgow Declaration on Climate Action in Tourism, 28, 208

Global Family Travels, 32, 211, 212–213

Global Sustainable Tourism Council, 31, 70–71

GoKinda, 77

Gold Coast (Australia), 205, 206

golf, learning while traveling, 202–203

Gorilla Friendly Pledge, 26

gorilla tourism, 126–127, 226–227

Great Barrier Reef (Australia), 132, 172, 188

Great Divide Trail (Canada), 164

Great Southern Rail (Australia), 46

Greece, 204, 228–229

Green Pearls, 77

Green School/Green Camp, 34

greenwashing, 13, 31–32

group hiking and trekking excursions, 126–128

group tours, size of, 29

Guyana, 213

H

haggling for souvenirs, 92–94

hand luggage, 65, 68

harpy eagles, 157

Hawai'i, USA, 23, 188, 204–205

healthcare volunteers, 188–189

heritage items, as souvenirs, 100

hiking

    getting started with shorter walks, 163

    incorporating wildlife watching, 125–129

    long-distance treks, 163–167

    overview, 162

    sustainable, 167–168

Himalaya Yoga Valley, 206

Hinduism, 104

Holi festivals, 106

homestays, 71–73, 104–105

Hong Kong, 51

humpback whales, 132–133

hybrid car travel, 49–50

hygiene products, 65

I

Icelandic Pledge, 24

icons, explained, 3

Il Sasso language school (Italy), 197

imported souvenirs, 89

Inca Trail (Peru), 165

India, 49, 140–141, 205–206

Indigenous peoples. See First Nations peoples

Indigenous Tourism Association of Canada (ITAC), 116, 117

Indonesia, 104, 146–147, 205, 213–214

insurance, travel, 30, 180

InterContinental Maldives Maamunagau Resort, 133

International Driving Permit (IDP), 50

International Whaling Commission, 131

Intrepid Travel, 30, 31

Israel, 77

Italy, 44, 197

ivory souvenirs, 98

J

jacaranda tourism, 162

Japan

    flower-based tourism in, 161

    homestays in, 72, 105

    long-distance treks in, 167

    public transport in, 52

    train travel in, 47–48

Jarjeer Mule and Donkey Refuge (Morocco), 144–145

Jordan, 145

K

Kenya, 75
Kima Surf, 205
Kissimee, Florida (USA), 157
koala cuddling, 134–136
kopi luwak, 84, 138
Kumano Kodo trail (Japan), 167

L

Lampang Elephant Hospital (Thailand), 139–140
Land's End to John O'Groats trek (UK), 164
language, learning local, 108–109, 220
language schools, 109, 196–197
Laos, 127
lavender fields, visiting, 161
laws, respecting local, 102–109, 220
learning while traveling
    art and cultural tours, 200–202
    language schools, 196–197
    overview, 195–196
    photography tours and workshops, 199–200
    Road Scholar, 198–199
    sports, 202–206
less-known locations, 21–22, 54–55, 220
Lindblad Expeditions, 41
lion encounters, 124, 151
local, eating like, 82–83
local businesses, buying from, 222
local community
    families, staying with, 104–105
    importance of safari employment for, 123
    meaningful interaction with, 104–108
    questions to ask accommodations about, 78–79
    in regenerative tourism, 210–215
    travel provider support for, 29
local events, attending, 106–108
local language, learning, 108–109, 220
local laws and customs, respecting, 102–109, 220
local vacations, choosing, 18–19
local walking groups, 163
locally made items, buying, 88–90, 222
lodging. See accommodations
long-distance treks, 163–167
luggage, 57, 58–59, 65–67
lupin tourism, 162
luxury hotels, 75–77

M

Machu Picchu (Peru), 19
Malaysia, 225–226
Maldives, 133
Manakin Nature Tours, 157
manta rays, swimming with, 133
Manta Trust, 133
Maori culture, 117
marine conservation projects, 188
marine life
    aquariums, 145–148
    swimming with, 132–134
    whale watching, 129–132
marine parks, 151
Matariki festivals (New Zealand), 108, 169
Maya Bay, Thailand, 20, 159
medical volunteers, 188–189
medicines harming animals, 98–99
Mente Argentina, 201
Mexico, 143, 197
Milford Track (New Zealand), 165
minke whales, 132
Minneapolis, Minnesota (USA), 53–54, 173, 174
Monument Valley (USA), 74
Morocco, 144–145

Mount Hagen Show (Papua New Guinea), 106–107
mountain biking, 176
mountain gorilla tourism, 126–127, 226–227
Much Better Adventures, 128
museums, buying souvenirs at, 89

N

Nakasendo Way (Japan), 167
NamibRand Nature Reserve (Namibia), 169
national parks, 54
nature, protecting when traveling, 54–55
nature-based travel
  birdwatching, 155–157
  botanical tourism, 160–162
  choosing, 154–155
  cycling, 172–176
  dark sky places, 168–170
  diving, 157–160
  hiking and trekking, 162–168
  overview, 153–154, 220
  sailing, 170–172
nature-positive travel, 214–215
nearby destinations, choosing, 18–19
Neolithic standing stones, 21
nesting season, birdwatching during, 157
net zero concept, 208
Netherlands, 51, 161
New Zealand
  dark sky places in, 169
  flower-based tourism in, 162
  indigenous cultural tours in, 117, 202
  long-distance treks in, 165–166
  Matariki festivals in, 108, 169
  possum fur products in, 97
  regenerative tourism in, 210–211, 212
  rodeos in, 144

as sustainable destination, 225
sustainable tourism pledge in, 25, 210–211
train travel in, 47
wildlife charities in, 121
Night Riviera Sleeper, 45
night trains, 42, 43, 44, 45
Nightjet, 44
Niue, 169

O

off the beaten track travel, 54–55
offseason travel, 14, 20–21, 220
offset companies, 13
offsetting carbon footprint, 12–13, 30, 39, 217–218
Ol'au Palau app, 26
online resources page, 3–4, 17
open-range zoos, 148
orangutans, 225
organic food, 80
orphanage tourism, 192–193
Overland Track (Australia), 166
overnight trains, 42, 43, 44, 45
over-tourism, 19–20, 41, 209, 220

P

Pacific Northwest Trail (USA), 163
pack animals, 144–145
Pack for a Purpose, 68
packing
  luggage, 58–59
  overview, 57–58
  reusable items, 62–64
  sustainable travel clothing, 59–62
  tips for, 67–68
  toiletries, 64–65
  traveling light, 57, 65–67

PADI (Professional Association of Diving Instructors), 158

Palau Pledge, 25–26

palm oil products, 96, 127–128, 225

pangolins, 85

Papua New Guinea, 106–108

Paros, Greece, 228–229

Patagonia (company), 58–59, 60–61

Patagonian toothfish, 85

payment for photographs, 111–112

peak season, avoiding, 20–21

Pebble Beach Links, 203

permission for photography, 111–112, 200

Peru, 19, 165, 185–186, 212–213

PETA, 81

Petra, Jordan, 145

Phi Phi Leh Island, Thailand, 20, 159

Philippines, 26

photography

   cultural sensitivities related to, 110–113

   tours and workshops, 199–200

picking flowers, 161

Pingxi Sky Lantern Festival (Taiwan), 106

Pinnawala Elephant Orphanage (Sri Lanka), 141

Pitcairn Island, 41

planning travel

   destination, choosing, 18–22

   family travel, 32–34

   overview, 17

   sustainable tourism pledges, 22–27

   travel provider, choosing, 27–32

plastic-free souvenirs, 94–95

pledges, sustainable tourism, 22–27, 210–211

PONANT, 41

popular destinations, 19–21

Portland, Oregon (USA), 53–54, 173

possum fur products, 97

Prague, Czech Republic, 51

Premier Travel Tasmania, 128

Professional Association of Diving Instructors (PADI), 158

public health volunteers, 188–189

public transport, 50–52, 219

Q

Queensland Rail (Australia), 47

R

rail trails, 175–176

The Ramblers, 163

recycled material souvenirs, 94, 95

Red Sea Mountain Trail (Egypt), 165

regenerative tourism, 210–215

religion, respecting, 103–104

religious buildings, photography in, 110

remote destinations, volunteering in, 184

Republic of the Congo, 127

ReShark, 146–147

responsible travel, 6–7, 8. See also sustainable travel

Responsible Travel, 28, 180, 187

restaurants. See dining

reusable items, packing, 62–64

Rewa Eco-lodge (Guyana), 213

Rewilding Argentina, 228

Road Scholar, 198–199

road-tripping, 49–50, 218

Rocky Mountaineer, 45, 46

rodeos, 142–144

Rooms for Change, 70

rosewood products, 100

Royal Canadian Pacific, 46

rubbish. See waste

Rubicon 3 Adventure, 171

Rwanda, 126–127, 226–227

S

sacred places, photography in, 110
safaris, 121–125
sailing, 170–172, 204
St Andrews Academy, 203
Sani Lodge (Ecuador), 75
Santa Claus Express (Finland), 44–45
sarongs, 62
Save the Ocean Pledge, 27
Scotland, 21, 164, 203, 229
scuba diving, 27, 157–160
sea (coastal) wolf-focused tours, 125
seabirds, 157
seafood, 80–81
Seafood Watch, 80–81
seahorse souvenirs, 99
seashells, 97
Sepik Crocodile Festival (Papua New Guinea), 107–108
Seven Stars in Kyushu train (Japan), 48
Shanghai, China, 51
shark fin soup, 84
ship travel, 38, 39–42
shoulder season travel. *See* offseason travel
similar locations, choosing, 21–22, 220
Sinai Trail (Egypt), 165
Singapore, 51
single-use plastics, 78, 94
Six Senses Shaharut resort (Israel), 77
SJ EuroNight, 44
skins, animal, 96–97
Skwachays Lodge and Residence (Canada), 74–75
Slovenia, 227–228
slow fashion, 60
slow travel, 13–14, 36–37, 221
Small Luxury Hotels of the World, 77
small ship travel, 40
snake wine, 98

snorkeling, 158, 160
Songkran Festival (Asia), 106
South Africa, 47, 124, 162
South Korea, 143
South Pacific Tourism Organisation, 117–118, 202
souvenirs
  bargaining, 92–94
  fakes, checking for, 90–92
  locally made items, 88–90, 222
  from nature, 168
  overview, 87–88
  plastic-free, 94–95
  that harm animals, avoiding, 95–99, 151
  things to watch out for, 99–100
Spain, 142–143, 197
Spanish language schools, 197
Spirit Bear Lodge (Canada), 75
sports, learning while traveling, 202–206
spotlighting tours, 128
Sri Lanka, 141–142, 205
STAR Project (ReShark), 146–147
Stockholm, Sweden, 52
Stonehenge (UK), 21
stray animals, 150
sunglasses, 61–62
sunscreen, 133–134, 160
surfing, learning while traveling, 204–205
sustainability reports for accommodations, 79
sustainable tourism pledges, 22–27, 210–211
sustainable travel
  benefits of, 14–15
  financial costs of, 11–14
  importance of, 7–11
  overview, 1–4, 5–6
  versus responsible travel, 6–7
  shifts in concepts of, 207–209
  tips for achieving, 217–222

Sustainable Wild Koala Watching Code, 135
Sweden, 52
swimming with marine life, 132–134

T

Taiwan, 52, 106
tall ship sailing, 172
Tandem, 109
Tangulia Mara (Kenya), 75
Tanzania, 124
textiles, as souvenirs, 99
Thailand
  cycling in, 174, 175
  elephant encounters in, 139–140, 142
  homestays in, 71
  over-tourism in Maya Bay, 20, 159
  respecting local laws and customs in, 103
  train travel in, 48
Tiaki Promise (New Zealand), 25, 210–211
TMP (Tun Mustapha Park), Malaysia, 226
toiletries, 64–65, 67, 78
Tokyo, Japan, 52
Tongariro Alpine Crossing (New Zealand), 165–166
Tourism Declares a Climate Emergency, 28
tourism pledges, 22–27, 210–211
Train No. 9 (Thailand), 48
train travel
  in Asia, 47–49
  in Australia, 46–47
  in Canada, 46
  in Europe, 43–45
  in New Zealand, 47
  overview, 38, 42–43
  slow travel, 14
  in South Africa, 47

as sustainable form of travel, 218
  in United Kingdom, 45
  in United States, 45–46
Trans Dinarica, 175
transportation. *See also* train travel
  biking, 52–54
  cruises, 38, 39–42
  flying, 38–39
  going off the beaten track, 54–55
  overview, 35–36
  public transport, 50–52
  road-tripping, 49–50
  slow travel, 36–37
  tips for achieving sustainable travel, 217–219
travel clothing, 59–62
travel insurance, 30, 180
travel products
  luggage, 58–59
  overview, 58
  reusable items, 62–64
  toiletries, 64–65
  travel clothing, 59–62
travel providers, 27–32, 221
traveling light, 57, 65–67
Traveling Spoon, 83
trekking. *See* hiking
tropical sea cucumbers, 84
tulips, viewing in Netherlands, 161
Tun Mustapha Park (TMP), Malaysia, 226
turtle products, 84, 97–98

U

Uganda, 127
Ulagalla hotel (Sri Lanka), 141–142
UNESCO World Heritage Sites, 20
United Kingdom (UK), 21, 45, 164. *See also* Scotland
United Nations World Tourism Organization (UNWTO), 28, 208, 209

United States of America (USA)
  cycle-friendly cities in, 53–54, 173–174
  dark sky places in, 168
  flower-based tourism in, 161
  Indigenous cultural tours in, 116–117, 202
  Indigenous festivals in, 108
  Indigenous peoples in, 114
  learning golf in, 203
  learning to surf in, 204–205
  long-distance treks in, 163
  rail trails in, 176
  regenerative tourism in, 211
  rodeos in, 144
  sustainable tourism pledges in, 23–24
  train travel in, 45–46
  urban hikes in, 163
  walrus tusk products in, 98
  Whale Heritage Site in, 131–132
untourist, 209
urban hikes, 163

V

Vacation with an Artist, 201
Venice Simplon Orient Express, 43–44
Via Alpina, 165
Via Dinarica, 164–165
VIA Rail, 46
Vietnam, 50
View Hotel (Utah, USA), 74
Volcanoes National Park (Rwanda), 127, 227
volunteering
  activity involved, picking, 185–189
  choices related to, 183
  common concerns about, 190–193
  deciding where to go, 184–185
  at home or abroad, 180–181
  interacting with communities by, 105
  operators, checking out, 189–190
  overview, 177
  paying for, 181–183
  research before, 179
  voluntourism, 178–183

W

walking groups, local, 163
walrus tusk products, 98
waste, 29, 167, 170–171, 222
Wat Phou, Laos, 21–22
water bottles, reusable, 63
WAZA (World Association of Zoos and Aquariums), 146, 147, 148
West Highland Way (Scotland), 164
whale captivity, 147–148, 151
Whale Heritage Site status, 131
whale meat, 84, 131
whale swims, 132–133
Whale Trail (North America), 132
whale watching, 129–132
Whitsunday Sailing School (Australia), 204
wildlife
  animal welfare policies, 29, 120
  animal-friendly pledges, 26
  animal-friendly tourism, 149–151, 222
  aquatic encounters, 129–134
  beasts of burden, 144–145
  bullfighting and rodeos, 142–144
  effect of COVID-19 pandemic on, 9
  elephant encounters, 138–142
  gorilla tourism, 126–127, 226–227
  hiking and trekking adventures, 125–129
  koala cuddling, 134–136
  orangutans, 225
  other steps to take to protect, 148–151
  overview, 119–120
  photography of, 200
  reputable tour, choosing, 120–121

wildlife *(continued)*
  safaris, 121–125
  souvenirs harming animals, 95–99, 151
  unethical experiences, 137–138
  volunteering on projects related to, 187–188, 191–192
  zoos and aquariums, 145–148
wildlife charities, 121
wolf-focused tours, 125
wood products as souvenirs, 100
Workaway, 183
World Animal Protection, 26, 29, 121, 137
World Association of Zoos and Aquariums (WAZA), 146, 147, 148
World Cetacean Alliance, 131
World Expeditions, 30, 185–186
World Naked Bike Ride, 173
World Nomads, 30

World Tourism Day Report (UNWTO), 209
World Travel and Tourism Council (WTTC), 214–215
World Wide Opportunities on Organic Farms (WWOOF), 72–73, 182–183
Worn Wear (Patagonia), 58–59, 60–61

Y
yacht travel, 36–37, 170
yoga, learning while traveling, 205–206

Z
zebra sharks, 146–147
zoos, 138, 145–148

About the Author

Lee Mylne is a passionate traveler who loves sharing her experiences with others. Born in New Zealand and a long-time resident of Australia, she's been traveling the world for most of her adult life and never tires of it. She's lived in six countries on four continents but now calls Brisbane, Australia, home. She's spent the past 30-something years specializing in travel and tourism, writing for magazines, newspapers, digital and online publications, and is the author or co-author of around a dozen guide books, including *Australia For Dummies* (2008).

Lee is a life member of the Australian Society of Travel Writers, and served three terms as the society's president. She holds a Doctor of Creative Industries degree from Queensland University of Technology in Brisbane. Learn more at www.leemylne.com and on her blog A Glass Half Full. Yep, you got it . . . she's a born optimist!

Dedication

For the next generation of travelers in my family, Ollie and Harper, with the hope that the world you will explore will be cared for by those who come before you and that you will appreciate, respect, and love it as you travel through it.

Author's Acknowledgments

Writing a book — any book — is never a solitary exercise. While the time at the keyboard is unavoidably the author's lot, many people help to make that possible.

First, I would like to thank Kelly Regan for putting forward my name for this project (and for keeping in touch remotely for all these years). And thank you, too, to Myka Carroll and Vicki Adang for guiding me through the early stages of getting back into the swing of writing a Dummies book!

The entire team at Wiley were helpful and supportive every step of the way — thank you in particular to Jennifer Yee and Chrissy Guthrie for your trust, confidence, and encouragement along the way. Thank you for publishing this book and for recognizing the need to spread the word about the importance of sustainable, responsible, and ethical travel. It is so important! My thanks, too, to Jennifer Connolly for her careful and meticulous editing and to Kerry Lorimer, whose knowledge of the world of sustainable travel was invaluable as technical editor on this book.

I am also grateful to photographer Ewen Bell for permission to quote from his beautiful and insightful book *ReIMAGINE*.

Over many years, fellow travelers have shared some of the adventures mentioned in this book with me, and I thank them for their companionship, friendship, and shared love of exotic places. I'm looking at you, Lee Atkinson, John Mylne, John Wright, Melissa MacCourt, and Paul, Joy, and Dan Wager (and anyone else who recognizes shared adventures in these pages).

Travel writers are often assisted by tourism organizations and operators. Some of the trips mentioned in this book would not have been the same with the support of wonderful people from: World Expeditions, G Adventures, Ayers Rock Resort, Tourism Authority of Thailand, Abercrombie & Kent, Tourism & Events Queensland, FNQ Nature Tours, Visit Finland, Morocco specialist By Prior Arrangement, and Taiwan Tourism, among others.

Heartfelt thanks too to my personal support team: Glen Cameron, Angelika Larcher, and Julie McGlone, who have kept me buoyant even when the going got tough during the writing of this book. And to my daughters, Sophie and Jess, who provided the reason to leave my desk from time to time for some family love.